George Gissing

The town traveller

George Gissing

The town traveller

ISBN/EAN: 9783337207366

Printed in Europe, USA, Canada, Australia, Japan

Cover: Foto ©Andreas Hilbeck / pixelio.de

More available books at **www.hansebooks.com**

THE
TOWN TRAVELLER

BY

GEORGE GISSING

METHUEN & CO.
36 ESSEX STREET, W.C.
LONDON
1898

CONTENTS

CHAPTER		PAGE
I.	Mr. Gammon Breakfasts in Bed	1
II.	A Missing Uncle	8
III.	The China Shop	16
IV.	Polly and Mr. Parish	28
V.	A Nondescript	38
VI.	The Head Waiter at Chaffey's	52
VII.	Polly's Wrath	63
VIII.	Mr. Gammon's Resolve	75
IX.	Polly's Defiance	88
X.	The Storming of the Fort	99
XI.	The Nose of the Trefoyles	110
XII.	Polly Condescends	121
XIII.	Gammon the Crafty	131
XIV.	Mr. Parish Pursues a Brougham	139
XV.	The Name of Gildersleeve	154
XVI.	An Ally in the Quest	165
XVII.	Polly Shows Weakness	178
XVIII.	Lord Polperro's Representative	192
XIX.	Not in the Secret	207
XX.	The Husband's Return	218

CONTENTS

CHAPTER		PAGE
XXI.	HIS LORDSHIP'S WILL	232
XXII.	NEW YEAR'S EVE	247
XXIII.	HIS LORDSHIP RETIRES	257
XXIV.	THE TRAVELLER'S FICKLENESS AND FRAUD	273
XXV.	THE MISSING WORD	287
XXVI.	A DOUBLE EVENT	298
XXVII.	THE TRAVELLER AT REST	307

THE TOWN TRAVELLER

CHAPTER I.

MR. GAMMON BREAKFASTS IN BED

MOGGIE, the general, knocked at Mr. Gammon's door, and was answered by a sleepy "Hollo?"

"Mrs. Bubb wants to know if you know what time it is, sir? 'Cos it's half-past eight an' more."

"All right!" sounded cheerfully from within. "Any letters for me?"

"Yes, sir; a 'eap."

"Bring 'em up, and put 'em under the door. And tell Mrs. Bubb I'll have breakfast in bed; you can put it down outside and shout. And I say, Moggie, ask somebody to run across and get me a *Police News* and *Clippings* and *The Kennel*—understand? Two eggs, Moggie, and three rashers, toasted crisp—understand?"

As the girl turned to descend a voice called to her from another room on the same floor, a voice very distinctly feminine, rather shrill, and a trifle imperative.

"Moggie, I want my hot water—sharp!"

"It ain't nine yet, miss," answered Moggie in a tone of remonstrance.

"I know that—none of your cheek! If you come up here hollering at people's doors, how can anyone sleep? Bring the hot water at once, and mind it *is* hot."

"You'll have to wait till it *gits* 'ot, miss."

"*Shall* I? If it wasn't too much trouble I'd come out and smack your face for you, you dirty little wretch!"

The servant—she was about sixteen, and no dirtier than became her position — scampered down the stairs, burst into the cellar kitchen, and in a high tearful wail complained to her mistress of the indignity she had suffered. There was no living in the house with that Miss Sparkes, who treated everybody like dirt under her feet. Smack her face, would she? What next? And all because she said the water would have to be '*otted*. And Mr. Gammon wanted his breakfast in bed, and—and—why, there now, it had all been drove out of her mind by that Miss Sparkes.

Mrs. Bubb, the landlady, was frying some sausages for her first-floor lodgers; as usual at this hour she wore (presumably over some invisible clothing) a large shawl and a petticoat, her thin hair, black streaked with grey, knotted and pinned into a ball on the top of her head. Here and there about the

MR. GAMMON BREAKFASTS

kitchen ran four children, who were snatching a sort of picnic breakfast whilst they made ready for school. They looked healthy enough, and gabbled, laughed, sang, without heed to the elder folk. Their mother, healthy too, and with no ill-natured face— a slow, dull, sluggishly-mirthful woman of a common London type—heard Moggie out, and shook up the sausages before replying.

"Never you mind Miss Sparkes; I'll give her a talkin' to when she comes down. What was it as Mr. Gammon wanted? Breakfast in bed? And what else? I never see such a girl for forgetting!"

"Well, didn't I tell you as my 'ead had never closed at the top!" urged Moggie in plaintive key. "How can I 'elp myself?"

"Here, take them letters up to him, and ask again; and if Miss Sparkes says anything don't give her no answer—see? Billy, fill the big kettle, and put it on before you go. Sally, you ain't a-goin' to school without brushin' your 'air? Do see after your sister, Janey, an' don't let her look such a slap-cabbage. Beetrice, stop that 'ollerin'; it fair mismerizes me!"

Having silently thrust five letters under Mr. Gammon's door, Moggie gave a very soft tap, and half whispered a request that the lodger would repeat his orders. Mr. Gammon did so with perfect good humour. As soon as his voice had ceased that of Miss Sparkes sounded from the neighbouring bedroom.

"Is that the water?"

For the pleasure of the thing Moggie stood to listen, an angry grin on her flushed face.

"Moggie!—I'll give that little beast what for! Are you there?"

The girl made a quick motion with both her hands as if clawing an enemy's face, then coughed loudly, and went away with a sound of stamping on the thinly-carpeted stairs. One minute later Miss Sparkes' door opened and Miss Sparkes herself rushed forth—a startling vision of wild auburn hair about a warm complexion, and a small, brisk figure girded in a flowery dressing-gown. She called at the full pitch of her voice for Mrs. Bubb.

"Do you hear me? Mrs. Bubb, have the kindness to send me up my hot water immejately! This moment, if you please!"

There came an answer, but not from the landlady. It sounded so near to Miss Sparkes that she sprang back into her room.

"Patience, Polly! All in good time, my dear. Wrong foot out of bed this morning?"

Her door slammed, and there followed a lazy laugh from Mr. Gammon's chamber.

In due time the can of hot water was brought up, and soon after it came a tray for Mr. Gammon,

MR. GAMMON BREAKFASTS 5

on which, together with his breakfast, lay the three newspapers he had bespoken. Polly Sparkes throughout her leisurely toilet was moved to irritation and curiosity by the sound of frequent laughter on the other side of the party wall—uproarious peals, long chucklings in a falsetto key, staccato bursts of mirth.

"That is the comic stuff in *Clippings*," she said to herself with an involuntary grin. "What a fool he is! And why's he staying in bed this morning? Got his holiday, I suppose. I'd make better use of it than that."

She came forth presently in such light and easy costume as befitted a young lady of much leisure on a hot morning of June. Meaning to pass an hour or two in quarrelling with Mrs. Bubb she had arrayed herself thus early with more care than usual, that her colours and perfumes might throw contempt upon the draggle-tailed landlady, whom, by-the-bye, she had known since her childhood. On the landing, where she paused for a moment, she hummed an air, with the foreseen result that Mr. Gammon called out to her.

"Polly!"

She vouchsafed no answer.

"Miss Sparkes!"

"Well?"

"Will you come with me to see my bow-wows this fine day?"

"No, Mr. Gammon, I certainly will not!"

"Thank you, Polly, I felt a bit afraid you might say yes."

The tone was not offensive, whatever the words might be, and the laugh that came after would have softened any repartee, with its undernote of good humour and harmless gaiety. Biting her lips to preserve the dignity of silence, Polly passed downstairs. Sunshine through a landing window illumined the dust floating thickly about the staircase and heated the familiar blend of lodging-house smells— the closeness of small rooms that are never cleaned, the dry rot of wall-paper, plaster, and old wood, the fustiness of clogged carpets trodden thin, the ever-rising vapours from a sluttish kitchen. As Moggie happened to be wiping down the front steps the door stood open, affording a glimpse of trams and omnibuses, cabs and carts, with pedestrians bobbing past in endless variety—the life of Kennington Road—all dust and sweat under a glaring summer sun. To Miss Sparkes a cheery and inviting spectacle—for the whole day was before her, to lounge or ramble until the hour which summoned her to the agreeable business of selling programmes at a fashionable theatre. The employment was precarious; even with luck in the way of tips it meant nothing very brilliant; but something had happened lately which made Polly in-

MR. GAMMON BREAKFASTS

different to this view of the matter. She had a secret, and enjoyed it all the more because it enabled her to excite not envy alone, but dark suspicions in the people who observed her.

Mrs. Bubb, for instance—who so far presumed upon old acquaintance as to ask blunt questions, and offer homely advice—plainly thought she was going astray. It amused Polly to encourage this misconception, and to take offence on every opportunity. As she went down into the kitchen she fingered a gold watch chain that hung from her blouse to a little pocket at her waist. Mrs. Bubb would spy it at once, and in course of the quarrel about this morning's hot water would be sure to allude to it.

It turned out one of the finest frays Polly had ever enjoyed, and was still rich in possibilities, when, at something past eleven, the kitchen door suddenly opened and there entered Mr. Gammon.

CHAPTER II.

A MISSING UNCLE

HE glanced at Mrs. Bubb, at the disorderly remnants of breakfast on the long deal table, then at Polly, whose face was crimson with the joy of combat.

"Don't let me interrupt you, ladies. Blaze away! if I may so express myself. It does a man good to see such energy on a warm morning."

"I've said all I'm a-goin' to say," exclaimed Mrs. Bubb, as she mopped her forehead with a greasy apron. "I've warned her, that's all, and I mean her well, little as she deserves it. Now, you Moggie, don't stand gahpin' there; git them breakfast things washed up, can't you? It'll be tea time agin before the beds is made. And what's come to *you* this morning?"

She addressed Mr. Gammon, who had seated himself on a corner of the table, as if to watch and listen. He was a short, thick-set man with dark, wiry hair roughened into innumerable curls, and similar whiskers ending in a clean razor-line half-way down the cheek. His eyes were blue and

A MISSING UNCLE

had a wondering innocence, which seemed partly the result of facetious affectation, as also was the peculiar curve of his lips, ever ready for joke or laughter. Yet the broad, mobile countenance had lines of shrewdness and of strength, plain enough whenever it relapsed into gravity, and the rude shaping of jaw and chin might have warned anyone disposed to take advantage of the man's good nature. He wore a suit of coarse tweed, a brown bowler hat, a blue cotton shirt with white stock and horse-shoe pin, rough brown leggings, tan boots, and in his hand was a dog-whip. This costume signified that Mr. Gammon felt at leisure, contrasting as strongly as possible with the garb in which he was wont to go about his ordinary business—that of commercial traveller. He had a liking for dogs, and kept a number of them in the back premises of an inn at Dulwich, whither he usually repaired on Sundays. When at Dulwich Mr. Gammon fancied himself in completely rural seclusion; it seemed to him that he had shaken off the dust of cities, that he was far from the clamour of the crowd, amid peace and simplicity; hence his rustic attire, in which he was fond of being photographed with dogs about him. A true-born child of town, he would have found the real country quite unendurable; in his doggy rambles about Dulwich he always preferred a northerly direction, and was never so happy as when sitting in the inn-parlour amid a group of friends whose voices rang the purest cockney. Even in his business he disliked engagements which took him far from London; his "speciality" (as he would have said) was town travel, and few men had had more varied experience in that region of enterprise.

"I'm going to have a look at the bow-wows," he replied to Mrs. Bubb. "Polly won't come with me; unkind of her, ain't it?"

"Mr. Gammon," remarked the young lady with a severe glance, "I'll thank you not to be so familiar with my name. If you don't know any better, let me tell you it's very ungentlemanly."

He rose, doffed his hat, bowed profoundly, and begged her pardon, in acknowledgment of which Polly gave a toss of the head. Miss Sparkes was neither beautiful nor stately, but her appearance had the sort of distinction which corresponds to these qualities in the society of Kennington Road; she filled an appreciable space in the eyes of Mr. Gammon; her abundance of auburn hair, her high colour, her full lips and excellent teeth, her finely-developed bust, and the freedom of her poses (which always appeared to challenge admiration and anticipate impertinence) had their effectiveness against a kitchen background, and did not entirely lose it when she flitted about the stalls at the theatre selling programmes. She was but two-and-twenty.

A MISSING UNCLE

Mr. Gammon had reached his fortieth year. In general his tone of intimacy passed without rebuke; at moments it had seemed not unacceptable. But Polly's temper was notoriously uncertain, and her frankness never left people in doubt as to the prevailing mood.

"Would you like a little bull-pup, Miss Sparkes?" he pursued in a conciliatory tone. "A lovely little button-ear? There's a new litter; say the word, and I'll bring you one."

"Thank you. I don't care for dogs."

"No? But I'm sure you would if you kept one. Now, I have a cobby little fox terrier—just the dog for a lady. No? Or a sweet little black-and-tan—just turning fifteen pounds, with a lovely neck and kissing spots on both cheeks. I wouldn't offer her to everybody."

"Very good of you," replied Miss Sparkes contemptuously.

"Why ain't you goin' to business?" asked the landlady.

"I'll tell you. We had a little difference of opinion yesterday. The governors have been disappointed about a new line in the fancy leather; it wouldn't go, and I told them the reason, but that wasn't good enough. They hinted that it was my fault. Of course, I said nothing; I never do in such cases. But—this morning I had breakfast in bed."

He spoke with eyes half closed and an odd vibration of the upper lip, then broke into a laugh.

"You're an independent party, you are," said Mrs. Bubb, eyeing him with admiration.

"It was always more than I could do to stand a hint of that kind. Not so long ago I used to lose my temper, but I've taken pattern by Polly—I mean Miss Sparkes—and now I do it quietly. That reminds me"—his look changed to seriousness—"do you know anyone of the name of Quodling?"

Polly—to whom he spoke—answered with a dry negative.

"Sure? Try and think if you ever heard your uncle speak of the name."

The girl's eyes fell as if, for some reason, she felt a momentary embarrassment. It passed, but in replying she looked away from Mr. Gammon.

"Quodling? Never heard it—why?"

"Why, there is a man called Quodling who might be your uncle's twin brother—he looks so like him. I caught sight of him in the City, and tracked him till I got to know his place of business and his name. For a minute or two I thought I'd found your uncle; I really did. Gosh! I said to myself, there's Clover at last! I wonder I didn't pin him like a bull terrier. But, as you know, I'm cautious—that's how I've made my fortune, Polly."

Miss Sparkes neither observed the joke nor

A MISSING UNCLE 13

resented the name; she was listening with a preoccupied air.

"You'll never find *him*," said Mrs. Bubb, shaking her head.

"Don't be so sure of that. I shan't lose sight of this man Quodling. It's the strangest likeness I ever saw, and I shan't be satisfied till I've got to know if he has any connection with the name of Clover. It ain't easy to get at, but I'll manage it somehow. Now, if I had Polly to help me—I mean Miss Sparkes——"

With a muttering of impatience the girl rose; in the same moment she drew from her belt a gold watch, and deliberately consulted it. Observing this Mrs. Bubb looked towards Mr. Gammon, who, also observant, returned the glance.

"I shan't want dinner," Polly remarked in an offhand way as she moved towards the door.

"Going to see Mrs. Clover?" Gammon enquired.

"I'm sick of going there. It's always the same talk."

"Wait till *your* 'usband runs away from you and stays away for five years," said Mrs. Bubb with a renewal of anger, "and then see what *you* find to talk about."

Polly laughed and went away humming.

"If it wasn't that I feel afraid for her," continued Mrs. Bubb in a lower voice, "I'd give that young woman notice to quit. Her cheek's getting past everything. Did you see her gold watch and chain?"

"Yes, I did; where does it come from?"

"That's more than *I* can tell you, Mr. Gammon. I don't want to think ill of the girl, but there's jolly queer goin's-on. And she's so brazen about it! I don't know what to think."

Gammon knitted his brows and gazed round the kitchen.

"I think Polly's straight," he observed at length. "I don't seem to notice anything wrong with her except her cheek and temper. She'll have to be taken down a peg one of these days, but I don't envy the man that'll have the job. It won't be me, for certain," he added with a laugh.

Moggie came into the room, bringing a telegram.

"For me?" said Gammon. "Just what I expected." Reading, he broadened his visage into a grin of infinite satisfaction. "'Please explain absence. Hope nothing wrong.' How kind of them, ain't it! Yesterday they chucked me; now they're polite. Reply-paid too; very considerate. They shall have their reply."

He laid the blank form on the table and wrote upon it in pencil, every letter beautifully shaped in a first-rate commercial hand:

"Go to Bath and get your heads shaved."

"You ain't a-goin' to send that!" exclaimed Mrs.

A MISSING UNCLE

Bubb, when he had held the message to her for perusal.

"It'll do them good. They're like Polly—want taking down a peg."

Moggie ran off with the paper to the waiting boy, and Mr. Gammon laughed for five minutes uproariously.

"Would you like a little bull-pup, Mrs. Bubb?" he asked at length.

"Not me, Mr. Gammon. I've enough pups of my own, thank you all the same."

CHAPTER III.

THE CHINA SHOP

MR. GAMMON took his way down Kennington Road, walking at a leisurely pace, smiting his leg with his doubled dog-whip, and looking about him with his usual wide-awake contented air. He had in perfection the art of living for the moment, no art in his case, but a natural characteristic, for which it never occurred to him to be grateful. Indeed, it is a common characteristic in the world to which Mr. Gammon belonged. He and his like take what the heavens send them, grumbling or rejoicing, but never reflecting upon their place in the sum of things. To Mr. Gammon life was a wonderfully simple matter. He had his worries and his desires, but so long as he suffered neither from headache nor stomach-ache, these things interfered not at all with his enjoyment of a fine morning.

He was in no hurry to make for Dulwich; as he walked along his thoughts began to turn in a different direction, and on reaching the end of Upper Kennington Lane he settled the matter by striking towards Vauxhall Station. A short railway journey

THE CHINA SHOP

and another pleasant saunter brought him to a street off Battersea Park Road, and to a china shop, over which stood the name of Clover.

In the window hung a card with an inscription in bold letters: "Glass, china, and every kind of fashionable ornament for the table for hire on moderate terms." Mr. Gammon read this with an appreciative smile, which, accompanied by a nod, became a greeting to Mrs. Clover, who was aware of him from within the shop. He entered.

"How does it go?"

"Two teas and a supper yesterday. A wedding breakfast this morning."

"Bravo! What did I tell you? You'll want a bigger place before the end of the year."

The shop was well stocked, the window well laid out; everything indicated a flourishing, though as yet a small, business. Mrs. Clover, a neat, comely, and active woman, with a complexion as clear as that of her own best china, chatted vivaciously with the visitor, whilst she superintended the unpacking of a couple of crates by a muscular youth and a young lady (to use the technical term), her shop assistant.

"Why are you off to-day?" she enquired presently, after moving to the doorway for more private talk.

Mr. Gammon made his explanation with spirit and humour.

"You're a queer man, if ever there was one," Mrs.

Clover remarked after watching him for a moment and averting her eyes as soon as they were met by his. "You know your own business best, but I should have thought——"

It was a habit of hers to imply a weighty opinion by suddenly breaking off; a form of speech known to the grammarians by a name which would have astonished Mrs. Clover. Few women of her class are prone to this kind of emphasis. Her friendly manner had a quietness, a reserve in its cordiality, which suited well with the frank, pleasant features of a matron not yet past her prime.

"It's all right," he replied, more submissively than he was wont to speak. "I shall do better next time; I'm looking out for a permanency."

"So you have been for ten years, to my knowledge."

They laughed together. At this point came an interruption in the shape of a customer who drove up in a hansom; a loudly-dressed woman, who, on entering the shop, conversed with Mrs. Clover in the lowest possible voice, and presently returned to her vehicle with uneasy glances left and right. Mr. Gammon, who had walked for some twenty yards, sauntered back to the shop, and his friend met him on the threshold.

"That's the sort," she whispered with a merry eye. "Eight-roomed 'ouse near Queen's Road Station.

Wants things for an at 'ome—teaspoons as well—couldn't I make it ninepence the two dozen! That's the kind of place where there'll be breakages. But they pay well, the breakages do."

"Well, I won't keep you now," said Gammon. "I'm going to have a peep at the bow-wows. Could I look in after closing?"

Mrs. Clover turned her head away, pretending to observe the muscular youth within.

"Fact is," he pursued, "I want to speak to you about Polly."

"What about her?"

"Nothing much. I'll tell you this evening."

Without more words he nodded and went off. Mrs. Clover stood for a moment with an absent expression on her comely face, then turned into the shop and gave the young man in shirt sleeves a bit of her mind about the time he was taking over his work.

She was anything but a bad-tempered woman. Her rating had no malice in it, and only signified that she could not endure laziness.

"Hot, is it? Of course it's hot. What do you expect in June? You don't mind the heat when you're playing cricket, I know."

"No, mum," replied the young giant with a grin.

"How many runs did you make last Saturday?"

"Fifty-three, mum, and caught out."

"Then don't go talking to me about the heat. Finish that job and run off with this filter to Mrs. Gubbins's."

Her life had not lacked variety. Married at eighteen, after a month's courtship, to a man of whom she knew next to nothing, she lived for a time in Liverpool, where her husband—older by ten years—pursued various callings in the neighbourhood of the docks. After the birth of her only child, a daughter, they migrated to Glasgow, and struggled with great poverty for several years. This period was closed by the sudden disappearance of Mr. Clover. He did not actually desert his wife and child; at regular intervals letters and money arrived from him addressed to the care of Mrs. Clover's parents, who kept a china shop at Islington; beyond the postmarks, which indicated constant travel in England and abroad, these letters (always very affectionate) gave no information as to the writer's circumstances. When Mrs. Clover had lived with her parents for about three years she was summoned by her husband to Dulwich, where the man had somehow established himself as a cab proprietor; he explained his wanderings as the result of mere restlessness, and with this cold comfort Mrs. Clover had to be content. By degrees they settled into a not unhappy life; the girl, Minnie, was growing up, the business might have been worse, everything

THE CHINA SHOP

seemed to promise unbroken domestic tranquillity, when one fine day Mr. Clover was again missing. Again he sent letters and money, the former written in a strangely mingled mood of grief and hopefulness, the remittance varying from half a sovereign to a ten-pound note. This time the letters were invariably posted in London, but in different districts. Clover declared that he was miserable away from home, and, without offering any reason for his behaviour, promised that he would soon return.

Six years had since elapsed. To afford herself occupation Mrs. Clover went into the glass and china business, assisted by her parents' experience, and by the lively interest of her friend Mr. Gammon. Minnie Clover, a pretty and interesting girl, was now employed at Doulton's potteries. All would have been well but for the harassing mystery that disturbed their lives. Clover's letters were still posted in London; money still came from him, sometimes in remittances of as much as twenty pounds. But handwriting and composition often suggested that the writer was either ill or intoxicated. The latter seemed not unlikely, for Clover had always inclined to the bottle. His wife no longer distressed herself. The first escapade she had forgiven; the second estranged her. She had resolved, indeed, that if her husband did again present himself, his home should not be under her roof.

The shop closed at eight. At a quarter past the house-bell rang and a small servant admitted Mr. Gammon, who came along the passage and into the back parlour where Mrs. Clover was wont to sit. As usual at this hour her daughter was present. Minnie sat reading; she rose for a moment to greet the visitor, spoke a word or two very modestly, even shyly, and let her eyes fall again upon the book. Considering the warmth of the day it was not unnatural that Mr. Gammon showed a very red face, shining with moisture; but his decided hilarity, his tendency to hum tunes and beat time with his feet, his noisy laughter and expansive talk, could hardly be attributed to the same cause. Having taken a seat near Minnie he kept his look steadily fixed upon her, and evidently discoursed with a view of affording her amusement; not altogether successfully it appeared, for the young girl — she was but seventeen — grew more and more timid, less and less able to murmur replies. She was prettier than her mother had ever been, and spoke with a better accent. Her features suggested a more delicate physical inheritance than Mrs. Clover's comeliness could account for. As a matter of fact she had her father's best traits, though Mrs. Clover frequently thanked goodness that in character she by no means resembled him.

Mr. Gammon was in the midst of a vivid description of a rat hunt, in which a young terrier had displayed astonishing mettle, when his hostess abruptly interposed.

"Minnie, I wish you'd put your hat on and run round to Mrs. Walker's for me. I'll give you a message when you're ready."

Very willingly the girl rose and left the room. Mr. Gammon, whose countenance had fallen, turned to the mother with jocose remonstrance.

"Now I call that too bad. What did you want to go sending her away for?"

"What does it matter?" was Mrs. Clover's reply, uttered good humouredly, but with some impatience. "The child doesn't want to hear about rats and terriers."

"Child? I don't call her a child. Besides, you'd only to give me a hint to talk of something else." He leaned forward, and softened his voice to a note of earnest entreaty. "She won't be long, will she?"

"Oh, I daresay not!"

A light tap at the door called Mrs. Clover away. She whispered outside with Minnie and returned smiling.

"Have you told her to be quick?'

Mrs. Clover did not answer the question. Sitting with her arms on the round table she looked Mr. Gammon steadily in the face, and said with decision:

"Never you come here again after you've been to Dulwich!"

"Why not?"

"Never mind. I don't want to have to speak plainer. If ever I have to——"

Mrs. Clover made her great effect of the pregnant pause. The listener, who had sobered wonderfully, sat gazing at her, his blue eyes comically rueful.

"She isn't coming back at all?" fell from his lips.

"Of course she isn't."

"Well, I'm blest if I thought you could be so unkind, Mrs. Clover."

She was silent for three ticks of the clock, an odd hardness having come over her face, then, flushing just a little, as if after an effort, she smiled again, and spoke in her ordinary tone.

"What had you to say about Polly?"

"Polly?—Polly be hanged! I half believe Polly's no better than she should be."

The flush on Mrs. Clover's face deepened and she spoke severely.

"What do you mean by saying such things?"

"I didn't mean to," exclaimed Gammon, with hasty penitence. "Look here, I really didn't; but you put me out. She had some presents given her, that's all."

"I know it," said Mrs. Clover. "She's been here to-day—called this afternoon."

THE CHINA SHOP

"Polly did?"

"Yes, and behaved very badly too. I don't know what's coming to the girl. If I had a temper like that I'd——"

What Mrs. Clover would do remained conjectural.

"It's a good thing," remarked the other, laughing. "Trust Polly to take care of herself. She cheeked you, did she?"

They discussed Miss Sparkes very thoroughly. There had been a battle royal in the afternoon, for the girl came only to "show off" and make herself generally offensive. Mrs. Clover desired to be friendly with her sister's daughter, but would stand no "cheek," and had said so.

"Polly's all right," remarked Mr. Gammon finally. "Don't you fret about her. She ain't that kind. I know 'em."

"Then why did you say just now——"

"Because you riled me, sending Minnie away."

Again Mrs. Clover reflected, and again she looked her friend steadily in the face.

"Why did you want her to stay?"

Mr. Gammon's heated visage glowed with incredible fervour. He shrugged his shoulders, shuffled his feet, and at length burst out with—

"Well, I should think you know. It isn't the first time I've showed it, I should think."

"Then I'm very sorry. I'm real sorry."

The words fell gently, and one might have thought that Mrs. Clover was softening the rejection of a tender proposal made to herself.

"You mean it's no good?" said the man.

"Not the least, not a bit. And never could be."

Mr. Gammon nodded several times, as if calculating the force of the blow, and nerving himself to bear it.

"Well, if you say it," he replied at length, "I suppose it's a fact—but I call it hard lines. Ever since I was old enough to think of marrying I've been looking out for the right girl—always looking out, and now I thought I'd found her. Hanged if it isn't hard lines! I could have married scores—scores; but do you suppose I'd have a girl that showed she was only waiting for me to say the word? Not me! That's what took me in Minnie. She's the first of that kind I ever knew—the only one. But, I say, do you mean you won't let me try? You surely don't mean that, Mrs. Clover?"

"Yes, I do. I mean just that, Mr. Gammon."

"Why? Because I haven't got a permanency?"

"Oh, no."

"Because I—because I go to Dulwich?"

"No."

"Why, then?"

"I can't tell you why, and I don't know why, but I mean it. And what's more"—her eyes sparkled—

THE CHINA SHOP

"if ever you say one such word to Minnie you never pass my door again."

This seemed to take Mr. Gammon's breath away. After a rather long silence he looked about for his hat, then for his dog-whip.

"I'll say good-night, Mrs. Clover. Hot, isn't it? Hottest day yet. I say, you're not riled with me? That's all right. See you again before long."

He did not make straight for home, but rambled in a circuit for the next hour. When darkness had fallen he found himself again near the china shop, and paused, for a moment only, by the door. On the opposite side of the street stood a man who had also paused in a slow walk, and who also looked towards the shop. But Mr. Gammon went his way without so much as a glance at that dim figure.

CHAPTER IV.

POLLY AND MR. PARISH

TWO first-rate quarrels in one day put Polly Sparkes into high good humour. On leaving her aunt's house in the afternoon she strolled into Battersea Park, and there treated herself to tea and cakes at a little round table in the open air. Mrs. Clover, though the quarrel was prolonged until four o'clock, had offered no refreshments, which seemed to Miss Sparkes a very gross instance of meanness and inhospitality.

At a table near to her sat two girls, for some reason taking a holiday, who conversed in a way which proved them to be "mantle hands," and Polly listened and smiled. Did she not well remember the day when the poverty of home sent her, a little girl, to be "trotter" in a workroom? But she soon found her way out of that. A sharp tongue, a bold eye, and a brilliant complexion helped her on, step by step, or jump by jump, till she had found much more agreeable ways of supporting herself. All unimpeachable, for Polly was fiercely virtuous, and put

POLLY AND MR. PARISH

a very high value indeed upon such affections as she had to dispose of.

The girls were appraising her costume; she felt their eyes and enjoyed the envy in them. Her hat, with its immense bunch of poppies; her blouse of shot silk in green and violet; her gold watch, carelessly drawn out and returned to its pocket. "Now what do you think I am? A real lady, I'll bet!" She caught a whisper about her hair. Red, indeed! Didn't they wish they had anything like it! Polly could have told them that at a ball she graced with her presence not long ago her hair was done up with no less than seventy-two pins. Think of that! Seventy-two pins!

She munched a cream tart, and turned her back upon the envious pair.

Back to Kennington Road by omnibus, riding outside, her eyes and hair doing execution upon a young man in a very high collar, who was, she saw, terribly tempted to address her, but, happily for himself, could not pluck up courage. Polly liked to be addressed by strange young men; experience had made her so skilful in austere rebuke.

She rested in her bedroom, as stuffy and disorderly a room as could have been found in all Kennington Road. Moggie, the general, was only allowed to enter it in the occupant's presence, otherwise who knew what prying and filching might go on? She paid a very low rent, thanks to Mrs. Bubb's good nature, but the strained relations between them made it possible that she would have to leave, and she had been thinking to-day that she could very well afford herself a room in a better neighbourhood; not that, all things considered, she desired to quit this house, but Mrs. Bubb took too much upon herself. Mrs. Bubb was the widow of a police officer; one of her children was in the Police Orphanage at Twickenham, and for the support of each of the others she received half a crown a week. This, to be sure, justified the good woman in a certain spirit of pride; but when it came to calling names and making unpleasant insinuations——! If a young lady cannot have a harmless and profitable secret, what is the use of being a young lady?

On the way to her duties at the theatre, about seven o'clock, she entered a little stationer's shop in an obscure street, and asked with a smile whether any letter had arrived for her. Yes, there was one addressed in a careless hand to "Miss Robinson." This, in another obscure street hard by, she opened. On half a sheet of notepaper was printed with pen and ink the letters *W. S. T.*—that was all. Polly had no difficulty in interpreting this cipher. She tore up envelope and paper, and walked briskly on.

There was but a poor "house" this evening. Commission on programmes would amount to very little indeed; but the young gentleman with the weak eyes, who came evening after evening, and must have seen the present piece a hundred times or so, gave her half a crown, weeping copiously from nervousness as he touched her hand. He looked about seventeen, and Polly, who always greeted him with a smile of sportive condescension, wondered how his parents or guardians could allow him to live so recklessly.

She left half an hour before the end of the performance with a girl who accompanied her a short way, talking and laughing noisily. Along the crowded pavement they were followed by a young man, of whose proximity Miss Sparkes was well aware, though she seemed not to have noticed him— a slim, narrow-shouldered, high-hatted figure, with the commonest of well-meaning faces set just now in a tremulously eager, pursuing look. When Polly's companion made a dart for an omnibus this young man, suddenly red with joy, took a quick step forward, and Polly saw him beside her in an attitude of respectful accost.

"Awfully jolly to meet you like this."

"Sure you haven't been waiting?" she asked with good humour.

"Well—I—you said you didn't mind, you know; didn't you?"

"Oh, I don't mind!" she laughed. "If you've nothing better to do. There's my 'bus."

"Oh, I say! Don't be in such a hurry. I was going to ask you "—he panted—"if you'd come and have just a little supper, if you wouldn't mind."

"Nonsense! You know you can't afford it."

"Oh, yes, I can—quite well. It would be awfully kind of you."

Polly laughed a careless acceptance, and they pressed through the roaring traffic of cross-ways towards an electric glare. In a few minutes they were seated amid plush and marble, mirrors and gilding, in a savoury and aromatic atmosphere. Nothing more delightful to Polly, who drew off her gloves and made herself thoroughly comfortable, whilst the young man—his name was Christopher Parish—nervously scanned a bill of fare. As his bearing proved, Mr. Parish was not quite at home amid these splendours. As his voice and costume indicated, he belonged to the great order of minor clerks, and would probably go dinnerless on the morrow to pay for this evening's festival. The waiter overawed him, and after a good deal of bungling, with anxious consultation of his companion's appetite, he ordered something, the nature of which was but dimly suggested to him by its name. Having accomplished this feat he at once became hilarious, and began to eat large quantities of dry bread.

Quite without false modesty in the matter of eating and drinking, Polly made a hearty supper. Christopher ate without consciousness of what was before him, and talked ceaselessly of his good fortune in getting a berth at Swettenham's, the great house of Swettenham Brothers, tea merchants.

"An enormous place—simply enormous! What do you think they pay in rent?—three thousand eight hundred pounds a year! Could you believe it? Three thousand eight hundred pounds! And how many people do you think they employ? Now just guess, do; just make a shot at it!"

"How do I know? Two or three hundred, I dessay."

Christopher's face shone with triumph.

"One thousand—three hundred—and forty-two! Could you believe it?"

"Oh, I dessay," Polly replied, with her mouth full.

"Enormous, isn't it? Why, it's like a town in itself!"

Had his own name been Swettenham he could hardly have shown more pride in these figures. When Polly enquired how much *they* made a year he was unable to reply with exactitude, but the mere thought of what such a total must be all but overcame him.

Personally he profited by his connection with the great firm to the extent of two pounds a week, an advance of ten shillings on what he had hitherto earned. And his prospects! Why, they were limitless. Once let a fellow get into Swettenham's——!

"You're not doing so bad for a single man," remarked Polly, with facetious malice in her eye. "But it won't run to a supper like this very often."

"Oh — well — not often, of course." His voice quavered into sudden despondency. "Just now and then, you know. Have some cheese?"

"Don't mind—gorgonzoler."

He paid the bill right bravely and added sixpence for the waiter, though it cost him as great a pang as the wrenching of a double tooth. A rapid calculation told him that he must dine at the Aërated Bread Shop for several days to come. Whilst he was thus computing Polly drew out her gold watch. It caught his eye, he stood transfixed, and his stare rose from the watch to Polly's face.

"Just after eleven," she remarked airily, and began to hum.

Christopher had but a silver watch, an heirloom of considerable antiquity, and the chain was jet. Sunk of a sudden in profoundest gloom he led the way to the exit, walking like a shame-faced plebeian who had got into the room by mistake. Polly's spirits were higher than ever. Just beyond the electric glare she thrust her arm under that of her mute companion.

"You don't want me to git run over, do you?"

Parish had a thrill of satisfaction, but with difficulty he spoke.

"Let's get out of this crowd—beastly, isn't it?"

"I don't mind a crowd. I like it when I've someone to hang on by."

"Oh, I don't mind it, I like just what you like. What time did you say it was, Miss Sparkes?"

"Just eleven. Time I was gettin' 'ome. There'll be a 'bus at the corner."

"I hoped you were going to walk," urged Christopher timidly.

"S'pose I might just as well—if you'll take care of me."

It was a long time since Polly had been so gracious, so mild. All the way down Whitehall, across the bridge, and into Kennington Road she chatted of a hundred things, but never glanced at the one which held complete possession of Christopher's mind. Many times he brought himself all but to the point of mentioning it, yet his courage invariably failed. The risk was too great; it needed such a trifling provocation to disturb Polly's good humour. He perspired under the warmth of the night and from the tumult of his feelings.

"You mustn't meet me again for a week," said Polly when her dwelling was within sight.

"Why not?"

"Because I say so—that's enough, ain't it?"

"I say—Polly——"

"I've told you you're not to say 'Polly,'" she interrupted archly.

"You're awfully good, you know—but I wish——"

"What? Never mind; tell me next time. Ta-ta!"

She ran off, and Christopher had no heart to detain her. For five minutes he hung over the parapet at Westminster, watching the black flood and asking what was the use of life. On the whole Mr. Parish found life decidedly agreeable, and after a night's rest, a little worry notwithstanding, he could go to the City in the great morning procession, one of myriads exactly like him, and would hopefully dip his pen in the inkpots of Swettenham Bros.

Moggie, the general, was just coming from the public-house with two foaming jugs, one for Mrs. Bubb, the other for Mr. and Mrs. Cheeseman, her first-floor lodgers. Miss Sparkes passed her disdainfully, and entered with the aid of a latch-key. From upstairs sounded a banjo, preluding; then the sound of Mr. Cheeseman's voice chanting a popular refrain:—

> "Come where the booze is cheaper,
> Come where the pots 'old more,
> Come where the boss is a bit of a joss,
> Come to the pub next door!"

Polly could not resist this invitation. She looked in at the Cheesemans' sitting-room and enjoyed half an hour of friendly gossip before going to bed.

CHAPTER V.

A NONDESCRIPT

SCARCELY had quiet fallen upon the house—it was half an hour after midnight—when at the front door sounded a discreet but resolute knocking. Mrs. Bubb, though she had retired to her chamber, was not yet wholly unpresentable; reluctantly, and with wonder, she went to answer the untimely visitor. After a short parley through the gap of the chained door she ascended several flights and sought to arouse Mr. Gammon—no easy task.

"What's up?" shouted her lodger in a voice of half-remembered conviviality. "House on fire?"

"I hope not indeed. There wouldn't have been much chance for you if it was. It's your friend Mr. Greenacre, as says he must see you for a minute."

"All right; send him up, please. What the dickens can he want at this time o' night!"

Mr. Gammon having promised to see his visitor out again, with due attention to the house door,

A NONDESCRIPT

the landlady showed a light whilst Mr. Greenacre mounted the stairs. The gas-jet in his friend's bedroom displayed him as a gaunt, ill-dressed man of about forty, with a long unwholesome face, lank hair, and prominent eyes. He began with elaborate apologies, phrased and uttered with more refinement than his appearance would have led one to expect. No; he would on no account be seated. Under the circumstances he could not dream of staying more than two, or at most three, minutes. He felt really ashamed of himself for such a flagrant breach of social custom; but if his friend would listen patiently for one minute—nay, for less.

"I know what you're driving at," broke in Gammon good-humouredly, as he sat in bed with his knees up. "You've nowhere to sleep—ain't that it?"

"No, no; I assure you no!" exclaimed the other, with unfailing politeness. "I have excellent lodgings in the parish of St. Martin's-in-the-Fields; besides, you don't imagine I should disturb you after midnight for such a trivial cause! You have heard of the death of Lord Bolsover?"

"Never knew he was living," cried Gammon.

"Nonsense, you are an incorrigible joker. The poor fellow died nearly a week ago. Of course I must attend his funeral to-morrow down at Hitchin; I really couldn't neglect to attend his funeral. And here comes my difficulty. At present I'm driving a 'Saponaria' van, and I shall have to provide a substitute, you see. I thought I had found one, a very decent fellow called Grosvenor, who declares, by-the-bye, that he can trace his connection with the aristocratic house—interesting, isn't it? But Grosvenor has got into trouble to-day—something about passing a bad half-crown—a mere mistake, I'm quite sure. Now I've been trying to find someone else—not an easy thing; and as I *must* have a substitute by nine to-morrow, I came in despair to you. I'm *sure* in your wide acquaintance, my dear Gammon——"

"Hold on, what's 'Saponaria'?"

"A new washing powder; only started a few days. Big vans, painted vermilion and indigo, going about town and suburbs distributing handbills and so on."

"I see. But look here, Greenacre, what's all this rot about Lord Bolsover?"

"My dear Gammon," protested the other. "I really can't allow you to speak in that way. I make all allowance for the hour and the circumstances, but when it comes to the death of a dear friend——"

"How the devil come you to be his friend, or he yours?" shouted Gammon in comical exasperation.

A NONDESCRIPT 41

"Why, surely you have heard me speak of him. Yet, perhaps not. It was rather a painful subject. The fact is, I once gave the poor fellow a severe thrashing; it was before he succeeded to the title; I was obliged to do it. Poor Bolsover confessed afterwards that he had behaved badly (there was a lady in the case), but it put an end to our intimacy. And now he's gone, and the least I can do is to attend his funeral. That reminds me, Gammon, I fear I shall have to borrow a sovereign, if it's quite convenient to you. There's the hire of the black suit, you see, and the fare to Hitchin. Do you think you could?"

He paused delicately, whereupon Gammon burst into a roar of laughter which echoed through the still house.

"You're the queerest devil I know," was the remark that followed. "It's no use trying to make out what you're really up to."

"I have stated the case in very clear terms," replied Greenacre solemnly. "The chief thing is to find a substitute to drive the Saponaria van."

"What sort of animal in the shafts?"

"Two—a pair of Welsh cobs—good little goers."

"By jingo!" shouted Gammon, "I'll tool 'em round myself. I'm off for to-morrow, and a job of that kind would just suit me."

Greenacre's face brightened with relief. He began

to describe the route which the Saponaria van had to pursue.

"It's the south-east suburbs to-morrow, the main thoroughfares of Greenwich, Blackheath, Lewisham, and all round there. There are certain shops to call at to drop bills and samples; no order-taking. Here's the list. At likely places you throw out a shower of these little blue cards. Best is near a Board School when the children are about. I'm greatly obliged to you, Gammon; I never thought you'd be able to do it yourself. Could you be at the stable just before nine? I'd meet you and give you a send-off. Bait at—where is it?" He consulted the note-book. "Yes, Prince of Wales's Feathers, Catford Bridge; no money out of pocket; all settled in the plan of campaign. Rest the cobs for an hour or so. Get round to the stables again about five, and I'll be there. It's very kind of you; I'm very greatly obliged. And if you *could*—without inconvenience——"

His eyes fell upon Gammon's clothing, which lay heaped on a chair. On the part of the man in bed there was a moment's hesitation, but Gammon had never refused a loan which it was in his power to grant. In a few minutes he fulfilled his promise to Mrs. Bubb, seeing Greenacre safely out of the house, and making fast the front door again; then he turned in and slept soundly till seven o'clock.

All went well in the morning. The sun shone and

there was a pleasant north-west breeze; in high spirits Gammon mounted the big but light van, which seemed to shout in its brilliancy of red and blue paint.

It was some time since he had had the pleasure of driving a pair. Greenacre had not overpraised the cobs; their start promised an enjoyable day. He was not troubled by any sense of indignity; unfailing humour and a vast variety of experience preserved him from such thoughts. As always he threw himself into the business of the moment with conscientious gusto; he had Saponaria at heart, and was as anxious to advertise the new washing powder as if the profits were all his own. At one spot where a little crowd chanced to gather about the van he delivered an address, a fervid eulogy of Saponaria, declaring his conviction (based on private correspondence) that in a week or two it would be exclusively used in all the laundries of the Royal Family.

At one shop where he was instructed to call he found a little trap waiting, and as he entered there came out a man whom he knew by sight, evidently a traveller, who mounted the trap and drove off. The shopkeeper was in a very disagreeable mood and returned Gammon's greeting roughly.

"Something wrong?" asked Gammon with his wonted cheeriness.

"Saw that chap in the white 'at? I've just told him str'ight that if he comes into this shop again I'll kick 'im. I told him str'ight—see?"

"Did you? I like to hear a man talk like that. It shows there's something in him. Who is the fellow? I seem to remember him somehow."

"Quodlings' traveller. And he's lost them my orders. And I shall write and tell 'em so. I never did like that chap; but when he comes in 'ere, with his white 'at, telling me how to manage my own business, and larfin', yis larfin', why, I've done with him. And I told him str'ight," etc.

"Quodlings', eh?" said Gammon reflectively. "They're likely to be wanting a new traveller, I should say."

"They will if they take my advice," replied the shopkeeper. "And that I shall give 'em, 'ot and strong."

As he drove on Gammon mused over this incident. The oil and colour business was not one of his "specialities," but he knew a good deal about it, and could easily learn what remained. The name of Quodling interested him, being that of the man in the City who so strikingly resembled Mr. Clover; who, moreover, was probably connected in some way with the oil and colour firm. It might be well to keep an eye on Quodlings'—a substantial concern, likely to

A NONDESCRIPT 45

give one a chance of the "permanency" which was, on the whole, desirable.

He had a boy with him to hold the horses, a sharp lad, whose talk gave him amusement when he was tired of thinking. They found a common interest in dogs. Gammon invited the youngster to come and see his "bow-wows" at Dulwich, and promised him his choice out of the litter of bull terriers. With animation he discoursed upon the points of this species of dog — the pure white coat; the long, lean, punishing head, flat above; the breadth behind the ears, the strength of back. He warned his young friend against the wiles of the "faker," who had been known to pipeclay a mottled animal and deceive the amateur. Altogether the day proved so refreshing that Gammon was sorry when its end drew near.

Greenacre was late for his appointment at the stables; he came in a suit of black, imperfectly fitting, and a chimney-pot hat some years old, looking very much like an undertaker's man. His appearance seemed to prove that he really had attended a funeral, which renewed Gammon's wonder. As a matter of course they repaired to the nearest eating-house to have a meal together— an eating-house of the old fashion, known also as a coffee-shop, which Gammon greatly preferred to any kind of restaurant. There, on the narrow seats with high wooden backs, as uncomfortable a sitting as could be desired, with food before him of worse quality and worse cooked than any but English-speaking mortals would endure, he always felt at home, and was pleasantly reminded of the days of his youth, when a supper of eggs and bacon at some such resort rewarded him for a long week's toil and pinching. Sweet to him were the rancid odours, delightfully familiar the dirty knives, the twisted forks, the battered teaspoons, not unwelcome the day's newspaper, splashed with brown coffee and spots of grease. He often lamented that this kind of establishment was growing rare, passing away with so many other features of old London.

More fastidious, Greenacre could have wished his egg some six months fresher, and his drink less obviously a concoction of rinsings. But he was a guest, and his breeding did not allow him to complain. Of the funeral he shrank from speaking; but the few words he dropped were such as would have befitted a genuine grief. Gammon even heard him murmur, unconsciously, "poor Bolsover."

Having eaten they wended their way to a little public-house, with a parlour known only to the favoured few, where Greenacre, after a glass or two of rum—a choice for which he thought it necessary to apologise — began to discourse upon a topic peculiarly his own.

"I couldn't help thinking to-day, Gammon, what a strange assembly there would be if all a man's relatives came to his funeral. Nearly all of us must have such lots of distant connections that we know nothing about. Now a man like Bolsover — an aristocrat, with fifty or more acknowledged relatives in good position—think how many more there must be in out-of-the-way places, poor and unknown. Aye, and some of them not so very distant kinsfolk either. Think of the hosts of illegitimate children, for instance—some who know who they are, and some who don't."

This was said so significantly that Gammon wondered whether it had a personal application.

"It's a theory of mine," pursued the other, his prominent eyes fixed on some far vision, "that every one of us, however poor, has some wealthy relative, if he could only be found. I mean a relative within reasonable limits, not a cousin fifty times removed. That's one of the charms of London to me. A little old man used to cobble my boots for me a few years ago in Ball's Pond Road. He had an idea that one of his brothers, who went out to New Zealand and was no more heard of, had made a great fortune; said he'd dreamt about it again and again, and couldn't get rid of the fancy. Well, now, the house in which he lived took fire, and the poor old chap was burnt in his bed, and so his name got into the newspapers. A day or two after I heard that his brother—the one he spoke of—had been living for some years scarcely a mile away, at Stoke Newington—a man rolling in money, a director of the British and Colonial Bank."

"Rummy go!" remarked Gammon.

"When I was a lad," pursued the other, after sipping at his refilled glass, "I lived just by an old church in the City, and I knew the verger, and he used to let me look over the registers. I think that's what gave me my turn for genealogy. I believe there are fellows who get a living by hunting up pedigrees; that would just suit me, if I only knew how to start in the business."

Gammon looked up and asked abruptly:

"Know anybody called Quodling?"

"Quodling? No one personally. But there's a firm of Quodling, brushmakers or something."

"Oil and colourmen?"

"Yes, to be sure. Quodling? Now I come to think of it—why do you ask?"

"There's a man in the City called Quodling, a silk broker. For private reasons I should like to know something about him."

Greenacre gazed absently at his friend, like one who tries to piece together old memories.

"Lost it," he muttered at length in a discontented tone. "Something about a Mrs. Quodling and a lawsuit—big lawsuit that used to be talked about when I was a boy. My father was a lawyer, you know."

"Was he? It's the first time you ever told me," replied Gammon with a chuckle.

"Nonsense! I must have mentioned it many a time. I've often noticed, Gammon, how very defective your memory is. You should use a mnemonic system. I made a splendid one some years ago; it helped me immensely."

"I could have felt sure," said Gammon, "that you told me once your father was a coal merchant."

"Why, so he was—later on. Am I to understand, Gammon, that you accuse me of distorting facts?"

With the end of his third tumbler there had come upon Greenacre a tendency to maudlin dignity and sensitiveness; he laid a hand on his friend's arm and looked at him with pained reproach.

"Gammon! I was never inclined to mendacity, though I confess to mendicity I have occasionally fallen. To you, Gammon, I could not lie; I respect you, I admire you, in spite of the great distance

between us in education and habits of mind. If
I thought you accused me of falsehood, my dear
Gammon, it would distress me deeply. Assure me
that you don't. I am easily put out to-day. The
death of poor Bolsover—my friend before he succeeded to the title. And that reminds me. But for
a mere accident I might myself at this moment have
borne a title. My mother, before her marriage,
refused the offer of a man who rose to wealth and
honours, and only a year or two ago died a baronet.
Well, well, the chances of life; the accidents of
birth!"

He shook his head for some minutes, murmuring
inarticulate regrets.

"I think I'll just have one more, Gammon."

"I think not, old boy. Where did you say you
lived?"

"Oh, that's all right. Most comfortable lodgings
in the parish of St. Martin's-in-the-Fields. If you
have the slightest doubt of my veracity, leave me,
Gammon; I beg you will leave me. I—in fact,
I have an appointment with a gentleman I met at
poor Bolsover's funeral."

With no little difficulty Gammon led him away,
and by means of an omnibus landed him at length
near St. Martin's Church. No entreaty could induce
the man to give his address. He protested that a
few minutes' walk would bring him home, and as he

seemed to have sobered sufficiently, Gammon left him sitting on the church steps—a strange object in his borrowed suit of mourning and his antiquated top hat.

CHAPTER VI.

THE HEAD WAITER AT CHAFFEY'S

POLLY SPARKES had a father. That Mr. Sparkes still lived was not known to the outer circles of Polly's acquaintance; she never spoke of her family, and it was not easy to think of Polly in the filial relation. For some years she had lived in complete independence, now and then exchanging a letter with her parent, but seeing him rarely. Not that they were on ill terms, unpleasantness of that kind had been avoided by their satisfaction in living apart. Polly sometimes wished she had a father "to be proud of"—a sufficiently intelligible phrase on Polly's lips; but for the rest she thought of him with tolerance as a good, silly sort of man, who "couldn't help himself"—that is to say, could not help being what he was.

And Mr. Sparkes was a waiter, had been a waiter for some thirty years, and would probably pursue the calling as long as he was fit for it. In this fact he saw nothing to be ashamed of. It had never occurred to him that anyone could or should be ashamed of the position; nevertheless, Mr. Sparkes was a dis-

THE HEAD WAITER 53

appointed, even an embittered man; and that for a subtle reason, which did credit to his sensibility.

All his life he had been employed at Chaffey's. As a boy of ten he joined Chaffey's in the capacity of plate washer; zeal and conduct promoted him, and seniority made him at length head-waiter. In those days Chaffey's was an eating-house of the old kind, one long room with "boxes"; beef its staple dish, its drink a sound porter at twopence a pint. How many thousand times had Mr. Sparkes shouted the order "One ally-mode!" The chief, almost the only, variant was "One 'ot!" which signified a cut from the boiled round, served of course with carrots and potatoes, remarkable for their excellence. Mid-day dinner was the only meal recognized at Chaffey's; from twelve to half-past two the press of business kept everyone breathless and perspiring. Before and after these hours little if anything was looked for, and at four o'clock the establishment closed its doors.

But it came to pass that the proprietor of Chaffey's died, and the business fell into the hands of a young man with new ideas. Within a few months Chaffey's underwent a transformation; it was pulled down, rebuilt, enlarged, beautified; nothing left of its old self but the name. In place of the homely eating-house there stood a large hall, painted and gilded and set about with mirrors, furnished with marble tables and cane-bottomed chairs,—to all appearances a restaurant on the Franco-Italian pattern. Yet Chaffey's remained English, flagrantly English, in its viands and its waiters. The new proprietor aimed at combining foreign glitter with the prices and the entertainment acceptable to a public of small means. Moreover, he prospered. The doors were now open from nine o'clock in the morning to twelve at night. There was a bar for the supply of alcoholic drinks—the traditional porter had always been fetched from a neighbouring house—and frivolities such as tea and coffee were in constant demand.

This change told grievously upon Mr. Sparkes. At the first mention of it he determined to resign; but the weakness in his character shrank from such a decided step, and he allowed himself to be drawn into a painfully false position. The proprietor did not wish to lose him. Mr. Sparkes was a slim, upright, grave-featured man, whose deportment had its market value; his side-whiskers and shaven lip gave him a decidedly clerical aspect, which, together with long experience and a certain austerity of command, well fitted him for superintending the younger waiters. His salary was increased, his "tips" represented a much larger income than heretofore. At the old Chaffey's every diner gave him a penny, whilst at the new he often received twopence, and customers were much more numerous. But every copper he pouched cost Mr. Sparkes a pang of

THE HEAD WAITER 55

humiliation; his "thank you, sir," had the urbanity which had become mechanical, but more often than not he sneered inwardly, despising himself and those upon whom he waited.

To one person alone did he exhibit all the bitterness of his feelings, and that was Mrs. Clover, the sister of his deceased wife. With her he occasionally spent a Sunday evening in the parlour behind the china shop, and there would speak the thoughts that oppressed him.

"It isn't that I've any quarrel with the foreign rest'rants, Louisa. They're all right in their way. They suit a certain public, and they charge certain prices. But what I do think is mean and low—mean and low—is to be neither one thing nor the other; to make a sort of show as if you was 'igh-clawss, and then have it known as you're the cheapest of the cheap. Potatoes! That I should live to see Chaffey's 'anding out such potatoes! They're more like food for pigs, and I've known the day when Chaffey's 'ud have thrown 'em at the 'ead of anybody as delivered 'em such offal. It isn't a place for a self-respecting man, and I feel it more and more. If a shopboy wants to take out his sweetheart and make a pretence of doing it grand, where does he go to? Why, to Chaffey's. He couldn't afford a real rest'rant; but Chaffey's looks the same, and Chaffey's is cheap. To hear 'em ordering roast fowl and camumbeer cheese to follow—it fair sickens me. Roast fowl! a old 'en as wouldn't be good enough for a real rest'rant to make inter soup! And the camumbeer! I've got my private idea, Louisa, about what that camumbeer is made of. And when I think of the Cheshire and the Cheddar we used to top up with! It's 'art-breaking."

From a speaker with such a countenance all this was very impressive. Mrs. Clover shook her head and wondered what England was coming to. In return she would tell of the people who came to her shop to hire cups and saucers just to make a show when they had a friend to tea with them. There was much of the right spirit in both these persons, for they sincerely despised shams, though they were not above profiting by the snobberies of others. But Mrs. Clover found amusement in the state of things, whereas Mr. Sparkes grew more despondent the more he talked, and always added with a doleful self-reproach :

"If I'd been half a man I should have left. They'd have taken me on at Simpkin's, I know they would, or at the Old City Chop House, if I'd waited for a vacancy. Who'd take me on now? Why, they'd throw it in my face that I came from Chaffey's, and I shouldn't have half a word to say for myself."

It was very seldom that he received a written

THE HEAD WAITER 57

invitation from his sister-in-law, but he heard from her in these hot days of June that she particularly wished to see him as soon as possible. The message, he thought, must have some reference to Mrs. Clover's husband, whose reappearance at any moment would have been no great surprise, even after an absence of six years. Mr. Sparkes had a strong objection to mysterious persons; he was all for peace and comfort in a familiar routine, and for his own part had often hoped that the man Clover was by this time dead and buried. Responding as soon as possible to Mrs. Clover's summons, he found that she wished to speak to him about his daughter. Mrs. Clover showed herself seriously disturbed by Polly's recent behaviour; she told of the newly-acquired jewellery, of the dresses in which Miss Sparkes went "flaunting," of the girl's scornful refusal to answer natural enquiries.

"The long and the short of it is, Ebenezer, you ought to see her, and find out what's going on. There may be nothing wrong, and I don't say there is; but that watch and chain of hers wasn't bought under twenty pounds—that I'll answer for, and it's a very queer thing, to say the least of it. What business was it of mine, she asked. I shouldn't wonder if she says the same to you; but it's your plain duty to have a talk with her, don't you think so now?"

To have a talk with Polly, especially on such a subject, was no easy or pleasant undertaking for Mr. Sparkes, who had so long resigned all semblance of parental authority. But as a conscientious man he could not stand aside when his only surviving daughter seemed in peril. After an exchange of post cards a meeting took place between them on the Embankment below Waterloo Bridge, for neither father nor child had anything in the nature of a home beyond the indispensable bedroom, and their only chance of privacy was in the open air. Having no desire to quarrel with her parent (it would have been so very one-sided and uninspiriting) Polly began in a conciliatory tone.

"Aunt Louisa's been making a bother, has she? Just like her. Don't you listen to her fussicking, dad. What's all the row about? I've had a present given to me; well, what of that? You can look at it for yourself. I can't tell you who give it me, 'cos I've promised I wouldn't; but you'll know some day, and then you'll larff. It ain't nothing to fret your gizzard about; so there. I'm old enough to look after myself, and if I ain't I never shall be; so there."

This did not satisfy Mr. Sparkes. He saw that the watch and chain were certainly valuable, and he could not imagine how the girl had become honourably possessed of them, save as the gift of an

THE HEAD WAITER 59

admirer; but the mere fact of such an admirer's exacting secrecy implied a situation of danger.

"I don't like the look of it, Polly," he remarked, with a nervous attempt to be severe.

"All right, dad; then don't like the look of it. The watch is good enough for me."

It took Mr. Sparkes two or three minutes to understand this joke. Whilst he was reflecting upon it a thought suddenly passed through his mind, which startled him by its suggestiveness.

"Polly!"

"Well?"

"It ain't your uncle Clover, is it?"

The girl laughed loudly as if at a preposterous question.

"Him? Why, I've as good as forgot there was such a man! What do you mean? Why, I shouldn't know him if I saw him. What made you think of that?"

"Oh, I don't know. Who knows when and where he may turn up, or what he'll do?"

"That's a good 'un! My uncle Clover indeed! Whatever put that into your 'ead?"

Her ejaculations of wonder and disdain continued until the close of the interview, and Mr. Sparkes went his way, convinced that Polly was being pursued by some wealthy man, probably quite unprincipled—the kind of man who frequents "proper rest'rants" and sits in the stalls at "theaytres," where, doubtless, Polly had made his acquaintance. After brooding a day or two on this idea he procured a sheet of the cheapest note-paper and sat down in his bedroom, high up at Chaffey's, to compose a letter for his daughter's behoof.

"DEAR POLLY,

"I write you these few lines to say that the more I think about you and your way of carrying on the less I like the look of it, and the sooner I make that plain to you the better for both of us, and I'm sure you'll think the same. You are that strong-headed, my girl; but listen to the warnings of experience, who have seen a great deal of the wicked world, and cannot hope to see much more of it at my present age. There will come a day when you will wish that you could hear of me by a note to Chaffey's, but such will not be. Before it's too late I take up the pen to say these few words, which is this: I have always been a respectable and a saving man, which I hope to be until I am no more. What I mean to say is this, Chaffey's is not what it used to be. But I have laid by, and when it comes to the solemn hour then Mr. Walker has promised to make my will. All I want to say is that there may be more than you think for, and if you are respectable I think it most likely all will be yours. But listen to this, if you disgrace yourself, my girl, not one halfpenny nor yet one sixpennypiece will you receive from

"Your affectionate father,
"EBENEZER SPARKES.

"P.S.—This is wrote in a very serious mind."

THE HEAD WAITER 61

This epistle at once pleased and angered Polly. Though a greedy, she was not a mercenary young woman; she had little cunning, and her vulgar ambitions were consistent with a good deal of honest feeling. To do her justice, she had never considered the possibility that her father might have money to bequeath; his disclosure surprised her, and caused her to reflect for the first time that Chaffey's head-waiter had long held a tolerably lucrative position, whilst his expenses must have been trivial; so much the better for her. On the other hand, she strongly resented his suspicions and warnings. In the muddled obscurity of Polly's consciousness there was a something which stood for womanly pride. She knew very well what dangers perpetually surrounded her, and she contrasted herself with the girls who weakly, or recklessly, threw themselves away. Divided thus between injury and gratitude she speedily answered her father's letter, writing upon a sheet of scented grass-green note-paper, deeply ribbed, which made her pen blot, splutter, and sprawl far more than it would have done on a smooth surface.

"Dear Dad,

"In reply to yours, what I have to say is, Aunt Louisa and Mrs. Bubb are nasty cats, and I don't thank them for making a bother. It is very kind of you about your will, though I'm sure, if you believe me, I don't want not yet to see you in your grave; and what I do think is, you might have a better opinion of your daughter, and not think all the bad things you can turn your mind to. And if it is me that dies first, you will be sorry for the wrong you done me. So I will say no more, dear dad.

"From your loving
"POLLY."

CHAPTER VII.

POLLY'S WRATH

POLLY posted her letter on the way to the theatre. This evening she had a private engagement for ten o'clock, and on setting forth to the appointed place she looked carefully about her to make sure that no one watched or followed her. Christopher Parish was not the only young man who had a habit of standing to wait for her at the theatre door. Upon him she could lay her commands with some assurance that they would be observed, but others were less submissive, and at times had given her trouble. To be sure, she could always get rid of importunate persons by the use of her special gift, that primitive sarcasm which few cared to face for more than a minute or two; but with admirers Polly wished to be as far as possible gracious, never coming to extremities with one of them until she was quite certain that she thoroughly disliked him. Finding the coast clear (which after all slightly disappointed her) she walked sharply into another street, where she hailed a passing hansom, and was driven to Lincoln's Inn Fields.

Here, on the quiet pavement shadowed by the College of Surgeons, she lingered in expectancy. Ten was striking, but she looked in vain for the figure she would recognize—that of a well-dressed, middle-aged man, with a white silk comforter about his neck, and drawn up so as to hide his mouth. Twice she had met him here, and on each occasion he was waiting for her when she arrived. Five minutes passed—ten minutes. She grew very impatient and, as a necessary consequence, very angry. To avoid unpleasant attention from the few people who walked by, she had to pace backwards and forwards as if going about her business. When the clocks chimed the first quarter Polly was in a turmoil of anger, blended with disappointment and apprehension. She could not have made a mistake. The message she had received was "W. S. T.," which meant "Wednesday same time." Some accident must have interfered. At twenty minutes past ten she had lost all hope. She must go home, and wait for a possible communication on the morrow.

Swinging her skirts, clenching her fists, and talking silently at a great rate, she walked in the direction of Chancery Lane. At a corner someone going in the opposite direction caught sight of her and stopped.

POLLY'S WRATH

Polly was so preoccupied that she would not have noticed the figure had it merely passed; by stopping it drew her attention, and she beheld Christopher Parish.

"Why, Miss Sparkes!"

He held out his hand, but to no purpose. Polly had her eyes fixed upon him, and they flashed with hostility.

"What do you mean by it?"

"Mean by what?"

The young man was astonished; his hand dropped, and he trembled before her.

"How dare you spy after me? Nasty little wretch!"

"Spy after you, Miss Sparkes? Why, I hadn't the least idea of anything of the kind; I swear I hadn't! I was just taking a walk——"

"Oh, yes! Of course! You're always taking a walk, aren't you? And you always come just this way 'cause it's nice and convenient for Lambeth Road, ain't it? I've a good mind to call a p'liceman and give you in charge for stopping me in the street!"

"Well, did ever anybody hear such a thing as this?" exclaimed Mr. Parish, faint in voice and utterly at a loss for protestations at all effective. "I tell you I was only taking a walk—that's to say, I've been with a friend."

"A friend? Oh, yes, of course. What friend?"

"It's somebody you don't know; his name——"

"Oh, of course, I don't know him! And I don't know you either after to-night, so just remember that, Mr. Parish. The idea! If I can't take two steps without being followed and spied upon! And you call yourself a gentleman. Get out of my way, please. If you want to follow and spy, you're quite at liberty to do so. P'r'aps it'll ease your nasty little mind. Don't talk to me! What business have you got to stop me in the street, I'd like to know? If you're not careful I shall send a complaint to your employers, and then you'll have plenty of time to go taking walks."

She turned from him and pursued her way, but not so quickly as before. Christopher, limp with misery, tried to move off in another direction, but in spite of himself he was drawn after her. By Chancery Lane and along the Strand he kept her in sight, often with difficulty, for he durst not draw nearer than some twenty yards. At Charing Cross she stopped, and by her movements showed that she was looking for an omnibus. Parish longed to approach, quivered with the ever-recurrent impulse, but his fear prevailed. In a more lucid state of mind he would probably have remarked that Polly allowed a great many omnibuses to go by, and that she was surely waiting much longer than she need have done. But

POLLY'S WRATH 67

at length she jumped in and disappeared, whereupon Mr. Parish spent all the money he had with him on a large brandy and soda, hoping it would make him drunk.

The door of the house in Kennington Road stood open; in the passage Mr. Gammon and Mr. Cheeseman were conversing genially. They nodded to Polly, but did not speak. Passing them to the head of the kitchen stairs she called to Mrs. Bubb, and that lady's voice summoned her to descend.

"Are you alone?" asked Miss Sparkes sharply.

"There's only Mrs. Cheeseman."

Polly went down into the kitchen, where Mrs. Cheeseman, a stout woman of slatternly appearance, was sitting with her legs crossed and a plate of shrimps in her lap.

"Have a srimp, Polly?" began Mrs. Bubb, anxious to dismiss the memory of recent discord.

"Thank you, Mrs. Bubb, if I have a fancy for srimps I can afford to buy them for myself."

"Well, you *are* nasty! Ain't she real obstropolous, Mrs. Cheeseman? I never knew a nastier tempered girl in all my life, that I never did. There's actially no living with her."

"Now set down, Polly," urged the stout woman in an unctuous voice. "Set down, do, an' tike things easy. You'll worrit your sweet self to death before you're many years older if you go on like this."

"I'm much obliged to you, Mrs. Cheeseman," answered Polly, holding herself very stiff; "but I didn't come here to set down, nor to talk neither. But I'm glad you're here, because you'll be a witness to what I say. I've come to give Mrs. Bubb a week's notice. She's often enough told me that she wants to keep her house respectable, and I'm sure she'll be glad to get rid of people as don't suit her. It's the first time I was ever told that I disgraced a 'ouse, and I hope it'll be the last time too. When I pay my rent to-morrow morning you'll please to understand, Mrs. Bubb, that I've given a week's notice. I may be a disgrace, but I daresay there's people as won't be ashamed to let me a room. And that's what I came to say, and now I've said it, and Mrs. Cheeseman is a witness."

This was spoken so rapidly that it left Polly breathless and with a very high colour. The elder women looked at each other, and Mrs. Cheeseman, with a shrimp in her mouth, resumed the attempt at pacification.

"Now, see 'ere, Polly. You're a young gyell, my dear, and a 'andsome gyell, as we all know, and you've only one fault, which there ain't no need to mention it. And we're all fond of you, Polly, that's the fact. Ain't we all fond of her, Mrs. Bubb?"

POLLY'S WRATH 69

"Oh, yes, she's very fond of me!" exclaimed the girl. "And so is my Aunt Louisa. And to show it they go telling everybody that I ain't respectable, that I'm a disgrace to a decent 'ouse. D'you think I'll stand it?" Of a sudden she changed from irony to fierceness. "What do you mean by it, Mrs. Bubb? Did you never hear of people being prosecuted for taking away people's characters? Just you mind what you're about, Mrs. Bubb. I give you fair warning, and that's all I have to say to you."

Having relieved her feelings with these and a few more verbal missiles, Polly ran up the kitchen steps. In the passage the two men were still conversing; at sight of Polly they stopped with an abruptness which did not escape her observation. No doubt, she said to herself, they had been talking about her. No doubt, too, they had their reasons for letting her go by as before without a word. Only when she was half-way up the first flight of stairs did Mr. Cheeseman call to her a "Goodnight, Miss Sparkes," to which she made no reply whatever.

On the morrow she called at the little stationer's shop, but no letter awaited her. She decided to be again at the rendezvous that evening, lest there should have been some mistake in her cipher message; but she lingered near the College of

Surgeons in vain. Polly's heart sank as she went home, for to-night there was no one to quarrel with. Mrs. Bubb and all the lodgers had shown that they meant to hold aloof, not even Moggie would look at her or speak a word. It was quite an unprecedented state of things, and Polly found it disagreeable.

There was only one consolation, and that a poor one. She had received a letter from Christopher Parish, a letter of abject remonstrance and entreaty. He grovelled at her feet. He talked frantically of poison and the river. If she would but meet him and hear him in his own defence! And Polly, quite meaning to do so, gave herself the pleasure of appearing obdurate for a couple of days.

At the theatre she examined every row of spectators in stalls and dress-circle, having her own reason for thinking that she might discover a certain face. But no such fortune befell her, and still no letter came.

At home she suffered increasing discomfort. For one thing she had to seek her meals in the nearest coffee-shop instead of going down into Mrs. Bubb's kitchen and gossiping as she ate at the family deal table, amid the dirt and disorder which custom had made pleasant. When in the house she locked herself in her bedroom, reading the kind of print that interested her, or lying in sullen idleness on

POLLY'S WRATH

the bed. Numerous as were her acquaintances elsewhere, they did not compensate her for the loss of domestic habit. As the week drew on she bethought herself that she must look for new lodgings. In giving notice to Mrs. Bubb she had not believed for a moment that it would come to this; she felt sure that her old friend would make up the quarrel and persuade her to stay. Nothing of the kind; for once she was taken most literally at her word. There were moments when Polly felt disposed to cry.

It vexed her much more than she would have thought to miss the jocose greetings of her neighbour, Mr. Gammon. As usual he sang in his bedroom of a morning, as usual he shouted orders and questions to Moggie, but for her he had never a word. She listened for him as he came out of the room, and once so far humbled herself as to affect a cough in his hearing. Mr. Gammon paid no attention.

Then she raged at him—of course, *sotto voce*. Many were the phrases of abuse softly hurled at him as he passed her door. The worst of it was that none of them seemed really applicable; her vision of the man defeated all such contumely. She had never disliked Mr. Gammon; oddly enough she seemed to think of him with a more decided friendliness now that his conduct demanded her enmity. She asked herself whether he really believed any harm of her. It looked very much as if he did, and the thought sometimes kept her awake for fully a quarter of an hour.

It was the last day but one of her week. To-morrow she must either submit to the degradation of begging Mrs. Bubb's leave to remain, or pack her boxes and have them removed before nightfall. Worry had ended by giving her a slight headache, a very rare thing indeed. Moreover, it rained, and breakfast was only obtainable by walking some distance.

"Oh, the beasts!" Polly exclaimed to herself, as she pulled on her boots, meaning the inhabitants of the house all together.

Mr. Gammon opened his door and shouted down the staircase.

"Moggie! Fry me three eggs this morning with the bacon—do you hear?"

Three eggs! Fried with bacon! And all comfortably set out at the end of the kitchen table. And to think that she might be going down to breakfast at the same time, with Mr. Gammon's jokes for a relish!

"Oh, the wretches! The mean, selfish brutes!"

She stamped about the floor to ease her nerves as she put on a common hat and an old jacket. She

POLLY'S WRATH

unlocked her door with violence, banged it open, and slammed it to again. From the staircase window she saw that the rain was falling more heavily, and she could not wait, for she felt hungry—after hearing about those three eggs. If she met anyone down below!

And, as chance had it, she met Mrs. Cheeseman just coming up to her room from the kitchen with a dish of sausages. The woman grinned and turned her head away. Polly had never been so tempted to commit an assault; she thought with a burning brain how effective would be one smart stroke on the dish of sausages with the handle of her umbrella.

Still hot from this encounter in the passage she came face to face with Mrs. Bubb. The landlady seemed to hesitate, but before Polly had gone by she addressed her with exaggerated politeness.

"Good morning, Miss Sparkes. So I s'pose we're losing you to-morrow?"

"Yes, you are," Polly replied, from a parched throat, glaring at her enemy.

"Oh, then I'll put the card up!"

"Do! I wouldn't lose no time about it. And listen to this, Mrs. Bubb. Next time you see your friend Mrs. Clover, you may tell her that if she wants to know where her precious 'usband is she's not to ask *me*, 'cos I wouldn't let her know, not if she was on her death-bed!"

Having uttered this surprising message, with point and emphasis worthy of its significance, Polly hastened from the house. And Mrs. Bubb stood looking after her in bewilderment.

CHAPTER VIII.

MR. GAMMON'S RESOLVE

CONVINCED that his life was blighted, Mr. Gammon sang and whistled with more than usual vivacity as he dressed each morning. It was not in his nature to despond; he had received many a knock-down blow, and always came up fresher after it. Mrs. Clover's veto upon his tender hopes with regard to Minnie had not only distressed, but greatly surprised him; for during the last few months he had often said to himself that, whether Minnie favoured his suit or not, her mother's goodwill was a certainty. His advances had been of the most delicate, no word of distinct wooing had passed his lips; but he thought of Minnie a great deal, and came to the decision that in her the hopes of his life were centred. It might be that Minnie had no inkling of his intentions; she was so modest, so unlike the every-day girls who tittered and ogled with every marriageable man; on that very account he had made her his ideal. And Mrs. Clover would help him as a mother best knows how. The shock of learning that Mrs. Clover would do no such thing utterly confused his mind. He still longed for Minnie, yet seemed of a sudden hopelessly remote from her. He could not determine whether he had given her up or not; he did not know whether to bow before Mrs. Clover, or to protest and persevere. He liked Mrs. Clover far too much to be angry with her; he respected Minnie far too much to annoy her by an unwelcome courtship; he wished, in fact, that he had not made a fool of himself that evening, and wanted things to be as they were before.

In the meantime he occupied himself in looking out for a new engagement. Plenty were to be had, but he aimed at something better than had satisfied him hitherto. He must get a "permanency"; at his age it was time he settled into a life of respectable routine. But for his foolish habit of living from hand to mouth, now in this business, now in that, indulging his taste for variety, Mrs. Clover would never, he felt sure, have "put her foot down" in that astonishing way. The best thing he could do was to show himself in a new light.

Thanks to his good nature, his practicality, and the multitude of his acquaintances, all manner of shiftless or luckless fellows were in the habit of looking to him for advice and help. As soon

MR. GAMMON'S RESOLVE 77

as they found themselves adrift they turned to Gammon. Every day he had a letter asking him to find a "berth" or a "billet" for some out-at-elbows friend, and in a surprising number of cases he was able to make a useful suggestion. It would have paid him to start an employment agency; as it was, instead of receiving fees, he very often supplied his friends' immediate necessities out of his own pocket. The more he earned the more freely he bestowed, so that his occasional strokes of luck in commerce were of no ultimate benefit to him. No man in his position had a larger credit, for weeks at a time he could live without cash expenditure; but this was seldom necessary.

By a mental freak which was characteristic of him he nursed the thought of connecting himself with Messrs. Quodling and Son, oil and colour merchants. Theirs was a large and sound business, both in town and country. It might not be easy to become traveller to such a firm, but his ingenious mind tossed and turned the possibilities of the case, and after a day or two spent in looking up likely men—which involved a great deal of drinking in a great variety of public resorts—he came across an elderly traveller who had represented Quodlings on a northern circuit, and who boasted a certain acquaintance with Quodling the senior. Thus were things set in train. At a second meeting with the venerable bagman—who had a wonderful head for whisky—Gammon acquired so much technical information, that oil and colours might fairly be set down among his numerous "specialities." Moreover, his friend promised to speak a word for him in the right quarter when opportunity offered.

"By the way," Gammon remarked carelessly, "are these Quodlings any relation to Quodling the silk broker in the City?"

His companion smiled over the rim of a deep tumbler, and continued to smile through a long draught.

"Why do you ask?"

"No particular reason. Happen to know the other man—by sight."

"They're brothers — Quodling senior and the broker."

"What's the joke?" asked Gammon, as the other still smiled.

"Old joke—very old joke. The two men just as unlike as they could be—in face, I mean. I never took the trouble to enquire about it, but I've been told there was a lawsuit years ago, something to do with the will of Lord somebody, who left money to old Mrs. Quodling—who wasn't old then. Don't know the particulars, but I'm told that something turned on the likeness of the younger boy to the man who made the will—see?"

MR. GAMMON'S RESOLVE 79

"Ah! Oh!" muttered Gammon reflectively.

"An uppish, high-notioned fellow, Quodling the broker. Won't have anything to do with his brother. He's nothing much himself; went through the court not very long ago."

Gammon promised himself to look into this story when he had time. That it could in any way concern him he did not seriously suppose, but he liked to track things out. Some day he would have another look at Quodling the broker, who so strongly resembled Mrs. Clover's husband. Both of them, it seemed, bore a likeness to some profligate aristocrat. Just the kind of thing to interest that queer fish Greenacre.

In the height of the London season nothing pleased Gammon more than to survey the streets from an omnibus. Being just now a man of leisure he freely indulged himself, spending an hour or two each day in the liveliest thoroughfares. It was a sure way of forgetting his cares. Sometimes he took a box place and chatted with the driver, or he made acquaintances, male and female, on the cosy cross seats just broad enough for two. The London panorama under a sky of June feasted his laughing eyes. Now he would wave a hand to a friend on the pavement or borne past on another 'bus; now he would chuckle at a bit of comedy in real life. Huge hotels and brilliant shops vividly impressed

him, though he saw them for the thousandth time;
a new device in advertising won his ungrudging
admiration. Above all he liked to find himself in
the Strand at that hour of the day when east and
west show a double current of continuous traffic,
tight wedged in the narrow street, moving at a mere
footpace, every horse's nose touching the back of the
next vehicle. The sun could not shine too hotly;
it made colours brighter, gave a new beauty to the
glittering public-houses, where names of cooling
drinks seemed to cry aloud. He enjoyed a "block,"
and was disappointed unless he saw the policeman
at Wellington Street holding up his hand whilst the
cross traffic from north and south rolled grandly
through. It always reminded him of the Bible story
—Moses parting the waters of the Red Sea.

He was in the full enjoyment of this spectacle
when an odour of cloves breathed across his face, and
a voice addressed him.

"Isn't that you, Mr. Gammon? Well, if I didn't
think so!"

The speaker was a young woman, who, with a
male companion, had just mounted the 'bus and
seated herself at Gammon's back. Facing round
he recognized her as a friend of Polly Sparkes, Miss
Waghorn by name, who adorned a refreshment bar
at the theatre where Polly sold programmes. With
a marked display of interesting embarrassment Miss

MR. GAMMON'S RESOLVE

Waghorn introduced him to her companion, Mr. Nibby, who showed himself cordial.

"I've often heard talk of you, Mr. Gammon; glad to meet you, sir. I think it's Berlin wools, isn't it?"

"Well, it was, sir, but it's been fancy leather goods lately, and now it's going to be something else. You are the Gillingwater burners, I believe, sir?"

Mr. Nibby betrayed surprise.

"And may I ask you how you know that?"

"Oh, I've a good memory for faces. I travelled with you on the Underground not very long ago, and saw the name on some samples you had."

"Now, that's what I call smart observation, Carrie," said the Gillingwater burners, beaming upon Miss Waghorn.

"Oh, we all know that Mr. Gammon's more than seven," replied the young lady with a throaty laugh, and her joke was admirably received.

"Business good, sir?" asked Gammon.

"Not bad for the time of year, sir. Is it true, do you know, that Milligan of Bishopsgate has burst up?"

"I heard so yesterday; not surprised; business very badly managed. Great shame, too, for I know he got it very cheap, and there was a fortune in it. Two years ago I could have bought the whole concern for a couple of thousand."

"You don't say so!"

Mr. Gammon was often heard to remark that he could have bought this, that, or the other thing for something paltry, such as a couple of thousands. It was not idle boasting, such opportunities had indeed come in his way, and, with his generous optimism, he was content to ignore the fact that only the money was wanting.

"What's wrong with Polly Sparkes?" enquired the young lady presently, again sending a waft of cloves into Gammon's face.

"That's what I want to know," he answered facetiously.

"She's awful cut up about something. I thought you was sure to know what it was, Mr. Gammon. She says a lot of you has been using her shimeful."

"Oh, she does, does she?"

"You should hear her talk! Now it's her landlydy—now it's her awnt—now it's I don't know who. To hear her—she's been used shimeful. She says she's been drove out of the 'ouse. I didn't think it of *you*, Mr. Gammon."

At the moment the 'bus was drawing slowly near to a popular wine-shop. Mr. Nibby whispered to Miss Waghorn, who dropped her eyes and looked demure; whereupon he addressed Gammon.

"What do you say to a glass of dry sherry, sir?"

"Right you are, sir!"

MR. GAMMON'S RESOLVE 83

So the omnibus was stopped to allow Miss Waghorn to alight, and all three turned into the wine-shop. Dry sherry not being to Miss Waghorn's taste she chose sweet port, drinking it as one to the manner born, and talking the while in hoarse whispers, with now and then an outburst of shrill laughter. The dark narrow space before the counter or bar was divided off with wooden partitions as at a pawnbroker's; each compartment had a high stool for the luxuriously inclined, and along the wall ran a bare wooden bench. Not easily could a less inviting place of refreshment have been constructed; but no such thought occurred to its frequenters, who at this hour were numerous. Squeezed together in a stifling atmosphere of gas and alcohol, with nothing to look at but the row of great barrels whence the wine was drawn, these merry folk quenched their midsummer thirst and gave their wits a jog, and drank good fellowship with merciless ill-usage of the Queen's English. Miss Waghorn talked freely of Polly Sparkes, repeating all the angry things that Polly had said, and persistingly wanting to know what the "bother" was all about.

"It's for her own good," said Gammon with significant brevity.

He did not choose to say more or to ask any questions which might turn to Polly's disadvantage. For his own part he seldom gave a thought to the girl, and was far from imagining that she cared whether he kept on friendly terms with her or not. At his landlady's suggestion he had joined in the domestic plot for sending Polly "to Coventry"—a phrase, by-the-bye, which would hardly have been understood in Mrs. Bubb's household; he argued that it might do her good, and that in any case some such demonstration was called for by her outrageous temper. If Polly could not get on with people who were sincerely her friends and had always wished her well, let her go elsewhere and exercise her ill-humour on strangers. Gammon did not believe that she would go; day after day he expected to hear that the quarrel was made up, and that Polly had cleared her reputation by a few plain words.

But this was the last day save one of Polly's week, and as yet she had given no sign. On coming down into the kitchen to discuss his fried eggs and bacon he saw at once that Mrs. Bubb was seriously perturbed; with huffings and cuffings—a most unusual thing—she had just despatched her children to school, and was now in conflict with Moggie about a broken pie-dish, which the guilty general had concealed in the back-yard. A prudent man in the face of such tempers, Gammon sat down without speaking, and fell to on the viands which Mrs. Bubb—also silent—set before him. In

MR. GAMMON'S RESOLVE 85

a minute or two, having got rid of Moggie and closed the kitchen door, Mrs. Bubb came near and addressed him in a subdued voice.

"What d'you think? It's her uncle! It's Clover!"

"Eh? What is?"

"Why, it's him as 'as been giving her things."

"Has she said so?" asked Gammon, with eager interest.

"I met her as she was coming down just now and she was in a tearin' rage, and she says to me, she says, 'When you see my awnt,' she says, 'you tell her I know all about her 'usband, and that I wouldn't tell *her* anything not if she went down on her bended knees! There now!'"

The uneducated man may perchance repeat with exactness something that has been said to him, or in his hearing; for the uneducated woman such accuracy is impossible. Mrs. Bubb meant to be strictly truthful, but in the nature of things she would have gone astray, even had Polly's message taken a much simpler form than wrathful sarcasm gave to it. However, she conveyed the spirit of Polly's words, and Gammon was so excited by the report that he sprang up, overturning his cup of coffee.

"Oh, cuss it! Never mind; most's gone on to my trousers. She said that? And to think we never thought of it! Where is she? When'll she be back?"

"I don't know. But she says she's going to leave to-morrow, and looks as if she meant it, too. Hadn't I better send to Mrs. Clover?"

Gammon reflected.

"I tell you what, send and ask her to come here to-night; say it's very important. We'll have them face to face, by jorrocks, we will!"

"Polly mayn't be 'ome before half-past ten or eleven."

"Never mind. I tell you we'll have them face to face. If it comes to that, I'll pay for a cab for Mrs. Clover to go home in. Tell her to be here at eight. Stop. You mustn't have the trouble; I can very well go round myself. Yes, I'll go myself and arrange it."

"It may be a lie," remarked Mrs. Bubb.

"So it may be, but somehow I don't think so. The rummiest thing that that never came into my head! I shouldn't be a bit surprised if Clover ain't living in Belgrave Square, or some such place. Just the kind of thing that happens with these mysterious Johnnies. She'll have come across him somewhere, and he's bribed her to keep it dark—see? What a gooseberry I was never to think of it! We'll have 'em face to face!"

"Suppose Polly won't?"

"Won't? Gosh, but she *shall!* If I have to carry her downstairs, she shall! Think we're going to let her keep a thing like this to herself? You just wait and see. Leave it to me, that's all. Lucky there's only friends in the house. Polly likes a row, and by jorrocks she shall have one!"

CHAPTER IX.

POLLY'S DEFIANCE

CONTENT with her four lodgers, Mrs. Bubb reserved the rooms on the ground floor for her own use. In that at the back she slept with the two younger children; the other two had a little bed in the front room, which during the day-time served as a parlour. On occasions of ceremony —when the parlour was needed in the evening—the children slept in a bare attic next to that occupied by Moggie; and this they looked upon as a treat, for it removed them from their mother's observation, and gave opportunities for all sorts of adventurous pranks.

Thus were things arranged for to-night. Mrs. Bubb swept and garnished her parlour for the becoming reception of a visitor whom she could not but "look up to." Mrs. Clover's origin was as humble as her own, and her education not much better, but natural gifts and worldly circumstances had set a distance between them. Partly, perhaps,

POLLY'S DEFIANCE 89

because she was the widow of a police constable Mrs. Bubb gave all due weight to social distinctions; she knew her "place," and was incapable of presuming. With Polly Sparkes she did not hesitate to use freedom, for Polly could not pretend to be on a social level with her aunt, and as a young girl of unformed character, naturally owed deference to an experienced matron who took a kindly interest in her.

There had been some question of inviting Mr. Sparkes, but Mr. Gammon spoke against it. No; let Polly have a fair chance, first of all, of unbosoming herself before her aunt and her landlady. If she refused to do so, why then other steps must be taken.

Gammon passed the day in high spirits, which, with the aid of seasonable beverages, tended to hilarious excitement. The thing was going to be as good as a play. In his short dialogue with Mrs. Clover he withheld from her the moving facts of the case, telling her only that her niece was going to quit Mrs. Bubb's, and that it behoved her to assist in a final appeal to the girl's better feelings. His own part in the affair was merely, he explained, that of a messenger, sent to urge the invitation. Mrs. Clover willingly consented to come. Not a word passed between them with reference to their last conversation, but Mr. Gammon made it plain that he nursed no resentment, and the lady of the china shop behaved very amicably indeed.

At six o'clock Polly came home to dress for the theatre. She left again, having spoken to no one. Soon afterwards Gammon, who in fact had watched for her departure, entered the house and held a conversation with Mrs. Bubb in the parlour, where already the table was laid for supper at half-past eight. Scarcely had eight struck when Mrs. Clover, who had alighted from an omnibus, sounded her pleasant rat-tat—self-respecting, and such as did credit to the house, but with no suggestion of arrogance. As her habit was she kissed Mrs. Bubb—a very kindly and gracious thing to do. She asked after the children, and was sorry she could not see them. In her attire Mrs. Clover preserved the same happy medium as in her way of plying the knocker; it was sufficiently elaborate to show consideration for her hostess, yet not so grand as to overwhelm by contrast. She looked, indeed, so pleasant, and so fresh, and so young that it was as difficult to remember the troubles of her life as it was to bear in mind that she had a daughter seventeen years of age. Mr. Gammon, who made up a trio at the supper table, put on his best behaviour. It might perhaps have been suspected that he had quenched his thirst more often than was needful on a day of showers and falling temperature, but at supper he drank only two

POLLY'S DEFIANCE

glasses of mild ale, and casually remarked, as he poured out the second, that he had serious thoughts of becoming a total abstainer.

"You might do worse than that," said Mrs. Clover meaningly, but with good nature.

"You think so? Say the word, Mrs. Clover, and I'll do it."

"I shan't say the word, because I know you couldn't live without a glass of beer. There's no harm in that. But when——"

The remark was left incomplete.

"Hush!" came from Mrs. Bubb in the same moment. "Wasn't that the front door?"

All listened. A heavy step was ascending the stairs.

"Only Mr. Cheeseman," said the landlady with a sigh of agitation. "Of course it couldn't be Polly yet."

Not till the repast was comfortably despatched did Mr. Gammon give a sign that it might now be well to inform Mrs. Clover of what had happened. He nodded gravely to Mrs. Bubb, who with unaffected nervousness, causing her to ramble and stumble for many minutes in mazes of circumlocution, at length conveyed the fact to her anxious listener that Polly Sparkes had said something or other which implied a knowledge of Mr. Clover's whereabouts. Committed to this central fact, and urged by Mrs. Clover's growing impatience, the good woman came out at length with her latest version of Polly's remarkable utterance.

"And what she said was this, Mrs. Clover. When next you goes tale-telling to my awnt, she says—just as nasty as she could—when next you goes making trouble with my Awnt Louisa, she says, you can tell her, she says, that there's nobody but me knows where her 'usband is, and what he's a-doin' of; but I wouldn't let *her* know, she says, not if it was to save her from death and burial in the workus! That's what Polly said to me this very morning, and the words made that impression on my mind that I shall never forget them to the last day of my life."

"Did you ever!" exclaimed or rather murmured Mrs. Clover, for she was astonished and agitated. Her face lost its wholesome tone for a moment, her hands moved as if to repel something, and at length she sat quite still gazing at Mrs. Bubb.

"And don't you think it queer," put in Mr. Gammon, "that we never hit on that?"

"I'm sure I should never have thought of such a thing," replied Mrs. Clover heavily, despondently.

"And who knows," cried Mrs. Bubb, "whether it's true after all? Polly's been that nasty, how if she's made it up just to spite us?"

Mrs. Clover nodded, and seemed to find relief.

"I shouldn't a bit wonder. How should Polly

know about him? It seems to me a most unlikely thing, the most unlikely thing I ever heard of. I shall never believe it till she's proved her words. I won't believe it—I can't believe it—never!"

Her voice rose on tremulous notes, her eyes wandered disdainfully. She looked at Gammon and immediately looked away again. He, as though in answer to an appeal, spoke with decision.

"What we're here for, Mrs. Clover, is to put Polly face to face with you and so get the truth out of her. That we will do, cost what it may. We're not going to have that girl making trouble and disturbance just to please herself. I don't want to poke myself into other people's business, and I'm sure you won't think I do."

"Of course not, Mr. Gammon. 'Tain't likely I should think so of you."

'You know me better. I was just going to say that I'm a man of business, and perhaps I can help to clear up this job in a business-like way. That's what I'm here for. If I didn't think I could be of some use to you I should make myself scarce. What I propose is this, Mrs. Clover. When Polly comes in—never mind how late it is, I'll see you safe 'ome— let her get upstairs just as usual. Then you go up to her door and you knock and you just say, 'Polly, it's me, and I want a word with you; let me come in, please?' If she lets you in, all right; have a talk and see what comes of it. If she won't let you in just come down again and let us know, and then we'll think what's to be done next."

This suggestion was approved, and time went on as the three discussed the mystery from every point of view. At about ten o'clock Mrs. Bubb's ear caught the sound of a latch-key at the front door. She started up, her companions did the same. By opening the door of the parlour an inch or two it was ascertained that a person had entered the house and gone quickly upstairs. This could only be Polly, for Mr. and Mrs. Cheeseman were together in their sitting-room above, their voices audible from time to time.

"Now then, Mrs. Clover," said Gammon, "up you go. Don't be nervous; it's only Polly Sparkes, and she's more call to be afraid of you than you of her."

"I should think so, indeed," assented Mrs. Bubb. "Don't give way, my dear. Whatiever you do, don't give way. I'm sure I feel for you. It's fair crool, it is."

Mrs. Clover said nothing, and made a great effort to command herself. Her friends escorted her to the foot of the stairs. Mr. and Mrs. Cheeseman had their door ajar, knowing well what was in progress, for the landlady had not been able to keep her counsel at such a dramatic crisis; but fortunately Mrs. Clover was unaware of this. With light, quick foot she mounted the flight of stairs and knocked softly at Polly's door.

"Well? Who's that?" sounded in a careless voice.

"It's me, Polly—your Aunt Louisa. Will you let me come in?"

"What do you want?"

The tone of the enquiry was not encouraging, and Mrs. Clover delayed a moment before she spoke again.

"I want to speak to you, Polly," she said at length, with firmness. "You know what it's about. Let me come in, please."

"I've got nothing to say to you about anything," answered Polly, in a tone of unmistakable decision "You're only wasting your time, and the sooner you go 'ome the better."

She spoke near to the door, and with her last word sharply turned the key. Only just in time, for Mrs. Clover was that moment trying the handle when she heard the excluding snap. Natural feeling so much prevailed with her that she gave the door a shake, whereat her niece laughed.

"You're a bad, wicked, deceitful girl!" exclaimed Mrs. Clover hotly. "I don't believe a word you said, not a word! You're going to the bad as fast as ever you can, and you know it, and you don't care, and I'm sure I don't care! Somebody ought to box your ears soundly, miss. I wouldn't have such a temper as yours not for untold money. And when you want a friend, and haven't a penny in the world, don't come to me, because I won't look at you, and won't own you. And remember that, miss!"

Again Polly laughed, this time in high notes of wrathful derision. Before the sound had died away Mrs. Clover was at the foot of the staircase, where Gammon and Mrs. Bubb awaited her.

"It's all a make-up," she declared vehemently. "I won't believe a word of it. She's made fools of us—the nasty, ill-natured thing!"

Trembling with excitement she was obliged to sit down in the parlour, whilst Mrs. Bubb hovered about her with indignant consolation. Gammon, silent as yet, stood looking on. As he watched Mrs. Clover's countenance his own underwent a change; there was a ruffling of the brows, a working of the lips, and in his good-humoured blue eyes a twinkling of half-amused, half-angry determination.

"Look here," he began, thrusting his hands into his side pockets. "You've come all this way, Mrs. Clover, to see Polly, and see her you shall."

"I don't want to, Mr. Gammon! I couldn't——"

"Now steady a bit—quiet—don't lose your head. Whether you want to see her or not, I want you to, and what's more you shall see her. If Polly's trying to make fools of us she shan't have all the fun; if she's telling the truth she shall have a fair chance of proving it; if she's lying we'll have a jolly good try to make her jolly well ashamed of herself. See here, Mrs. Bubb, will you do as I ask you?"

"And what's that, Mr. Gammon?" asked the landlady, eager to show her spirit.

"You go up to Polly's room, and you say this: 'Miss Sparkes,' you say, 'you've got to come downstairs and see your aunt. If you'll come, quite well and good; if you won't, I just got to tell you that the lock on your door is easy forced, and expense shan't stand in the way.' Now you just go and say that."

Mrs. Bubb and Mrs. Clover exchanged glances. Both were plainly impressed by this masculine suggestion, but they hesitated.

"I don't want to make an upset in the house," said Mrs. Clover. "There isn't a word of truth in what she said; I feel sure of that, and it's no use."

"If you ask me," Gammon interposed, "I'm not at all sure about that. It seems to me just as likely as not that she has come across Mr. Clover—just as likely as not!"

Angry agitation again took hold of Polly's aunt, who was very easily swayed by an opinion from Mr. Gammon. The landlady, too, gave willing ear to his words.

"Do you mean," she asked, "that we should really break the door open?"

"I do; and what's more—I'll pay the damage. Go up, Mrs. Bubb, and just say what I told you; and let's see how she takes it."

Mrs. Clover began a faint objection, but Mrs. Bubb did not heed it. Her face set in the joy of battle, she turned from the room and ran upstairs.

CHAPTER X.

THE STORMING OF THE FORT

MR. and Mrs. Cheeseman, squeezed together at their partly-open door, were following the course of events with a delighted eagerness which threatened to break all bounds of discretion. Their grinning faces signalled to Mrs. Bubb as she went by, and she, no less animated, waved a hand to them as if promising richer entertainment. The next minute she was heard parleying with Miss Sparkes. Polly received her, as was to be expected, with acrimonious defiance.

"Oh, it's you, is it, Mrs. Bubb! Go and clean up your dirty kitchen. It'll take you all your time."

There needed but this to fire the landlady to extremities. Her answer rang through the house. Dirty kitchen, indeed! And how many meals had Miss Sparkes eaten there at cost price—aye, often for nothing at all! And who was it as made most dirt, coming in at all hours of the day and night from running about the streets?

"Very well, my lady! Are you going to turn that key or not? That's all I want to know."

"I'll have pity on your ignorance," replied Polly, "and tell you more than that. I'm going to bed, and going to try to get to sleep if there's any chance of it in a 'ouse like this, which might be a 'sylum for inebriates."

Mrs. Bubb laughed, the strangest laugh ever heard from her respectable lips. Words were needless, and in a few seconds she panted before her friends downstairs.

"She says she's a-goin' to bed. Of all the shimeless creatures! Called me every nime she could turn her tongue to! And wouldn't open her door not if the 'ouse was burning. Do you hear her?"

Mr. Gammon buttoned his coat from top to bottom, smoothed his moustache and his side-whiskers, and had the air of a man who is in readiness for stern duty.

"I want both of you to come up with me," he said quietly.

Mrs. Clover began to look alarmed, even embarrassed.

"But perhaps she's really gone to bed."

"All right, she shall have time," he nodded, laughing. "I want both of you to come up to see fair play."

STORMING OF THE FORT

"But, Mr. Gammon, I shouldn't like——"

"Mrs. Clover, you've come here to see Polly, and you've a right to see Polly, and by jorrocks you shall see Polly! Follow me upstairs. I've said all that need be said; now to business."

They ascended; Gammon three steps at a stride, the others in a hurry and a flutter. Light streamed from the Cheesemans' room; the first-floor lodgers, incapable any longer of self-restraint, were out on the landing. On the next floor it was dark, but Mr. Gammon saw a gleam along the bottom of Polly's door. He knocked—the knock of a policeman armed with a warrant.

"Miss Sparkes!"

"Oh, it's you this time, is it? Come just to say good-night? You needn't have put yourself out."

"Miss Sparkes, are you in your proper dress?"

"What d'you mean?" Polly answered resentfully.

"You've been drinking again, I suppose."

"Not at all, my dear. I asked you for a good and sufficient reason. I'm going to break your door open, that's all, and I wish to give you fair warning. Are you dressed or not?"

"Impudent wretch! What are you doing here? What business is it of yours?"

"I'm the only strong man handy, that's all. Paid for the job, being out of work just now."

Mrs. Bubb tittered; Mrs. Cheeseman, down below, choked audibly.

"Will you answer that question or not? Very good; I give you till I've counted fifty, slow. When I say fifty, bang goes the bloomin' door."

Amid an awful silence, enveloped, as it were, by the dull rumbling of vehicles without, Mr. Gammon's voice began counting. He expected to hear Polly's key turn in the lock, so did Mrs. Bubb and Mrs. Clover. But the key moved not.

"Forty-eight—forty-nine—fifty!"

Gammon drew back to give himself impetus, and rushed against the door. With raised foot he struck it just by the handle, and the house seemed to quiver. A second assault was successful; with crash and splintering the lock yielded, the door flew open. At the far side of the room stood Polly, but in no attitude of surrender; she held a clothes brush, and as soon as the assailant showed himself flung it violently at his head. Another missile would have followed, but Gammon was too quick; with a red Indian yell of victory he crossed the floor at one bound and had Polly in his arms.

"Look out, ladies!" he shouted. "See fair play!"

Mrs. Bubb vented her emotions in "Oh my!"

STORMING OF THE FORT

and "Did you ever!" with little screams of excitement verging on sheer laughter. It avenged her delightfully to see Miss Sparkes gripped by the waist and hoisted for removal. But Mrs. Clover was evidently possessed by very different feelings. Drawing back, as if in alarm or shame, a glow on each cheek, she uttered an involuntary cry of protest.

"No, Mr. Gammon, I can't have that!"

It was doubtful whether the champion heard, for he unmistakably had his work set. Tooth and nail Polly contested every inch of ground. One moment her little fists were pummelling Gammon in the face, the next she tugged at his hair. Then again she scratched and kicked simultaneously, her voice meanwhile screaming insult and menace, which must have been audible in the neighbours' houses.

"Stop!" entreated Mrs. Clover. "Put her down at once!" she commanded. "Do you hear me, Mr. Gammon?"

Whether he did or not, the bold bagman paid no heed. He had at length a firmer grip of Polly with one of her arms imprisoned. He neared the head of the stairs, the women falling back before him.

"Mind what you're up to," he was heard to shout good-humouredly as ever. "If you trip me we shall both break our blessed necks."

How dare you!" shrieked the voice of the captive, now growing hoarse. "I'll give you in charge the minute I get downstairs! Ugly beast, I'll give you all in charge!"

The descent began. But that Polly was slightly made, a man of Gammon's physique would have found it impossible to carry her down the stairs; as it was he soon began puffing and groaning. In spite of the risk Polly still struggled—two stair-railings were wrenched away on the first flight. Then appeared Mr. and Mrs. Cheeseman, red and perspiring with muffled laughter.

"You may laugh, you wretches!" Polly shrieked. "I'll give you all in charge, see if I don't. You've all took part in an assault—see what you'll get for it!"

After that she no longer resisted, except for an occasional kick on her bearer's shins. They reached the ground floor; they tottered into the parlour; close upon them followed Mrs. Bubb and Mrs. Clover. Set upon her feet, Polly seemed for a moment about to rush to the window; a second thought led her to the mirror over the mantelpiece, where, fiercely eyeing the reflected group behind her, she made shift to smooth her hair and arrange her dress. Gammon had sunk upon a chair and was mopping his forehead. He had suffered far more than Polly in the encounter,

STORMING OF THE FORT

and looked indeed, with wild hair, scratched face, burst collar, loose necktie, a startling object.

"Now, then!" the girl moved towards him, fists clenched, as if to renew hostilities. "What d'you mean by this? Just you tell me what you mean by it."

"As soon as I can get breath, my dear. I meant to bring you down to speak to your aunt, and I've done it—see?"

"I'm ashamed of you, Mr. Gammon," exclaimed Mrs. Clover severely. "I never thought you would go so far as this."

"Ashamed of him, are you?" shrieked the girl, turning furiously upon her relative. "Be ashamed of yourself! What do you call yourself, eh? A respectable woman? And you look on while your own niece is treated in this way. Why, a costermonger's wife wouldn't disgrace herself so. No wonder your 'usband run away from you!"

"Oh, this low, vulgar, horrid girl!" cried her aunt in a revulsion of feeling. "How she can be any relative of mine I'm sure I don't know."

"Ugh! you nasty, ungrateful young woman, you!" chimed in Mrs. Bubb. "To speak to your kind awnt like that, as has been taking your part when I'm sure I wouldn't 'a done! I'd like to see you put on bread and water till you owned up whether you've told lies or not."

Mrs. Clover was moved to the point of shedding tears, though her handkerchief soon stopped the flow.

"Polly," she said, raising her voice above the hubbub, "you've treated me that bad there's no words for it. But I can't believe you'll let me go away like this, without knowing whether you've really seen Mr. Clover or not. Just tell me, do."

"Oh, it's just tell you, is it! After you've had me knocked about and insulted by a dirty rough like that Gammon——"

"You've heard me say I never thought he meant to behave so. I wouldn't have had it for anything."

Whilst Mrs. Clover was speaking Gammon beckoned to the landlady, and together they retreated from the room, closing the door behind them. On the stairs stood Mr. and Mrs. Cheeseman eager for the latest news of the fray. At their invitation Mrs. Bubb and the hero of the evening stepped up, and for a quarter of an hour Mrs. Clover was left alone with her niece. Then the landlady's attention was called by a voice from below.

"I must be going, Mrs. Bubb; I'll say goodnight."

Quickly Mrs. Bubb descended; she saw at a glance that Polly's wrath had in no degree diminished, and that Mrs. Clover was no whit easier in mind; but both had become silent. Merely saying that she

STORMING OF THE FORT

would see her hostess again before long, the lady of the china shop took a hurried leave and quitted the house.

She had walked but a few yards when Mr. Gammon's voice sounded at her shoulder.

"I'll see you part of the way home," he said genially.

"I'm much obliged to you, Mr. Gammon," was Mrs. Clover's reply, "but I can find my own way."

"You'll let me see you into a 'bus, at all events."

"Please don't trouble; I'd much rather you didn't."

"Why?" asked Gammon bluntly.

"Because I had. I'll say good-night."

She stood still looking him in the face with cold displeasure; only for a moment though, as her eyes could not bear the honest look in his.

"Right you are," said Gammon with affected carelessness. "Just as you like. I won't force my company on anyone."

Mrs. Clover made the movement which in women of her breeding signifies a formal bow—hopelessly awkward, rigid, and self-conscious—and walked rapidly away. The man, not a little crestfallen, swung round on his heel.

"What's wrong now?" he asked himself. "It can't be about Minnie, for she was all right till after supper. And why it should make her angry because

I lugged that cat Polly downstairs is more than I can understand. Well, I shan't die of it."

On re-entering the house he found all quiet. Polly had returned to her chamber, Mrs. Bubb was in the Cheesemans' room. He went down into the kitchen, where the gas was burning, and sat till the landlady came down.

"I don't see as you did much good," was Mrs. Bubb's first remark, in the tone which signifies reaction after excitement. "It weren't worth breaking a door in, it seems to me."

Gammon hung his head.

"Didn't Polly tell her anything?"

"She stuck out she knew where the 'usband was, and that's all."

"How do you know?"

"Polly said so as she went upstairs, and 'oped her awnt 'ud sleep well on it."

"H'm! I suppose that's why I couldn't get a word out of Mrs. Clover. Have the door mended, Mrs. Bubb, and charge me with it. Got anything to drink handy?"

"That I 'aven't, Mr. Gammon, except water."

Gammon looked at his watch.

"Why, it's only just half-past eleven. Hanged if I didn't think it was past midnight! I must go round and get a drop of something."

When he came back from quenching his thirst the

house was in darkness. He strode the familiar ascent, and by Polly's door (barricaded inside with the chest of drawers) hummed a mirthful strain. As he jumped into bed the events of the evening all at once struck him in such a comical light that he uttered a great guffaw, and for the next ten minutes he lay under the bedclothes shaking with laughter.

CHAPTER XI.

THE NOSE OF THE TREFOYLES

AT noon next day a cab drove up to Mrs. Bubb's house; from it alighted Miss Sparkes, who, with the help of the cabman, brought downstairs a tin box, a wooden box, two bandboxes, and three newspaper bundles. With no one did she exchange a word of farewell; the Cheesemans' were out, the landlady and Moggie kept below stairs. So Polly turned her back upon Kennington Road, and shook the dust thereof from her feet for ever.

Willingly she had accepted a proposal that she should share the room of her friend Miss Waghorn, who was to be married in a month's time to Mr. Nibby, and did not mind a little inconvenience. The room was on the third floor of a house at the north end of Shaftesbury Avenue; it measured twelve feet by fourteen. When Polly's bandboxes had been thrust under the bed and her larger luggage built up in a corner, there was nice standing room both for her and Miss Waghorn. The house contained ten rooms in all, and its population (including seven children) amounted to twenty-three. In this warm weather the atmosphere within doors might occasionally be a trifle close; but Shaftesbury Avenue is a fine broad street, and has great advantages of situation.

To Mr. Gammon's casual enquiry, Mrs. Bubb replied that she neither knew nor cared whither Polly had betaken herself. Himself having no great curiosity in the matter, and being much absorbed in his endeavour to obtain an engagement with the house of Quodling, he let Polly slip from his mind for a few days, until one morning came a letter from her. Positively, and to his vast surprise, a letter addressed to him by Miss Sparkes, with her abode fully indicated in the usual place. True, the style of the epistle was informal. It began :—

"You took advantage of me because there wasn't a man in the house to take my part, as I don't call that grinning monkey of a Cheeseman a man at all. If you like to call where I am now, I shall have the pleasure of introducing you to somebody that will give you the good hiding you deserve for being a coward and a brute.

"MISS SPARKES."

Gammon laughed over this for half an hour. He showed it to Mrs. Bubb, who was again on the old terms with him, and Mrs. Bubb wanted to exhibit it to Mrs. Cheeseman.

"No, don't do that," he interposed gently. "We'll keep it between ourselves."

"Why?"

"Oh, I don't know. The girl can't help herself; she was born that way, you know."

"I only hope she won't pay some rough to follow you at night and bash you," said Mrs. Bubb warningly.

"I don't think that. No, no; Polly's bark is worse than her bite any day."

On the evening of that day, about ten o'clock, he chanced to be in Oxford Street, and as he turned southward it occurred to him that he would so far act upon Polly's invitation as to walk down the Avenue and glance at the house where she lived. He did so, and it surprised him to see that she had taken up her abode in so mean-looking a place; he was not aware, of course, that Miss Waghorn found the quarters good enough for her own more imposing charms and not less brilliant wardrobe.

Walking on, at Cambridge Circus he came face to face with Miss Sparkes herself, accompanied by Miss Waghorn. To his hat salute and amiable smile Polly replied with a fierce averting of the look. Her friend nodded cheerfully, and they passed. Two minutes after he found Miss Waghorn beside him.

"Hallo! Left Polly?"

"I want you to come back with me, Mr. Gammon," replied the maiden archly. "I 'ear you've offended Miss Sparkes. I don't know what it is, I'm sure, and I don't ask to be told, 'cause it's none of my business; but I want to make you friends again, and I'm sure you'll apologise to her."

"Eh? Apologise? Why, of course I will; only too delighted."

"That's nice of you. I always said you were a nice man, ask Polly if I didn't."

"The same to you, my dear, and many of 'em! Come along."

As if wholly unaware of what was happening Polly had proceeded homewards, not so fast, however, but that the others overtook her with ease before she reached the house.

"How do you do, Miss Sparkes?" began her enemy, not without diffidence as she turned upon him. "I'm surprised to hear from Miss Waghorn that something I've said or done has riled you, if I may use the expression. I couldn't have meant it; I'm sure I 'umbly beg pardon."

Strange to say, by this imperfect expression of regret, Miss Sparkes allowed herself to be mollified. Presenting a three-quarter countenance with a forbearing smile, she answered in the formula of her class:

"Oh, I'm sure it's granted."

"There now, we're all friends again," said Carrie Waghorn. "Miss Sparkes is living with me for the present, Mr. Gammon. There'll be changes before long"—she looked about her with prudish embarrassment—" but, of course, we shall be seeing you again. Do you know the address, Mr. Gammon?"

She mentioned the number of the house, and carefully repeated it, whilst Polly turned away as if the conversation did not interest her. Thereupon Mr. Gammon bade them good-night, and went his way, marvelling that Polly Sparkes had all at once become so placable. Was it a stratagem to throw him off his guard and bring him into the clutches of some avenger one of these nights? One never knew what went on in the minds of such young women as Polly.

Next morning he had another surprise, a letter from his friend Greenacre, inviting him, with many phrases of studious politeness, to dine that day at a great hotel, the hour eight o'clock, and begging him to reply by telegram addressed to the same hotel. This puzzled Gammon, yet less than it could have done at an earlier stage of their acquaintance. He had abandoned the hope of explaining Greenacre's mysterious circumstances, and the attempt to decide whether his stories were worthy of belief or not. Half suspecting that he might be the victim of a hoax he telegraphed an acceptance, and thought no more of the matter until evening approached. Part of his day was spent in helping a distracted shopkeeper on the verge of failure to obtain indulgence from certain of his creditors; he also secured a place as errand boy for the son of a poor woman with whom he had lodged until her house was burnt down one Bank Holiday; and he made a trip to Hammersmith to give evidence at the police-court for a friend charged with assaulting a policeman. Just before eight o'clock, after a hasty wash and brush up at a public lavatory, he presented himself at the great hotel, where, from a lounge in the smoking-room, Greenacre rose to welcome him. Greenacre indubitably, but much better dressed than Gammon had ever seen him, and with an air of lively graciousness which was very impressive. The strange fellow offered not a word of explanation, but chatted as though their meeting in such places as this were an every-day occurrence.

"I have something interesting to tell you," he observed, when they were seated in the brilliant dining-room, with olives, sardines, and the like to toy with before the serious commencement of their meal. "You remember—when was it? not long ago—asking me about a family named Quodling?"

"Of course I do. It was only the other day at——"

"Ah, just so, yes," interposed Greenacre, suavely ignoring the locality. "You know my weakness for looking up family histories. I happened to be talking with my friend Beeching yesterday—Aldham Beeching, you know, the Q.C.—and Quodling came into my head. I mentioned the name. It was as I thought. I had, you know, a vague recollection of Quodling as connected with a lawsuit when I was a boy. Beeching could tell me all about it."

"Well, what was it?"

"Queer story. A Mrs. Quodling, a widow, or believed to be a widow, came in for a large sum of money under the will of Lord Polperro, the second baron—uncle, I am told, of his present lordship. This will was contested by the family; a very complicated affair, Beeching tells me. Mrs. Quodling, whose character was attacked, declared that she knew Lord Polperro in an honourable way, and that he had taken a great interest in her children—two young boys. Now these boys were produced in court, then it was seen—excellent soup this—that they bore little if any resemblance to each other; and at the same time it was made evident, by exhibition of a portrait, that the younger boy had a face with a strong likeness to the testator, and many witnesses declared the same. Interesting, isn't it?"

"For the widow," remarked Gammon.

"Uncommonly awkward, though she gained her case for all that. Polperro, it seems, had a shady reputation—heavy drinker, and so on. There were strong characteristics—some peculiarity of the nose. The old chap used to say that there was the nose of the Bourbons and the nose of the Trefoyles, his family name."

"What name?"

"Trefoyle. Cornish, you know. Rum lot they always seem to have been. Barony created by George III. for some personal service. The first Polperro is said to have lived a year or two as a gipsy, and at another time as a highwayman. There's a portrait of him, Beeching tells me, in somebody's history of Cornwall, showing to perfection the Trefoyle nose."

"Same as Quodling's, then," exclaimed Gammon. "Quodling, the broker?"

"Precisely. I would suggest, my dear fellow, that you don't speak quite so loud. Francis Quodling was the boy who so strongly resembled the Lord Polperro of the lawsuit. Nose with high arch, and something queer about the nostril."

"Yes! and hanged if it isn't just the same as——"

A deprecatory gesture from his friend stopped Gammon on the point of uttering the name "Clover."

Again he had sinned against the proprieties by unduly raising his voice, and he subsided in confusion.

"You were going to say?" murmured the host politely.

"Oh, nothing. There's a man I know has just the same nose, that's all."

"That's very interesting. And considering the Polperro reputation, it wouldn't surprise me to come across a good many such noses. You remember my favourite speculation. It comes in very well here, doesn't it. Is all this information of any service to you?"

"Much obliged to you for your trouble. I don't know that I can make any use of it; but yes, it does give a sort of hint."

On reflection Gammon decided to keep the matter to himself. He had set his mind on discovering Mrs. Clover's husband, and was all the more determined to perform this feat since the recent events in Kennington Road. Mrs. Clover had treated him unkindly; he would prove to her that this had no effect upon his zeal in her service. Polly Sparkes was making fun of him, and the laugh should yet be on his side. Greenacre, with his mysterious connections, might be of use, but must not be allowed to run away with the credit of the discovery. As for these stories about Lord Polperro, it might turn out that Clover was illegitimately related to the noble family—no subject for boasting, though possibly an explanation of his strange life. If Polly were really in communication with him—Ho, ho! Very good! Ha, ha!

"What now?" asked Greenacre.

"Nothing! Queer fancy I had."

After dinner they smoked together for an hour, the host talking incessantly, and for the most part in a vein of reminiscence. To hear him one would have supposed that he had always lived in the society of distinguished people; never a word referring to poverty or mean employment fell from his lips.

"Poor Bolsover!" he remarked. "Did I tell you that I had a very kind letter from his widow?"

"I haven't seen you since."

"Ah no, to be sure. I wrote, or rather I left a card at the town house. Charming letter in reply. The poor lady is still quite young. She was a Thompson of Derbyshire. I never knew the family at all well."

Gammon mused, and it occurred to him in his knowledge of the world that Greenacre's connection with the house of Bolsover might be that of a begging-letter writer. There might have been some slight acquaintance in years gone by between this strange fellow and young Lord Bolsover—subsequently made a source of profit. Perchance, Greenacre's prosperity at this moment resulted from a skilful appeal to the widowed lady.

Inclined to facetiousness by a blend of choice beverages, Gammon could not resist a joke at the moment when he took leave.

"Been out with the Saponaria van to-day?" he enquired innocently.

Greenacre looked steadily at him with eyes of gentle reproach.

"I'm afraid I don't understand that allusion," he replied gravely. "Is it a current jest? I am not much in the way of hearing that kind of thing. By-the-bye, let me know if I can help you in any more genealogies."

"I will. So long, old man."

And with a wink — an undeniable wink, an audacious wink—Mr. Gammon sallied from the hotel.

Before going to bed he wrote a letter—a letter to Miss Sparkes. Would she see him the day after to-morrow, Sunday, if he strolled along Shaftesbury Avenue at ten a.m.? It would greatly delight him, and perhaps she might be persuaded to take a little jaunt to Dulwich and look at his bow-wows.

CHAPTER XII.

POLLY CONDESCENDS

THERE was time enough for Polly to reply to this invitation, but reply she did not. None the less, Gammon was walking about near her lodgings at ten o'clock on Sunday morning. It seemed to him that he once or twice perceived a face at an upper window, but at a quarter past the hour Miss Sparkes had not come forth. He was on the point of going boldly to the door when a recognizable figure approached—that of Mr. Nibby. The men hailed each other.

"Waiting for somebody?" enquired the representative of the Gillingwater burner, a twinkle in his eye.

To avoid the risk of complications Gammon avowed that he was looking out for Miss Sparkes, with whom he wanted a word on private business.

"First rate!" exclaimed Mr. Nibby. "She's coming along with Miss Waghorn and me to my brother's at 'Endon—the Blue Anchor; do you know it? Nice little property. You'll have to join us; first rate. I'm only afraid it may rine. Do you think it will rine?"

"May or may not," replied Gammon, staring at the clouds and thinking over the situation as it concerned himself. "If it's going to rine, it will, you know."

"That's true. I'll just let 'em know I'm here."

But at this moment the two young ladies came forth, blushing and resplendent. Hats were doffed and hands were shaken.

"Why, is that you, Mr. Gammon?" cried Carrie Waghorn when the ceremony was over, as if only just aware of his presence. "Well, this is a surprise, isn't it, Polly?"

Miss Sparkes seemed barely to recognize Mr. Gammon, but of necessity she took a place by his side, and walked on with a rhythmic tossing of the head, which had a new adornment — a cluster of great blue flowers, unknown to the botanist, in the place of her every-day poppies.

"If you don't want me," remarked Gammon, glancing at her, "you've only to say so, and I'm off."

Polly looked up at the sky, and answered with a question.

"Do you think it's going to rine?"

"Shouldn't wonder."

"Well, you are polite."

POLLY CONDESCENDS

"What's the rine got to do with politeness? I say, why didn't you answer my letter?"

"I pay no attention to impertinence," replied Miss Sparkes haughtily.

"Oh, that's it? Never mind; we shall get on better presently. I say, Polly, do you see you've left marks on my face?"

Polly set her lips and kept a severe silence.

"I don't mind 'em," Gammon continued. "Rather proud of 'em. If anybody asks me how I got the scratches——"

The girl looked sharply at him.

"Do you mean to say you'd tell? Well, if you call that gentlemanly——"

"Wouldn't tell the truth, Polly, not for as many kisses as there are scratches, my dear."

Polly bridled—young women of her class still bridle—but looked rather pleased. And Gammon chuckled to himself, thinking that all went well.

The rain came, but for all that they had a day of enjoyment, spent chiefly in an arbour, not quite rain proof, on the skittle-ground behind the Blue Anchor at Hendon. Continuous was the popping of corks, and frequent were the outbursts of hilarity. Polly did not abandon her reserve with Mr. Gammon; now and then she condescended to smile at his sallies of wit, whereas she screamed at a joke from others. The landlord of the Blue

Anchor was a widower of about thirty, and had some claims to be considered a lady's man; to him Polly directed her friendly looks and remarks with a freedom which could not but excite attention.

"Is that the fellow that's going to give me a thrashing?" Gammon asked of her at length in an aside.

"Don't be a silly," she answered, turning her back.

"Because, if so, I'd better get the start of him There's a convenient bit of ground here."

He spoke with such seeming seriousness that Polly showed alarm.

"Don't be a silly, Mr. Gammon. If you misbehave yourself, I'll never speak to you again."

"Well, what I want to know is, am I to be on guard? Am I to mind my eye whenever I'm near you?"

He spoke as if with a real desire to be relieved from apprehension. At this moment their companions had drawn apart, and they could converse unheard.

"You know very well what you deserve," replied Polly, looking askance at him. "And if such a thing ever was to happen again—well, you'd see, that's all."

Therewith the peace, or at all events the truce, was concluded, and Miss Sparkes allowed herself to meet Mr. Gammon's advances with frankness and appreciation. The fact that he did unmistakably make advances secretly surprised her, but not more than Gammon was surprised to find himself coming into favour.

A few days later the opportunity for which he waited came to pass, and he was invited to an interview with Quodling and Son; that is to say, with a person who was neither Quodling nor Quodling's son, but held a position of authority at their place of business in Norton Folgate. Whenever the chance was given him of applying personally for any post that he desired, Mr. Gammon felt a reasonable assurance of success. Honesty was written broadly upon his visage; capability declared itself in his speech. He could win the liking and confidence of any ordinary man of business in ten minutes. It happened, fortunately, that the firm of Quodling needed just such a representative. As Gammon knew, they had been unlucky in their town traveller of late, and they looked just now more to the "address," the personal qualities, of an applicant for the position, than to his actual acquaintance with their business, which was greatly a matter of routine. Mr. Gammon was accepted on trial, and in a day or two began his urban travels.

Particular about the horses he drove, Gammon

saw with pleasure the young dark-bay cob, stylishly harnessed, which pawed delicately as he mounted the neat little trap put at his disposal. It is the blessedness of a mind and temper such as his that the things which charm at the beginning of life continue to give pleasure, scarce abated, as long as the natural force remains. At forty years of age Gammon set off about his business with all the zest of a healthy boy. The knowledge he had gained, all practical, and, so to speak, for external application, could never become the burden of the philosopher; if he had any wisdom at all it consisted in the lack of self-consciousness, the animal acceptance of whatever good the hour might bring. He and his bay cob were very much on the same footing; granted but a method of communication and they would have understood each other. Even so with his "bow-wows," as he called them. He rose superior to horse and dog mainly in that one matter of desire for a certain kind of female companionship; and this strain of idealism, naturally enough, was the cause of almost the only discontent he ever knew.

Joyously he rattled about the highways and byways of greater London. The position he had now obtained was to become a "permanency"; to Quodling and Son he could attach himself, making his services indispensable. One of these days—not

POLLY CONDESCENDS

just yet—he would look in at Mrs. Clover's and see whether she still kept in the same resentful mind towards him. It was an odd thing that nowadays he gave more thought to Mrs. Clover than to Minnie. The young girl glimmered very far away, at a height above him; he had made a mistake and frankly recognized it. But Mrs. Clover, his excellent friend of many years, shone with no such superiority, and was not above rebuke for any injustice she might do him. Probably by this time she had forgotten her fretfulness, a result of overstrung nerves. She would ask his pardon—and ought to do so.

He thought of Polly Sparkes, but always with a peculiar smile, inclining to a grimace. Polly had "come round" in the most astonishing way. But she would "come round" yet more before he had done with her. His idea was to take Polly to Dulwich and show her the bow-wows; he saw possibilities of a quiet meal together at the inn. The difficulty was to reassure her natural tremors, without losing the ground he had gained by judicious approaches.

About the middle of July he prevailed upon her to accept his invitation, and to come alone, though Polly continued to declare that she hated dogs, and that she had never in her life gone to so remote and rural a spot as Dulwich without a "lady friend" to keep her in countenance.

"Everything must have a beginning," said Gammon merrily.

"If you let those people know, I'll never speak to you again."

She referred to Mrs. Bubb and her household, of whom she had never ceased to speak with animus.

"Honour bright, they shan't hear a whisper of it."

So on a Sunday morning they made the journey by omnibus for the sake of the fresh air, Polly remarking again and again on her great condescension, reaffirming her dislike of dogs, and declaring that if a drop of rain fell she would turn about homeward forthwith. None the less did she appear to find pleasure in Mr. Gammon's society. If his gossip included a casual mention of some young lady, a friend of his, she pressed for information concerning that person, and never seemed quite satisfied with what she was told about her. Slyly observant of this, her companion multiplied his sportive allusions, and was amused to find Polly grow waspish. Then again he soothed her with solid flattery; nothing of the kind was too gross for Polly's appetite. And so conversing they shortened the journey to remote Dulwich.

With gathered skirts and a fear, partly real but more affected, Miss Sparkes entered the yard where Gammon's dogs were kept. (As a matter of fact he shared in their ownership with the landlord of the public-house, a skilful breeder.) When puppies gambolled about her she woke the echoes with a scream. From a fine terrier, a "game" dog whose latest exploit was the killing of a hundred rats in six minutes, she backed trembling, and even put out a hand to Gammon as if for protection. Polly's behaviour, indeed, was such as would have been proper in a fine lady forty years ago, the fashion having descended to her class just as fashions in costume are wont to do at a shorter interval. When Gammon begged her to feel the "feather" of a beautiful collie she at length did so with great timidity, and a moment after, to show how doggy she was becoming, she spoke of the "feather" of a little black-and-tan, whereat Gammon smiled broadly. On the whole they much enjoyed themselves, and had a good appetite at dinner time.

The meal was laid for them in a small private room, which smelt principally of stale tobacco and stale chimney soot. The water-bottle on the table was encrusted with a white enamel advertisement of somebody's whisky, and had another such recommendation legible on its base. The tray used by the girl in attendance was enamelled with the name of somebody's brandy. On the walls hung three brightly-coloured calendars, each an advertisement: one of sewing machines, one of a popular insurance office, one of a local grocery business. The other mural adornments were old coloured pictures of race-horses and faded photographs of dogs. A clock on the mantelpiece (not going) showed across its face the name of a firm that dealt in aërated waters.

Coarse and plentiful were the viands, and Polly did justice to them. She had excellent teeth, a very uncommon thing in girls of her kind; but Polly's parents were of country origin. With these weapons she feared not even the pastry set before her, which it was just possible to break with an ordinary fork.

Towards the end Gammon grew silent and meditative. He kept gazing at the windows as if for aid in some calculation. When Polly at last threw down her cheese-knife, glowing with the thought that she had dined well at somebody else's expense, he leaned forward on the table, looked her in the eyes, and began a momentous dialogue.

CHAPTER XIII.

GAMMON THE CRAFTY

"WHAT did you want to do such a silly thing as that for?"

Polly stared in astonishment.

"What d'you mean?"

"Why did you let out to Mrs. Clover what you knew?"

The girl's colour deepened by a shade (it was already rich), and her eyes grew alarmed, suspicious, watchful.

"I didn't let out what I knew," she answered rather confused.

It was Gammon's turn to watch keenly.

"Not all, of course not," he remarked slyly. "But why couldn't you keep it to yourself that you'd met him?"

Polly's eyes wandered. Gammon smiled with satisfaction.

"I'd have kept that to myself," he said in a friendly way. "I know how it was, of course; you got riled and came out with it. A great pity.

She had all but forgot him; now she'll never rest till she's found him out. And you might have seen how much more to your advantage it was to keep a thing like that quiet."

Unwonted mental disturbance was playing tricks with Polly's complexion. She evidently feared to compromise herself, and at the same time desired to know all that was in her companion's mind.

"What business is it of yours?" was the crude phrase that at length fell from her lips, uttered half-heartedly, between resentment and jesting.

"Well, there's the point," replied Gammon, with a laugh. "Queer thing, but it just happens to be particular business of mine."

Polly stared. He nodded.

"There's such a thing, Polly, as going halves in a secret. I've been wondering these last few days whether I should tell you or not. But we're getting on so well together—eh? Better than I expected, for one. I shouldn't feel I was doing right, Polly, if I took any advantage of you."

She was growing excited. Her wiles had given way before superior stratagem, and perhaps before something in herself that played traitor.

"You mean you know about him?" she asked, almost confidentially.

"Not all I want to—yet. He's a sharp customer. But considerably more than you do, Polly, my dear."

"I don't believe you!"

"That has nothing to do with it. Suppose you ask me a question or two. I might be able to tell you something you would like to know."

It was said, of course, without any suspicion of the real state of things; but Gammon saw at once that he had excited an eager curiosity.

"You know where he is, then?" asked Polly.

"Well—we'll say so."

"Where? When did you see him last?"

"We're going too quickly, old girl. The question is, When did *you* see him last?"

"Ah! you'd like to know, wouldn't you?"

Gammon burst out laughing, ever the surest way of baffling a silly woman. Polly grew hot with anger, then subsided into mortification. She knew the weakness of her position, and inclined ever more to make an ally of the man who had overcome her in battle and carried her off in his arms.

"And the other question is," Gammon proceeded, as if enjoying a huge joke, "When did you see him first?"

"I suppose you know?" she murmured reluctantly.

"Let us suppose I do. And suppose I am trying to make up my mind about the best way of dealing with the little affair. As I told you, I wish Mrs. Clover didn't know about it; but that's your doing. Our friend, Mr. C., wouldn't thank you."

"He knows, then, does he?" cried Polly.

"Mr. C. knows a great many things, my dear. He was not born yesterday. Now, see here, Polly. We're both of us in this, and we'd better be straight with each other. I am no friend of Mr. C., but I am a friend of yours, and if you can help me to get a bit tighter hold of him—— Yes, yes, I'll tell you presently. The question is, whether I can depend upon what he says. Of course, I know all about you; I want to know more about him. Now, is it true that you saw him first at the theatre?"

Polly nodded, and Gammon congratulated himself on his guess.

"And—he wasn't alone?"

"No."

"Just what I thought."

"He says he was alone—eh?" asked Polly with eagerness.

"I guess why. Now who was with him, old girl?"

A moment's sulky hesitation and Polly threw away all reserve.

"There was two ladies—if they were ladies; at all events, they was dressed like it. Oldish, both of 'em. One was a foreigner. I know that because I heard her speak; and it wasn't English. The other one spoke back to her in the same way, but I heard her speak English too. And she was the one as sat next to him."

GAMMON THE CRAFTY 135

"Good, Polly, we're getting on. And how did you notice him?"

"Well, it was like this," she began to narrate with vivacity. "I offered him a programme—see?—and he gave me half a sovereign and looked up at me, as much as to say he'd like change. And I'd no sooner met his eyes than I knew him. How could I help? He don't look to have changed a bit. And I saw as he knew me. I saw it by a queer sort of wink he give. And then he looked at me frightened like—didn't he just! Of course, I didn't say nothing, but I kept standing by him a minute or two. And I'd forgot all about the change till he said to me, with a sort of look, 'You may keep that,' he said, and I says, 'Thank you, sir,' and nearly laughed."

"Not a bad tip, eh, Polly?"

"Oh, I've had as good before," she replied, with a brief return to the old manner.

"No doubt he enjoyed himself that evening. He kept spying round for you, didn't he?"

"I saw him look once or twice, and I give him a look back, but I couldn't do much more then; I said to myself I'd keep my eye on him to see if he came out after the first act. And sure enough he did, and there was me standing in his way, and he put his hand out to give me something, and just nodded and went on. It wasn't money, but a bit of paper twisted up and something wrote on it in pencil."

"I thought so, and where were you to meet him?"

"Well, I knew there couldn't be no harm, him being my own uncle," Polly replied with the air of repelling an accusation.

"Of course not; who said there was?"

"Well, it was Lincoln's Inn Fields, the next night. And there he was, sure enough, with his face half hid as if he was ashamed of himself, as well he might be. And he begins with saying as he was very ill and he didn't think he'd live long. But I wasn't to think as he forgot me, and when he died I should find myself provided for. And I wasn't to say a word to nobody or he'd take my name out of his will at once."

Gammon laughed.

"It's all right, Polly. Don't be afraid. All between me and you. But I'll bet he didn't tell you where he was living?"

She shook her head.

"Of course not, I knew that," said Gammon, with a mysterious air. "Well, go on. He met you again, didn't he?"

"Once more, only once."

"Yes, and gave you little presents and told you to be a good gyurl and never disgrace your uncle. Oh,

GAMMON THE CRAFTY

I know him! But he took precious good care not to let you know where he lived."

"But you know?" she exclaimed.

"No fear, Polly. You shall, too, if you have patience, though I don't say it'll be just yet."

A few more questions, and the girl had told everything—Mr. Clover's failure to keep the third appointment and her fruitless watchings since then.

"He got a bit timid, Polly, you see," exclaimed Gammon. "And he was right, too; you couldn't keep it to yourself, you see. You spoil everything with that temper of yours, my dear. Don't be cross, my beauty; it don't matter much, comes to the same thing in the end. Now just look here, Polly. You haven't seen those two ladies again, nor either one of them?"

"You're wrong there," she cried triumphantly.

"Hollo! Steady, Polly. It wasn't the foreigner then?"

"How did you know?"

Gammon chuckled over his good luck.

"Never mind. We'll come to that another time. Who was she with, my dear?"

"Another lady and gentleman, much younger than her. I stood near 'em as long as I could and listened with all my ears, but I couldn't hear nothing any use. But I saw as they went away in a private kerridge, all three together; I saw that much."

"And found where they went to?"

"Go along. How could I?"

"Might have been managed, Polly," he answered musingly. "Never mind, better luck next time. What you've got to do, my angel, is to find where that lady lives—the one that sat next our friend, you know, not the foreigner. Keep your eyes open, Polly, and be smart, and if you tell me where she lives then I shall have something more to say to you. It's between me and you, my beauty. You just bring me that little bit of information and you won't regret it."

CHAPTER XIV.

MR. PARISH PURSUES A BROUGHAM

CHRISTOPHER PARISH lived at home, that is to say, he was not a lodger under an alien roof, like the majority of such young men in London, but abode with his own people—his mother, his elder brother, and his brother's wife. They had a decent little house in Kennington, managed—rather better than such houses generally are—by Mrs. Parish the younger, who was childless, and thus able to devote herself to what she called "hyjene," a word constantly on her lips and on those of her husband. Mr. Theodore Parish, aged about five-and-thirty, was an audit clerk in the offices of a railway company, and he loved to expatiate on the hardship of his position, which lay in the fact that he could not hope for a higher income than one hundred and fifty pounds, and this despite the trying and responsible nature of the duties he discharged. After dwelling upon this injustice he would add, with peculiar gravity, that really in certain moods one all but inclined to give a hearing to the arguments of socialistic agitators. In other moods, and these more frequent, Mr. Parish indulged in native optimism, tempered by anxiety in matters of "hyjene." He was much preoccupied with the laundry question.

"Now, are you quite sure, Ada, that this laundress is a conscientious woman? Does she manage her establishment on modern principles? I beg you will make a personal inspection. If ever a laundress refuses to let you make a personal inspection be sure there is something wrong. Just think how vital it is, this washing question. We send our clothes, our personal garments, to a strange house to be mixed with——"

And so on at great length, Mrs. Theodore listening patiently and approvingly. With equal solicitude did they discuss the food upon their table.

"Theo, I shall have to change our baker."

"Ah, indeed! Why?"

"I hardly like to tell you, but perhaps I had better. I have only just found out that a sewer-trap quite close to his shop gives out a most offensive *affluvia*, especially in this hot weather. The air must be full of germs. I hardly know whether we ought to eat even this loaf. What do you think?"

Everyone's dinner was spoilt. Theodore declared that really, when one considered the complicated

PURSUING A BROUGHAM 141

and expensive machinery of local government, if sewer traps and *affluvias* were allowed to exist in the immediate neighbourhood of bakers' shops, why it really made one inclined to think and ask whether there might not be something in the arguments of the Socialists.

Christopher one day brought home some knick-knack which he had bought from a City pedlar, one of those men who stand at the edge of the pavement between a vigilant police and a menacing vehicular traffic. It amused his sister-in-law, who showed it to her husband. Theodore having learnt whence it came was not a little concerned.

"Now, if that isn't like Christopher! When will that boy learn ordinary prudence? The idea of buying things from a man whose clothes more likely than not reek with infection! Dear me! Has he never reflected where those fellows live? Destroy the thing at once and wash your hands very carefully, I beg. I do hope you haven't been making pastry or lemonade? As if the inevitable risks of life were not enough."

It was, of course, utterly unsuspected by the elder members of the household that Christopher had "formed a connection," in so innocent a sense, with a young woman who sold programmes and took tips at the theatre. That connection had come about in the simplest way. One Sunday evening, a year ago, Christopher was returning from Clapham Common on the top of a crowded tram, and next to him sat a girl with a fresh colour, whom he eyed with respectfully furtive admiration. This young person had paid her fare, but carelessly dropped the ticket, and it chanced that an inspector who came on board at a certain point raised the question whether she had really paid. The conductor weakly expressed a doubt, suggesting that this passenger had ascended with two or three other people since his last collection of fares. Here was a chance for young Mr. Parish, who could give conscientious evidence. Very hot in the face, he declared, affirmed, and asseverated that the young lady was telling the truth, and his energy at length prevailed. Of course, this led to colloquy between the two. Polly Sparkes, for she it was, behaved modestly but graciously. It was true she had exhibited short temper in her passage with the officials, but Christopher thought this a becoming spirit. In his eyes she was lovely, and could do nothing amiss. When she alighted he did so too, frowning upon the conductor by way of final rebuke. Their ways appeared to be the same, as if inadvertently they walked together along Kennington Road. And so pleasant was their conversation that Polly went some way past Mrs. Bubb's before saying that she must bid her new companion good-bye. Trembling at his audacity, Christopher humbly put the question whether he might not hope to see the young lady again; and Polly laughed and tittered, and said she didn't know, but *p'r'aps*. Thereupon Mr. Parish nervously made an offering of his name and address, and Polly, tittering again, exclaimed that they lived quite near each other, and playfully made known the position of her dwelling. So were the proprieties complied with, and so began the enslavement of Christopher.

He had since told all there was to tell about his family and circumstances, Polly in return throwing out a few vague hints as to her own private affairs. Christopher would have liked to invite her to his home, but lacked courage; his mother, his brother, and Mrs. Theodore—what would they say? The rigour of their principles overawed him. He often thought of abandoning his home, but neither for that step had he the necessary spirit of independence. Miss Sparkes no longer seemed to him of virtues compact; he sadly admitted in his wakeful hours that she had a temper; he often doubted whether she ever gave him a serious thought. But the fact remained that Polly did not send him about his business, and at times even seemed glad to see him, until that awful night when, by deplorable accident, he encountered her near Lincoln's Inn. That surely was the end of everything. Christopher, after tottering home he knew not how, wept upon his pillow. Of course he was jealous as well as profoundly hurt. Not without some secret reason had Polly met him so fiercely, brutally. He would try to think of her no more; she was clearly not destined to be his.

For a full fortnight he shunned the whole region of London in which Polly might be met. He was obliged, of course, to pass each night in Kennington, but he kept himself within doors there. Then he could bear his misery no longer. Three lachrymose letters had elicited no response; he wrote once more, and thus:—

"DEAREST MISS SPARKES,

"If you do not wish to be the cause of my death I hereby ask you to see me, if only for the very shortest space of time. If you refuse I know I shall do something rash. To-night and to-morrow night at half-past ten I will be standing at the south end of Westminster Bridge. The *river* will be near me if *you* are not; remember that.

"Yours for now and eternity,

"C. J. P."

To this dread summons Polly at length yielded. She met Christopher, and they paced together on the embankment in front of St. Thomas's Hospital. It rained a little, and was so close that they both dripped with perspiration.

"P'r'aps I was a bit short with you," Polly admitted after listening to her admirer's remonstrances, uttered in a choking voice. "But I can't stand being spied after, and spied after I won't be."

"I have told you, Polly, at the very least sixty or seventy times, that I've never done such a thing, and wouldn't, and couldn't. It never came into my 'cad."

"Well, then, we won't say no more about it, and don't put me out again, that's all."

"But there's something else, Polly. You know very well, Polly, what a lot I think of you, don't you now?"

"Oh, I dessay," she replied with careless indulgence.

"Then why won't you let me see you oftener, and —and that kind of thing, you know?"

This was vague, but perfectly intelligible to the hearer. She gave an impatient little laugh.

"Oh, don't be silly! Go on!"

"But it isn't silly. You know what I mean. And you said——"

"There you go, bringing up what I said. Don't worry me. If you can't talk quiet and friendly we'd better not see each other at all. I shouldn't wonder if that was best for both of us."

Polly had never been less encouraging. She seemed preoccupied, and spoke in an idle, inattentive way.

Her suggestion that they should "part friends," though she returned upon it several times, did not sound as if it were made in earnest, and this was Christopher's one solace.

"Will you meet me reg'lar, once a week," he pleaded, "just for a talk?"

"No, it's too often."

"I know what that means," exclaimed the young man in the bitterness of his soul. "There's somebody else. Yes, that's it; there's somebody else."

"Well, and what if there was?" asked Polly, looking far away. "I don't see as it would be any business of yours."

"Oh, just listen to that!" cried Christopher. "That's how a girl talks to you when she knows you're ready to jump into the river! It's my belief that girls haven't much feeling."

The outrageous audacity of this avowal saved the speaker from Polly's indignation. She saw that he was terribly driven, and, in spite of herself, once more softened towards him; for Polly had never disliked Mr. Parish; from the very first his ingenuous devotedness excited in her something, however elementary, of reciprocal feeling. She thought him comely to look upon, and had often reflected upon how pleasant it was to rule a man by her slightest look or word. To be sure, Christopher's worldly position was nothing to boast

PURSUING A BROUGHAM 147

of; but one knew him for the steady, respectable young clerk, who is more likely than not to advance by modest increments of salary. Miss Sparkes would have perceived, had she been capable of intellectual perception, that Christopher answered fairly well to one of her ideals. Others there were, which tended to draw her from him, but she had never yet deliberately turned her back upon the young man.

So now, instead of answering bitterness with wrath, she spoke more gently than of wont.

"Don't take on in that way, you'll only have a headache to-morrow. I can't promise to meet you regular, but you can write, and I'll let you know when I'm ready for a talk. There now, won't that do?"

Christopher had to make it do, and presently accepted the conditions with tolerable grace. Before they parted Polly even assured him that if ever there *was* anyone else she would deal honestly with him and let him know. This being as much as to say that he might still hope, Christopher cast away his thoughts of self-destruction, and went home with an appetite for a late supper.

Two months elapsed before anything of moment occurred in the relations thus established. Then at one of their brief meetings Polly delighted the young man by telling him that he might wait for her outside the theatre on a certain evening of the same week. Hitherto such awaitings had been strictly forbidden.

"Won't I, just!" cried Mr. Parish. "And you'll come and have some supper?"

"I can't promise; I may want to ask you to do something for me. Just you be ready, that's all."

He promised exultingly, and when the evening came took up his position a full hour before Polly could be expected to come forth.

Now this was the first night of a new piece at Polly's theatre, and she, long watching in vain for the reappearance of the lady whose address she was to discover for Mr. Gammon, thought it a very possible thing that a person who had been twice to see the old entertainment might attend the first performance of the new. Her mysterious uncle had never again communicated with her, and Polly began to doubt what Mr. Gammon's knowledge really was; but she had given her confidence beyond recall, and, though with many vicissitudes of feeling, she still wished to keep Gammon sole ally in this strange affair. Once or twice indeed she had felt disposed to tell Christopher that there was "someone else"; but nothing Gammon had said fully justified this, and Polly, though an emotional young woman, had a good deal of prudence. One thing was certain, she very much desired to bring her old enemy to the point of a declaration. How she would receive it when it came she could not wholly determine.

Her conjecture regarding the unknown lady was justified. Among the first who entered the stalls was a man whom Polly seemed to remember, and close behind him came first a younger lady, then the one for whom her eyes had searched night after night. In supplying them with programmes Polly observed and listened with feverish attention. The elder woman had slightly grizzled hair; her age could not be less than fifty, but she was in good health and spirits. With the intention of describing her to Gammon, Polly noticed that she had a somewhat masculine nose, high in the bridge.

A quarter of an hour before the end of the piece Polly, dressed for departure, came forth and discovered her faithful slave.

"Now listen to me," she said, checking his blandishments. "I told you there might be something to do for me, and there is."

Parish was all eagerness.

"There'll be three people coming out from the stalls, a gentleman and two ladies. I'll show you them—see? They'll drive off in a kerridge—see? And I want you to find out where they go."

Nothing could have been more startling to Christopher, in whose mind began a whirl of suspicions and fears.

"Why? What for?" he asked involuntarily.
Polly was short with him.

"All right, if you won't do it say so, and I'll ask somebody else. I've no time to lose."

He gasped and stammered. Yes, yes, of course he would do it. He had not dreamt of refusing. He would run after the carriage, however far.

"Don't be a silly. You'll have to take a 'ansom and tell the driver to follow—see?"

Yes, oh yes, of course. He would do so. He trembled with excessive nervousness, and but for the sharp, contemptuous directions given him by Miss Sparkes must have hopelessly bungled the undertaking. Indeed, it was not easy to carry out in the confusion before a theatre when the audience is leaving, and bearing in mind the regulations concerning vehicles. Their scheme was based upon the certainty that the carriage must proceed at a very moderate pace for some two or three hundred yards; within that limit or a very little beyond it—at all events, before his breath was exhausted—Christopher would certainly be able to hail a cab.

"Tell the cabby they're friends of yours," said Polly, "and you're going to the same 'ouse. You look quite respectable enough with your 'igh 'at. That's what I like about you; you always look respectable."

"But—but he will set me down right beside the people."

"Well, what if he does, gooseberry? Can't you just pay him quietly? They'll think you're for next door."

"But—but it may be a big house by itself somewhere."

"Well, silly. They'll think it's a mistake, that's all. What's the matter in the dark? You do as I tell you. And when you've got to know the address — you can take your time about that, of course—come back along Shaftesbury Avenue and give three knocks at the door, and I'll come down."

It flashed through Christopher's mind that he would be terribly late in getting home, but there was no help for it. If he refused this undertaking, or failed to carry it out successfully, Polly would cast him off. The gloom of a desperate mood fell upon him. He had the feeling of a detective or of a criminal, he knew not which; the mystery of the affair was a hideous oppression.

Even the initial step, that of watching the trio of strangers into their brougham, was not without difficulty. The pavement began to be crowded. Clutching her slave by the arm, Polly managed to hold a position whence she could see the people who descended the front steps of the theatre, and at length her energy was rewarded. The ladies she could not have recognized, for they were muffled against the night air, but their male companion she "spotted"—that was the word in her mind—with certainty.

"There! See those three? That's them," she whispered excitedly. "Off you go!"

And off he went, as if life depended upon it; his eyes on the brougham, his heart throbbing violently, moisture dropping from his forehead and making his collar limp. The carriage disengaged itself, the pace quickened, he began to run, and collided with pedestrians who cursed him. Now —now or never—a cab!

By good luck he plunged into a hansom wanting a fare.

"The carriage—friends of mine—that carriage!"

"Ketch 'em up?" asked the driver briskly.

"No—same 'ouse—follow!"

As he flung himself into the vehicle he seriously feared he was on the point of breaking a blood vessel, never had he been at such extremity of breath. But his eyes clung to the brougham in dread lest he should lose sight of it, or confuse it with another. The driver whipped his horse. Thank goodness, the carriage remained well in sight. But if there should come a block! A perilous point was Piccadilly Circus. Never, it seemed to him, had the streets of London roared with such a tumult of traffic. Right! The Circus was passed; now Piccadilly with its blessed quietness. What a speed they kept! Hyde Park Corner, Knightsbridge, and—what road was that? Christopher's geography failed him; he pretended to no familiarity with the West End. On swept his hansom in what he felt to be a most impudent pursuit; nay, for all he knew, it might subject him to the suspicion of the police. The cabby need not follow so close; why, the horse's nose all but touched the brougham now and then. How much further? How was he to get back? He could not possibly reach home till one in the morning.

The brougham made a sharp curve, the hansom followed. Then came a sudden stop.

CHAPTER XV.

THE NAME OF GILDERSLEEVE

A SQUARE—imposing houses about a space of verdure. That was what Christopher perceived as he looked wildly round, flung back the apron, jumped out. His position was awful; voices of the persons alighting from the brougham seemed to sound at his very ear; he had become one of the party; the man in evening dress stared at him. But even in this dread moment so bent was he on fulfilling his mission that he at once cast an eye over the front of the house to fix it in his memory. There was a magnificent display of flowers at every window; the houses immediately right and left had no flowers at all.

Then he fumbled for money. Coppers, a sixpence, a shilling, no other small change, and he durst not offer so little as eighteenpence. (However, Heaven be thanked! the people had gone in and the brougham was moving away.) In his purse he had half a sovereign.

NAME OF GILDERSLEEVE 155

"Got change?" he enquired as boldly as possible.

"How much?" returned the driver curtly, for he had noticed with curiosity that his fare exchanged no greeting with the carriage people and that the door was shut.

"Change for half a sovereign. Seven shillings would do."

"Ain't got it. See, fourpence in 'apence, that's all."

The man's eye began to alarm Christopher. He shook with indecision, he gulped down his bitterness, he handed the golden coin.

"All right; never mind change."

"Thanky, sir. Good-night."

And Mr. Parish was alone on the pavement. So grievously did he feel for the loss of that half-sovereign that for some moments he could think of nothing else. His heart burned against Polly. What had she got to do with those people in the big house? How could he be sure that it did not imply some shameful secret? And he must go throwing away his hard-earned money! Gladly he would have spent it on a supper for Polly; but to pay ten shillings for a half-crown drive! A whole blessed half-sovereign!

Another carriage drove up and stopped at the next house. Christopher remembered that he must discover the address, an easy matter enough. He found that the square was called Stanhope Gardens; he noted the number of the house with flowers. Then, weary, disgusted, he started on his eastward walk. Omnibuses, of course, there were none. The chance of a train at some underground station seemed too doubtful to think about; in any case he had no more money to waste.

On he plodded, heavily, angrily—Cromwell Road, Brompton Road, at last Piccadilly, and so into familiar districts, though he had never walked here so late at night. Of course there would be nasty questions to-morrow; Theodore would look grave, and Ada would be virtuously sour, and his mother —but perhaps they would not worry her by disclosing such things. Unaccustomed to express himself with violence, Christopher at about half-past twelve found some relief in a timid phrase or two of swearing.

When he reached Shaftesbury Avenue he was dog-tired. The streets had now become very quiet; he felt a doubt as to the possibility of knocking at a house door. But Polly had said he was to do so, be the hour what it might. The front of the house was dark, not a glimmer in any windows. Doubtfully he drew near and knocked thrice.

Minutes passed, nearly five, in fact, then he knocked again. He would wait five minutes more, and then—

NAME OF GILDERSLEEVE 157

But the door softly opened.

"That you?" said Polly's voice.

"Yes, it is."

She opened the door wide, and he saw by the light from the street that she was dressed as usual.

"How late you are! Well? Can't you speak?"

"I'm dead beat, that's the truth," he replied, leaning against the door-post. "Walked back all the way from South Kensington."

"Oh, it was there, was it?" said Polly, without heed to his complaint. "What's the address?"

"I tell you what, Polly," broke from Christopher's dry lips, "I think you might show a bit more feeling for a fellow when he's walked himself to death——"

"You might have took a cab just for this once."

"A cab! Why, the other one cost me half a sovereign!"

"Half a sovereign!" echoed Polly in amazement. "To South Kensington!"

It did not occur to Mr. Parish that such a detail might be left unmentioned. In these little matters there is a difference between class and class. Polly was not, of course, surprised at his letting her know what the mission had cost him, but the sum made her indignant.

"Well, he had you, that cabby!"

Christopher related the circumstances, still leaning in exhaustion against the door-post, and Miss Sparkes, who under no conceivable stress could have suffered herself to be so "done out of" a piece of gold, scarcely knew whether to despise or to pity him. After all a compassionate feeling prevailed, sure sign that there was something disinterested in her association with this young man.

"I'm very sorry," she said; "I never thought it 'ud cost you that much."

"I shouldn't care a bit," Christopher replied, "if you treated me better now I've got here."

Polly moved just a little nearer to him, ever so little, but the movement was appreciable. Unfortunately Christopher was too weary to notice it.

"What was the address?" she asked in an undertone, which, had but Mr. Parish understood, fitly accompanied that little movement.

He told her bluntly, and Polly repeated the words.

"And now I suppose I may say good-night," Christopher added, still with discontent.

"Well, thank you very much for getting me that address."

"But you won't tell me what you want it for?"

"I will some time. I can't just now. It's awful late, and we mustn't stand talking here."

Again she came one step nearer. Now if Christopher Parish had not lost half a sovereign, or if he had been less worn out, or if the mystery of the evening had not lain so heavy on his mind, assuredly he would have noticed this onward coming; for, as a rule, the young man was sensitive and perceptive enough, all things considered. Alas! he did not look into Polly's face, which in the dusk of the doorway had turned towards his.

"I'll be going then," he muttered. "Good-night. Jolly long walk before me still."

"I'm very sorry. I am, really."

"Oh, never mind! When shall I see you again?"

The crucial moment was past. Polly drew a step back and held the door.

"I'll write before long. Good-night, and thank you."

Mr. Parish plodded away down the avenue, saying to himself that he was blest if he'd be make a fool of like this much longer.

The next morning Polly wrote a line to Mr. Gammon, and two days later, on Sunday, they met in that little strip of garden on the Embankment which lies between Charing Cross Station and Waterloo Bridge. It was the first week of October; a cold wind rustled the yellowing plane trees, and open-air seats offered no strong temptation. The two conversed as they walked along. Polly had not mentioned in her letter any special reason for wishing to see Mr. Gammon, nor did she hasten to make known her discovery.

"Why do you wear a 'at like that on a Sunday?" she began by asking, tartly.

"Because it's comfortable, I suppose," answered Gammon, reflecting for the first time that it was not very respectful to come to this rendezvous in a "bowler." Polly had never mentioned the matter before, though she had thought about it. "You like the chimney-pot better?"

"Why, of course I do. On a Sunday, too, who wouldn't?"

"I'll bear it in mind, my dear. My chimney-pot wants ironing. Have it done to-morrow if I can find time."

Polly scrutinized the costume of a girl walking with a soldier, and asked all at once, indifferently:

"Do you know anybody called Gildersleeve?"

"Gildersleeve? Don't think so. No. Why?"

She searched his face to make sure that he did not simulate ignorance.

"Well, you wanted me to find out where that lady lived—you know—her as was with Mr. C—— at the theatre."

"And you've got it?" cried Gammon excitedly.

Yes, she had got it, and by consulting a directory at a public-house she had discovered the name of the family residing at that address. Gildersleeve? The name conveyed nothing to Mr. Gammon; none the less he was delighted.

"Good for you, Polly. But how did you do it?"

She put on an air of mystery. Never mind how; there was the address, if he could make any use of it. Gammon smiled provokingly.

"Some friend of yours, eh? You're well off for friends, Polly. I ask no questions, my dear; no business of mine. Much obliged to you, all the same."

"If you're so particular about who it was," said Polly, with her air of pique and propriety, "well, it's a boy. So you needn't look at me like that."

"A boy, eh?"

"Well, that's what *I* think him. He's a young clurk in the City as I've known long enough, and *I* think him a boy. Of course you're always ready to believe harm of me—that's nothing new. And if the truth was known, you go talkin' to Mrs. Bubb and them Cheesemans."

"I don't! I told you I shouldn't, and I don't!"

"You do!"

"It's a lie!"

"You're one yourself!" retorted Polly with heat.

Thereupon Mr. Gammon turned about and walked

off. Polly could not believe that he would really go. Scorning to look back she paced on for some minutes, but no familiar step approached her; when at length she looked round Mr. Gammon was nowhere to be seen. This extraordinary behaviour she attributed to jealousy, and so was not entirely displeased. But the idea of leaving her in the middle of the street, as one might say! Did one ever! And just after he'd got what he wanted.

"All right, old fellow! Wait till you want to see me again, that's all."

To have his word disbelieved was the one thing fatal to Gammon's temper. He strode off in a towering rage, determined to hold no more communication with Miss Sparkes, and blaming himself for having got into such an ambiguous position towards her. As if he had ever really cared one snap of the fingers for the red-headed spitfire! She to tell him to his face that his word was not to be trusted! He had never stood that yet, from man or woman!

At this rate he would presently have no female friends at all. Mrs. Clover he had not once seen since the evening at Mrs. Bubb's, and every day that went by put a greater distance between them. He understood her unfriendliness; she thought this the best way of destroying any hopes he might still entertain with reference to Minnie; yes, that

NAME OF GILDERSLEEVE 163

was the only possible explanation of her silence. It was too bad; Mrs. Clover might have put more faith in him. Now he would not visit her; he would not write. If she wished to see him again, let her acknowledge the wrong she had done him.

As for the muddle about her husband, be hanged to it! He would think no more about the business. Ten to one this address that Polly had obtained would be quite useless. How could he go to strangers (named Gildersleeve) and coolly enquire of them whether they knew a man named Clover? Of course they would have him kicked into the street, and serve him right.

Polly and her boy! A young City clerk, eh? Old enough to wear a chimney-pot, he'd be bound. Polly was fond of chimney-pots. There, he had done with her, and with Clover and Quodling and Gildersleeve, and all the rest of the puzzle.

As he suddenly entered the house Moggie ran to him up the kitchen stairs.

"There's been a gentleman for you, Mr. Gammon."

"Oh! Who was it?"

"Mr. Greenacres, driving a trap, and the 'orse wouldn't stand still, and he said he'd see you some other time."

"Greenacre, eh? All right."

He sat for a quarter of an hour in his bedroom, unable to decide how he should spend the rest of the day. After all, perhaps, he ought not to have abandoned Polly so abruptly. In her own way she had been doing him a kindness, and as for her temper, well, she couldn't help it.

He would go to Dulwich and see the bow-wows.

CHAPTER XVI.

AN ALLY IN THE QUEST

COMMERCIALLY he was doing well. Quodling and Son were more than satisfied with him. Excellent prospects lay ahead, and this time it would assuredly be his own fault if he had not secured the "permanency" so much desired for him by Mrs. Clover.

By-the-bye, would this make any difference? What if he let Mrs. Clover know of his greatly improved position? She might reconsider things. And yet, as often as he thought of Minnie, he felt that her mother's objection corresponded too well with the disposition of the girl. Minnie was not for him. Well and good, he would find somebody else.

Polly Sparkes? Polly be hanged! Why did her eyes and her teeth and her rosy cheeks keep plaguing him? He had told himself times innumerable that he cared not a snap of the fingers for Polly and all her highly-coloured attractions.

If only he had not been such a fool as to treat her shabbily last Sunday morning! He felt sorry, and couldn't get rid of the vexation.

It worried him this afternoon as he left Quodlings' in Norton Folgate and walked towards the Bank. He was thinking, too, of a poor fellow with a large family for whom he had tried these last few days to find employment, without the usual success. In Threadneedle Street a hand arrested him.

"Just the man I wanted," said the voice of Mr. Greenacre. He was in an elegant overcoat, with a silk hat of the newest fashion. "You remember your promise?"

"What promise?"

"Nonsense! But we can't talk about it here. Come to the Bilboes. Don't know the Bilboes? What a mood you're in to-day."

Mr. Gammon flattered himself that he knew the City tolerably well, but with the place of refreshment to which his friend now led him he was totally unacquainted. It stood or lurked in a very obscure by-way between the Bank and St. Paul's, and looked externally by no means inviting; within, but for the absence of daylight at all times, it was comfortable enough, and peculiarly quiet—something between an old inn and a modern public-house, with several small rooms for eating, drinking, smoking, or any other legitimate occupation. The few men who were about had a prosperous appearance, and Gammon saw that they did not belong to his special world.

"What does the name mean?" he enquired, as they seated themselves under a gas-jet in a corner made cosy with a deep divan.

"Bilboes? Oh, I originated it in the days gone by. The proprietor was a man called William Bowes—you perceive? Poor little Jimmy Todd used to roar about it. The best-natured fellow that ever lived. You've heard me speak of him— second son of Sir Luke Todd. Died, poor boy, out in India."

"What promise of mine were you talking about?" asked Gammon, when an order for drinks had been given.

"Promise—promise? Nonsense! You're wool-gathering to-day, my dear boy. By-the-bye, I called at your place on Sunday. I was driving a very fresh pony, new to harness; promised to trot her round a little for a friend of mine. Thought you might have liked a little turn on the Surrey roads."

Greenacre chatted with his usual fluency, and seemed at ease in the world.

"You're doing well just now, eh?" said Gammon presently.

"Thanks; feel remarkably well. A touch of liver

now and then, but nothing serious. By-the-bye, anything I can do for you? Any genealogy?"

Gammon had drained his tumbler of hot whisky, and felt better for it. With the second he became more communicative. He asked himself why, after all, he should not hang on to the clue he had obtained from Polly, and why Greenacre should not be made use of.

"Know anything about a Gildersleeve?" he asked with a laugh.

His companion smiled cheerfully, looking at once more interested.

"Gildersleeve! Why, yes, there was a boy of that name—no, no; it was Gildersleeves, I remember. Any connection with Quodling?"

"Can't say. The people I mean live in Stanhope Gardens. I don't know anything about them."

"Like to?"

Gammon admitted that the name had a significance for him. A matter of curiosity.

"No harm in a bit of genealogy," said Greenacre. "Always interesting. Stanhope Gardens? What number?"

He urged no further question and gave no promise, but Gammon felt sure this time that information would speedily be forthcoming. Scarcely a week passed before Greenacre wrote to him with a request for a meeting at the Bilboes. As usual, the man of mystery approached his subject by indirect routes. Beginning with praise of London as the richest ground of romance discoverable in the world, he proceeded to tell the story of a cats'-meat woman who, after purveying for the cats at a West End mansion for many years, discovered one day that the master of the house was her own son.

"He behaved to her very handsomely. At this moment she is living in a pleasant little villa out Leatherhead way. You see her driving herself in a little donkey-carriage, and throwing bits of meat to pussy-cats at the cottage doors. Touch of nature that, isn't it? By-the-bye, you were speaking of a family named Gildersleeve."

He added this, absently looking about the little room, which just now they had to themselves.

"Know anything about them?" asked Gammon, eyeing him curiously.

"I was just going to say—ah, yes, to be sure, the Gildersleeves. Now I wonder, Gammon—forgive me, I can't help wondering—*why* this family interests you."

"Oh, nothing. I came across the name."

"Evidently." Greenacre's tone became a little more positive. "I'm sure you have no objection to telling me how and where you came across it."

Gammon had an uncomfortable sense of something unfamiliar in his friend. Greenacre had never spoken in this way to him; it sounded rather too imperative, too much the tone of a superior.

"I don't think I can tell you that," he said awkwardly.

"No? Really? I'm sorry. In that case I can't tell you anything that I have learnt. Yet I fancy it *might* be worth your while to exchange."

"Exchange?"

"Your information for mine, you know. What I have is substantial, reliable. I think you can trust me in matters of genealogy. Come now. Am I right in supposing this curiosity of yours is not altogether unconnected with your interest in Francis Quodling the silk broker? Nothing to me, Gammon; nothing, I assure you. Pure love of genealogical enquiry. Never made a penny out of such things in my life. But I have taken a little trouble, etc. As a matter of friendship—no? Then we'll drop the subject. By-the-bye have you a black-and-tan to dispose of?"

He passed into a vein so chatty and so amiable that Gammon began to repent of distrusting him. Besides, his information might be really valuable and could not easily be obtained in any other way.

"Look here, Greenacre, I don't see why I shouldn't tell you. The fact is, a man I used to know has disappeared, and I want to find him. He was seen

AN ALLY IN THE QUEST

at the theatre with a lady who lives at that house; that's the long and the short of it."

"Good. Now we're getting on in the old way. Age of the man about fifty, eh? And if I remember you said he was like Quodling in the face, Francis Quodling? Just so, h'm. I can assure you, then, that no such individual lives at the house we're speaking of."

"No, but perhaps——"

"One moment. The Gildersleeves are a young married couple. With them lives an older lady——"

Greenacre paused, meditating.

"The name of the missing man?" he added gently.

"Fellow called Clover."

"Clover—Clover? *Clo*——?"

Greenacre's first repetition of the name was mechanical, the next sounded a note of confused surprise, the third broke short in a very singular way, just as if his eyes had suddenly fallen on something which startled him into silence. Yet no one had entered the room, no face had appeared at the door.

"What's up?" asked Gammon.

The other regained his self-possession, as though he had for a moment wandered mentally from the subject they were discussing.

"Forgive me. What name did you say? Yes,

yes, Clover. Odd name. Tell me something about him. Where did you know him? What was he?"

Having gone so far, Gammon saw no reason for refusing the details of the story. With the pleasure that every man feels in narrating circumstances known only to a few, he told all he could about the career of Mrs. Clover's husband. Greenacre listened with a placidly smiling attention.

"Just the kind of thing I am always coming across," he remarked. "Every-day story in London. We must find this man. Do you know his Christian name?"

Mrs. Clover called him Mark.

"Mark? May or may not be his own, of course. And now, if you permit the question, who saw this man and recognized him in the theatre?"

Gammon gave a laugh. Then, fearing that he might convey a wrong impression, he answered seriously that it was a niece of Mrs. Clover, a young lady with whom he was on friendly terms, nothing whatever but friendly terms; a most respectable young lady—anxious, naturally, to bring Mrs. Clover and her husband together again, but discreet enough to have kept the matter quiet as yet. And he explained how it came about that this young lady knew only the address in Stanhope Gardens.

After reflecting upon that, Greenacre urged that

AN ALLY IN THE QUEST

it would be just as well not to take the young lady into their counsel for the present, to which his friend readily assented. And so, when they had chatted a little longer, the man of mystery rose "to keep an appointment." Gammon should hear from him in a day or two.

When ten days had gone by without the fulfilment of this promise Gammon grew uneasy. He could not communicate with Greenacre, having no idea where the man lived or where he was to be heard of; an enquiry at "The Bilboes" proved that he was not known there. One evening Gammon went to look for himself at the house in Stanhope Gardens; he hung about the place for half an hour, but saw nothing of interest or importance. He walked once or twice along Shaftesbury Avenue, but did not chance to meet Polly, and could not make up his mind to beg an interview with her. At the end of a fortnight Greenacre wrote, and that evening they met again at the obscure house of entertainment.

"It is not often," said Greenacre, in a despondent tone, "that I have found an enquiry so difficult. Of course it interests me all the more, and I shall go on with it, but I must freely confess that I've got nothing yet, absolutely nothing."

Gammon observed him vigilantly.

"Do you know what has occurred to me?" pursued

the other, with a half melancholy droop of the head. "I really begin to fear that the young lady, your friend, may have made a mistake."

"How can that be, when he met her twice and talked with her?"

"You didn't tell me that," replied Greenacre, as if surprised.

"No, I didn't mention it. I thought it was enough to tell you she spied him at the theatre."

He added a brief account of what had happened between Polly and her uncle, Greenacre listening as if this threw new light on the case.

"Then the mistake is mine. It's more interesting than ever. This puts me on my mettle, Gammon. Don't lose courage. I have a wonderful scent in this kind of thing. Above all, not a word to anybody—you understand the importance of *that?*"

"That's all right."

"I have a theory—oh, yes, there's a theory. Without a theory nothing can be done. I am working, Gammon, on the scientific principle of induction."

"Oh, are you!"

"Strictly; it has never failed me yet.—I can't stay now; appointment at 10.30. But you shall hear from me in a day or two."

AN ALLY IN THE QUEST

"I say," enquired Gammon, "what's your address now?"

"Address?—oh, address letters to this place. They'll be all right."

Another fortnight passed. It was now early in November; the weather gloomy, and by no means favourable to evening strolls. Gammon wanted much to see both Polly and Mrs. Clover; he had all but made up his mind to write to both of them, yet could not decide on the proper tone in either case. Was he to be humble to Mrs. Clover? Should he beg pardon of Polly? That kind of thing did not come easily to him.

On a day of thin yellow fog he returned about noon from seeing to a piece of business, the result of which he had to report at once to Mr. Quodling. He entered the clerk's office and asked whether 'the governor' was alone."

"No, he ain't," replied a friendly young man. "He's got a lord with him."

"A what?"

"A peer of the realm, sir! I had the honour of taking his ludship's card in—Lord Poll-parrot. Can't say I ever heard of him before."

"What d'you mean? See here, I'm in a hurry; no kid, Simpson."

"Well, it might be Poll-parrot. As a matter of fact, it's Lord Polperro."

Gammon gazed fixedly at the young man.

"Lord Polperro? By jorrocks!"

"Know him, Mr. Gammon?" asked another of the clerks.

"I know his name. All right, I'll wait."

Musing on the remarkable coincidence—which seemed to prove beyond doubt that there still existed some connexion between the family of Quodling and the titled house which he had heard of from Greenacre—he stood in the entrance passage, and looked out for five minutes through the glass door at the fog-dimmed traffic of Norton Folgate. Then a step sounded behind him. He moved aside and saw a man in a heavy fur-lined overcoat, with a muffler loose about his neck; a thin, unhealthy-looking man, with sharp eyes, rather bloodshot, which turned timidly this way and that, and a high-bridged nose. As soon as he caught sight of the face Gammon drew himself up, every muscle strung. The man observed him, looked again more furtively, stepped past to the door.

It took Gammon but a moment to dart into the clerk's room and ascertain that the person who had just gone out was Lord Polperro. A moment more and he was out in the street. The heavy-coated and muffled man was walking quickly southward; he waved his umbrella to a passing cab, which,

AN ALLY IN THE QUEST

however, did not pull up. Gammon followed for thirty yards. Again the man hailed a cab, and this time successfully. Just as he was about to step into the vehicle Gammon stood beside him.

"How do you do, Mr. Clover?"

CHAPTER XVII.

POLLY SHOWS WEAKNESS

IT was spoken with quiet confidence. Gammon smiled as he looked steadily into the pale, thin face, which at once grew mottled with a disturbance of the blood.

"You are making a mistake, sir," replied an indistinct voice, with an effort at dignity.

"Oh, no, not a bit of it. Not now I've heard you speak, Mr. Clover."

"I don't understand you, sir," sounded more clearly, the pallid visage now a muddy red and the eyes moist. "That is not my name. Be so good as to go your way."

"Certainly. I just wanted to make sure, that's all. No fuss. Good-morning, Mr. Clover."

Gammon drew back. He heard the order "Charing Cross," and the cab drove away.

After a moment or two of irresolution Gammon walked hurriedly back to the nearest public-house, where he called for a glass of bitter and the Directory.

With the former he slaked a decided dryness of the throat, the latter he searched eagerly in the section "Court." There it was! "Polperro, Lord, 16, Lowndes Mansions, Sloane Street, S.W. Junior Ramblers' Club. Trefoyle, Liskeard, Cornwall."

By jorrocks!

With thoughts tuned to anything but the oil and colour business he returned to Quodlings' and had his interview with the head of the firm. Mr. Quodling, senior, was a gruff, heavy-featured man, decidedly of coarse fibre; when moved he swore with gusto, and it did not take much to put him out. At present he was in an irritable mood, and, very unlike his habit, gave scant attention to the affair of which Gammon spoke. It would not have improved his temper had he known that the town traveller was amusing himself with the reflection that there was no trace of personal resemblance between him and his brother Francis, who, on the other hand, bore a very strong likeness indeed to—Lord Polperro.

As soon as he could get away Gammon despatched a telegram. It was to Miss Sparkes, whom he requested to meet him at the theatre door that night when she left. "Something very important to tell you."

This was done on a tell-tale impulse; it showed in what direction his thoughts and mind most readily turned just now. Thinking it over in the hours that followed he doubted whether, after all, he would tell Polly exactly what had happened; she could be useful to him in the way he intended without knowing more than she had discovered for herself. Doubt as to the identity of Lord Polperro with Mrs. Clover's husband he had none whatever—face, voice, trick of lips, and eyebrows made mistake an impossibility; but he must bring the man into a position where there would be no choice but to reveal himself, and, so far as Gammon knew, no one but Polly could help to that end. With Mrs. Clover he would communicate when the facts of the strange story were made plain; not yet awhile. And as for Greenacre, why, it was splendid to have got beforehand with that keen-scented fellow. The promise to keep silence held good only whilst their search might be hindered by someone's indiscretion. Now that the search was over he felt himself free to act as he chose.

But what an astounding discovery! Again and again, by jorrocks!

He was near the theatre long before his time. He had never waited so long or so impatiently for anyone since the days of his first sweethearting, twenty and odd years ago. When Polly at length came out she met him with a shyness and awkwardness which he fancied he perfectly understood.

"I want you to come with me where we can have a quiet talk," he said at once in a tone of eager

POLLY SHOWS WEAKNESS 181

cordiality. "It's too wet for walking; we'll have a cab."

Polly gazed at him in unfeigned surprise, and asked where they were to go. Not far, he replied; here was a cab; in with her. And before she could decide upon resistance Polly was seated by him. Gammon then explained that he had the use of a sitting-room at a coffee tavern; they would be there in a minute or two. There was good news for her, news that couldn't be told in the street or in a crowded restaurant.

"Did you get my letter?" she asked, shrinking as far from him as space allowed.

"Letter? When?"

"I posted it this morning," Polly answered in a timidly sullen voice.

He had not been home since breakfast-time. She had written to him? Now, wasn't that a queer thing! All yesterday he, too, had thought of writing, and to-day would have done so in any case. Never mind, the letter would be waiting for him. Was it nice? Was it sweet and amiable, like herself? Ha! ha! Ho! ho!

As he laughed the cab drew up with a jerk. Polly saw that she was in a familiar thoroughfare and in front of a respectable establishment, but it was not without a little distrust that she entered by the private door and went upstairs. A large room, so ugly and uncomfortable that it helped to reassure her, was quickly lighted. Gammon requested the woman in attendance to bring pen, ink, and paper, whereat Polly again stared her surprise.

"Come and sit over here," said Gammon, "away from the door. Now make yourself comfortable, old girl. Sure you won't have anything?"

The writing materials were brought; the door was closed.

"Now we're all right. A long time since we saw each other, Polly. Have you heard anything? Any more about Mr. C.?"

She shook her head.

"Well, look here now, I want you to write to him. You didn't believe me when I said I knew. Well, you'll believe me now. I want you to write to him, and to ask him to meet you *here*. If he won't come I know what to do next. But you just write a few lines, you know how. You want to see him at this coffee tavern at five o'clock to-morrow; he's to come to the private door and ask for Miss—let's say Miss Ellis—that'll do. I shall be here, but not in the room at first; I'll come in when you've had a little talk. I don't think he'll refuse to come when he sees you've got his address."

"What is the address?"

"Patience, my dear; wait till you've written the

POLLY SHOWS WEAKNESS 183

letter. I'll walk up and down the room whilst you do it."

He began pacing, but Polly made no movement towards the table. She was strangely sullen, or, perhaps, depressed; not at all like herself, even when in anger. She cast glances at her companion, and seemed desirous of saying something—of making some protest—but her tongue failed her.

"No hurry," Gammon remarked, after humming through a tune. "Think it out. Only a line or two."

"Are you telling me the truth about my letter?" she suddenly asked. "You haven't read it?"

"I assure you I haven't. That's a treat for when I get home."

Still she delayed, but before Gammon had taken many more steps she was seated at the table, and biting the end of the penholder.

"You'll have to tell me what to say."

"All right. Take the words down."

He dictated with all possible brevity. The letter was folded and enclosed. Only in the last few minutes had Gammon quite decided to share his knowledge with Polly. As she bent her head and wrote, something in the attitude—perhaps a suggestion of domesticity—appealed to his emotions, which were ready for such a juncture as this. After all there were not many girls prettier than Polly, or with more of the attractiveness of their sex. He looked, looked till he could not turn away.

"Now then for the address. I'll write it on this piece of paper, and you shall copy it."

Polly watched him, puzzled by the nervous grin on his face. She took the paper, on which he had written as legibly as he could—

"Lord Polperro,
    16, Lowndes Mansions,
        Sloane Street,
            S.W."

And having read it she stared at him.

"What d'you mean?"

"That's the address."

"Are you making a fool of me?" Polly exclaimed, angry suspicion flashing in her eyes.

"I tell you that's your uncle's address. Now be careful, Polly! I won't stand it a second time."

He was only half joking. Excitement tingled in him—the kind of excitement which might lead either to rage or caresses. He swayed now on one foot, now on the other, as if preparing for a dance, and his fists were clenched upon his hips.

"You mean to say that's his *real* name?" cried Polly, she, too, quivering and reddening.

"I do. Now mind, Polly; mind what you say, my girl! I won't stand it a second time."

POLLY SHOWS WEAKNESS 185

"Don't go on like a ijiot!" exclaimed the girl, starting up from her chair. "Of course I'll believe it if you tell me you're not kidding. And you mean to say he's a lord?"

"See for yourself."

"And his name ain't Clover at all? Then what's my awnt's name?"

"Why, Lady Polperro, of course! And Minnie is—well, I don't exactly know—Lady Minnie Polperro, I suppose. And you—no, I don't think it gives you a title; but, you see, you are the niece of Lord Polperro. Think of that, Polly; you've got a lord for your uncle—a peer of the realm!"

He came nearer and nearer as he spoke, his eyes distended with wild merriment, his arms swinging.

"And it's me that found it out, Polly! What have you got to say for it? Eh, old girl? What have you got to say?"

Polly uttered a scream of laughter and threw herself forward. Gammon's arms were ready; they clasped her and hugged her, she not dreaming of resistance—anything but that. Only when her face was very red, and her hat all but off, and her hair beginning to come loose, did she gently put him away.

"That'll do; that's enough."

"You mean it, don't you?" asked Gammon, tenderly enfolding her waist.

"I s'pose so; it looks like it. That'll do; let me git my breath. What a silly you are!"

"And were you fond of me all the time, Polly?" he whispered at her ear as she sat down.

"I dessay; how do I know? It's quite certain you wasn't fond of me, or you'd never have gone off like you did that Sunday."

"Why, I've been fond of you for no end of a time! Haven't I showed it in lots of ways? You must have known, and you did know."

"When you smashed my door in and fought me?" asked Polly with a shamefaced laugh.

"You don't think I'd have taken all that trouble if it hadn't been for the pleasure of carrying you downstairs?"

"Go along!"

"But there wasn't much love about you, Polly. You hit jolly hard, old girl, and you kicked and you scratched. Why, I've bruises yet!"

"Serve you right! Do let me put my 'air and my 'at straight."

"I say, Polly——" and he whispered something.

"I s'pose so—some day," was her answer, with head bent over the hat she was smoothing into shape.

"But won't you think yourself too good for me? Remember, you've got a lord for your uncle."

It returned upon both with the freshness of surprise; even Polly had quite lost sight of the startling fact during the last few minutes. They looked at the unaddressed letter; they gazed into each other's faces.

"You haven't gone and made a mistake?" asked Polly in an awed undertone.

"There now! You didn't think; you're beginning to be sorry."

"No, I'm not."

"You are; I can see it."

"Oh, all right; have it your own way! I thought you wouldn't be so sweet-tempered very long. You're all alike, you men."

"Why, it's you that can't keep your temper!" shouted Gammon. "I only wanted to hear you say it wouldn't make any difference, happen what might."

"And didn't I say it wouldn't?" shrilled Polly. "What more can I say?"

Strangely enough a real tear had started in her eye. Gammon saw it and was at once remorseful. He humbled himself before her; he declared himself a beast and a brute. Polly was a darling: far too good for him, too sweet and gentle and lovely. He ought to think himself the happiest man living, by jorrocks if he oughtn't! Just one more! Why, he liked a girl to have spirit! He wouldn't give tuppence farthing for fifty girls that couldn't speak up for themselves. And if she was the niece of a lord, why, she deserved it and a good deal more. She ought to be Lady Polly straight away; and hanged if he wouldn't call her so.

"Hadn't we better get this letter addressed?" Polly asked, very amiable again.

"Yes; it's getting late, I'm afraid."

Polly drew up to the table, but her hand was so unsteady that it cost her much trouble to manage the pen.

"I've wrote it awful bad. Does it matter?"

"Bad? Why it's beautifully written, Polly—Lady Polly, I mean. I've got a stamp."

She stuck it on to the envelope with an angle upwards; and Gammon declared that it was beautifully done; he never knew anyone stamp a letter so nicely. As she gazed at the completed missive Polly had a sudden thought which made a change in her countenance. She looked round.

"What is it?"

"He hasn't got another wife, has he?"

"Not likely," answered Gammon. "If so he's committed bigamy, and so much the worse for him. Your aunt must have been his first — it was so long ago."

"Couldn't you find out? Isn't there a book as gives all about lords and their families? I've heard so."

"I believe there is," replied the other thoughtfully. "I'll get a look at it somewhere. He's scamp enough for anything, I've no doubt. He comes of a bad lot, Polly. There's all sorts of queer stories about his father—at least, I suppose it was his father."

"Tell me some," said Polly with eagerness.

"Oh, I will some day. But now I come to think of it, I don't know when he became Lord Polperro. He couldn't, of course, till the death of his father. Most likely the old man was alive when he married your aunt. It's easy to understand now why he's led such a queer life, isn't it? I shouldn't a bit wonder if he went away the second time because his father had died. I'll find out about it. Would you believe, when I met him in the street and spoke to him, he pretended he'd never heard such a name as Clover!"

"You met him, did you? When?"

"Oh—I'll tell you all about that afterwards. It's getting late. We shall have lots of talk. You'll let me take you home? We'll have a cab, shall we? Lady Pollys don't walk about the streets on a wet night."

She stood in thought.

"I want you to do something for me."

"Right you are! Tell me and I'll do it like a shot, see if I don't."

His arm again encircled her, and this time Polly did not talk of her 'at or her 'air. Indeed, she bent her head, half hiding her face against him.

"You know that letter I sent you?"

"What's in it? Something nicey-picey?"

"I want you to let me go to the 'ouse with you—just to the door—and I want you to give me that letter back—just as it is—without opening it. You will, won't you, deary?"

"Of course I will, if you really mean it."

"I do, it was a *narsty* letter. I couldn't bear to have you read it now."

Gammon had no difficulty in imagining the kind of epistle which Polly would desire suppressed; yet, for some obscure reason, he would rather have read it. But his promise was given. Polly, in turn, promised to write another letter for him as soon as possible.

So they drove in a hansom, through a night which washed the fog away, to Kennington Road, and whilst Polly kept her place in the vehicle Gammon ran upstairs. There lay the letter on his dressing-table. He hastened down with it, and before handing it to its writer kissed the envelope.

"Go along!" exclaimed Polly, in high good humour, as she reached out with eager fingers.

Late as it was he accompanied her to Shaftesbury Avenue, and they parted tenderly after having come to an agreement about the next evening.

CHAPTER XVIII.

LORD POLPERRO'S REPRESENTATIVE

BY discreet enquiry Mr. Gammon procured an introduction to "Debrett," who supplied him with a great deal of information. In the first place he learnt that the present Lord Polperro, fourth of that title, was not the son, but the brother of the Lord Polperro preceding him, both being offspring, it was plain, of the peer whose will occasioned a law-suit some forty years ago. Granted the truth of scandalous rumour, which had such remarkable supports in facial characteristics, the present bearer of the title would be, in fact, half-brother to Francis Quodling. Again, it was discoverable that the Lord Polperro of to-day succeeded to the barony in the very year of Mrs. Clover's husband's second disappearance.

"Just what I said," was Gammon's mental comment as he thumped the aristocratic pages.

Now for the women. To begin with, Lord Polperro was set down a bachelor—ha! ha! Then he had one sister, Miss Adela Trefoyle, older than himself, and that might very well be the lady who was seen beside him at the theatre. Then again, though his elder brother's male children had died, there was living a daughter, by name Adeline, recently wedded to — by jorrocks ! — Lucian Gildersleeve, Esquire. Why, here was "the whole boiling of 'em !"

Mr. Gammon eagerly jotted down the particulars in his note-book, and swallowed the whisky at his side with gusto. Not once, however, had he asked himself why this man of guiles and freaks chose to mask under the name of Clover, an omission to be accounted for not by any lack of wit, but by mere educational defect. He could not have been further from suspecting that his utterance of the name Clover had given his genealogical friend a most important clue, and a long start in the search for the missing man.

Impatiently he awaited the early nightfall of the morrow. Business had to be attended to as usual ; but he went about with a bearing of extraordinary animation, now laughing to himself, now snapping his fingers, now (when he chanced to be out of people's sight) twirling round on one leg. Either of yesterday's events would have sufficed to exhilarate him ; together they whipped his blood and frothed his fancy. He had found Clover, who was a lord ! He had won the love of Polly Sparkes, who was the finest girl living ! Did ever the bagman of an oil and colour firm speed about his duties with such springs of excitement bubbling within him?

And Mrs. Clover? Ought she not to be told at once? Had he any right to keep to himself such a discovery as this? He knew, by police court precedent, that a false name in marriage did not invalidate the contract. Beyond shadow of doubt Mrs. Clover was Lady Polperro. And Minnie—why, suppose Minnie had favoured his suit, he would have been son-in-law of a peer! As it was, whom might not the girl marry! She would pass from the neighbourhood of Battersea Park Road to a house in Mayfair or Belgravia; from Doulton's and the china shop to unimaginable heights of social dignity. And who more fit for the new sphere? Mr. Gammon sighed, but in a moment remembered Polly and snapped his fingers.

A little before five o'clock he was hovering within sight of the coffee tavern, which already threw radiance into the murky and muddy street. In a minute or two he saw Polly and exchanged a quick word with her.

"Up you go! You'll find all ready. If he comes I shall see him, and I'll look in when you've had a little talk."

Polly disappeared, and Mr. Gammon again hovered. But who was this approaching? Of all unwelcome people at this moment, hanged if it wasn't Greenacre! What did the fellow want here? He was staring about him as if to make sure of an address. Worse than that, he stepped up to the private door of the coffee-tavern and rang the bell.

Shrinking aside into darkness, Gammon felt a shiver of unaccountable apprehension, which was quickly followed by a thrill of angry annoyance. What did this mean? The door had opened, Greenacre was admitted. What the devil did this mean? If it wasn't enough to make a fellow want to wring another fellow's neck!

He waited thirty seconds, thinking it was five minutes, then went to the door, rang, and entered.

"Who came in just now, miss?"

"The gentleman for the young lydy, sir."

"By jorrocks!"

Gammon mounted the stairs at break-neck speed and burst into the private sitting-room. There stood Polly, with her head up, looking pert indignation and surprise, and before her stood Greenacre, discoursing in his politest tone.

"What are you doing here?" asked Gammon breathlessly. "What are you up to, eh?"

"Ah, Gammon, how do you do? I'm glad you've dropped in. Let us sit down and have a quiet talk."

The man of mystery was very well dressed, very cool, more than equal to the situation. He took for granted the perfect friendliness of both Polly and

Gammon, smiled from one to the other, and as he seated himself, drew out a cigarette case.

"I'm sure Miss Sparkes won't mind. I have already apologised, Gammon, for the necessity of introducing myself. You, I am sure, will forgive me when you learn the position of affairs. I'm so glad you happened to drop in."

Declining a cigarette, Gammon stared about him in angry confusion. He had no words ready. Greenacre's *sang froid*, though it irritated him excessively, shamed him into quiet behaviour.

"When you entered, Gammon, I was just explaining to Miss Sparkes that I am here on behalf of her uncle, Lord Polperro."

"Oh, you are. And how do you come to know him?"

"Singular accident. The kind of thing that is constantly happening in London. Lord Polperro is living next door to an old friend of mine, a man I haven't seen for some seven or eight years till the other day. I happened to hear of my friend's address, called upon him, and there met his lordship. Now wasn't it a strange thing, Gammon? Just when you and I were so interested in a certain puzzle, a delightful bit of genealogy. Lord Polperro and I quite took to each other. He seemed to like my chat, and, in fact, we have been seeing a good deal of each other for a week or two."

"You kept this to yourself, Gammon."

"For a sufficient reason—anything but a selfish one. You, I may remark, also made a discovery and kept it to yourself."

"It was my own business."

"Certainly. Don't dream that I find fault with you, my dear fellow. It was the most natural thing in the world. Now let me explain. I grieve to tell you that Lord Polperro is in very poor health. To be explicit, he is suffering from a complication of serious disorders, among them disease of the heart." He paused to let his announcement have its full effect. "You will understand why I am here to represent him. Lord Polperro dare not, simply dare not, expose himself to an agitating interview; it might—it probably would—cost him his life. Miss Sparkes, I am sure you would not like to see your noble relative fall lifeless at your feet?"

Polly looked at Gammon, who, in spite of wrath, could not help smiling.

"He didn't do it in Lincoln's Inn Fields, Greenacre."

"He did not; but I very greatly fear that those meetings—of course I have heard of them—helped to bring about the crisis under which he is now suffering, as also did a certain other meeting which you will recollect, Gammon. Pray tell me, did Lord Polperro seem to you in robust health?"

"Can't say he did. Looked jolly seedy."

"Precisely. Acting on my advice he has left town for a few days. I shall join him to-morrow, and do my best to keep up his spirits. You will now see the necessity for using great caution, great consideration, in this strange affair. We can be quite frank with each other, Gammon, and of course we have no secrets from my new and valued friend—if she will let me call her so—Miss Polly Sparkes. One has but to look at Miss Sparkes to see the sweetness and thoughtfulness of her disposition. Come now, we are going to make a little plot together, to act for the best. I am sure we do not wish Lord Polperro's death. I am sure *you* do not, Miss Sparkes."

Polly again looked at Gammon, and muttered that of course she didn't. Gammon grinned. Feeling sure of his power to act independently, if need were, he began to see the jocose side of things.

"One question I should like to ask," continued Greenacre, lighting a second cigarette. "Has Mrs. Clover—as we will continue to call her, with an implied apology—been informed yet?"

"I haven't told her," said Gammon frankly.

"And I'm sure I haven't," added Polly, who had begun to observe Mr. Greenacre with a less hostile eye, and was recovering her native vivacity.

Greenacre looked satisfied.

"Then I think you have acted very wisely indeed

—as one might have expected from Miss Sparkes. I don't mean I shouldn't have expected it from you too, Gammon; but you and I are not on ceremony, old man. Now let me have your attention. We begin by admitting that Lord Polperro has put himself in a very painful position. Painful, let me tell you, in every sense. Lord Polperro desires nothing so much—nothing so much—as to be reunited to his family. He longs for the society of his wife and daughter. What more natural in a man who feels that his days are numbered! Lord Polperro bitterly laments the follies of his life; which are explained, Gammon, as you and I know, by the character he inherited. We know the peculiarities of the Trefoyle family. Some of them I must not refer to in the presence of a young lady such as Miss Sparkes." Polly looked at her toes and smirked. "But Lord Polperro's chief fault seems to have been an insuperable restlessness, which early took the form of a revolt against the habits and prejudices of aristocratic life. Knowing so much of that life myself, I must say that I understand him; that, to a certain extent, I sympathise with him. When a youth he desired the liberty of a plebeian station, and sought it under disguises. You must remember that at that time he had very little prospect of ever succeeding to the title. Let me give you a little genealogy."

"Needn't trouble," put in Gammon. "I know it all. Got it out of a book. I'll tell you afterwards, Polly."

"Ah, got it out of a book? Why, you are becoming quite a genealogist, Gammon. I need only say, then, that he did not give a thought to the title. He chose to earn his own bread, and live his own life, like ordinary mortals. He took the name of Clover. Of course, you see why."

"Hanged if I do," said Gammon.

"Why, my dear fellow, are not clover and trefoil the same things? Don't you see? Trefoyle. Only a little difference of accent."

"Never heard the word. Did you, Polly?"

"Not me."

"Ah! not unnatural. An out-of-the-way word." Greenacre hid his contempt beneath a smile. "Well now, I repeat that Lord Polperro longs to return to the bosom of his family. He has even gone in the darkness of the night to look at his wife's abode, and returned home in misery. A fact! At this moment —your attention, I beg—I am assisting him to form a plan by which he will be enabled to live a natural life without the unpleasantness of public gossip. I do not yet feel at liberty to describe our project, but it is ripening. What I ask you is this. Will you trust us? Miss Sparkes, have I your confidence?"

"It's all very well," threw in Gammon, before

Polly could reply. "But what if he drops down dead, as you say he might do? What about his family then?"

"Gammon," replied the other with great solemnity, "I asked whether I had your confidence. Do you, or do you not, believe me when I tell you that Lord Polperro has long since executed a will by which not only are his wife and his daughter amply—most amply—provided for, but even more distant relatives on his wife's side?"

He gazed impressively at Miss Sparkes, whose eyes twinkled as she turned with a jerk to Gammon.

"Look here, Greenacre," exclaimed the man of commerce, "let's be business-like. I may trust you, or I may not. What I want to know is, how long are we to wait before he comes to the shop down yonder and behaves like an honest man? Just fix a date, and I'll make a note of it."

"My dear Gammon——"

"Go ahead!"

"I cannot fix a date on my own responsibility. It depends so greatly on his lordship's health. I can only assure you that at the earliest possible moment Lady Polperro will be summoned to an interview with her husband. By-the-bye, I trust her ladyship is quite well?"

"Oh, she's all right," replied Gammon impatiently.

"And the Honourable Minnie Trefoyle—she, too, enjoys good health, I trust?"

Polly and Gammon exchanged a stare, followed by laughter, which was a little forced on the man's part.

"That's Miss Clover," he remarked. "Sounds queer, doesn't it?"

"That's her *real* name?" cried Polly.

"Indeed it is, Miss Sparkes," replied Greenacre. "But let me remind you—if it is not impertinent—that beauty and grace can very well afford to dispense with titles. I think, Gammon, you and I know a case in point."

Polly tossed her head and shuffled her feet, well pleased with the men's laughter.

"And if it comes to that," Greenacre pursued, "I don't mind saying, Gammon, that I suspect you to be a confoundedly lucky and enviable dog. May I congratulate him, Miss Sparkes?"

"Oh, you can if you like, Mr.—— I forget your name."

"I do so then, Gammon. I congratulate you, and I envy you. Heigh-ho! I'm a lonely bachelor myself, Miss Sparkes—no, hang it, Miss Polly. You may well look pityingly at me."

"I'm sure I didn't, Mr.—— I can't remember your name," answered Polly with a delighted giggle.

"See here, Greenacre," Gammon interposed genially,

"Miss Sparkes and I will have to talk this over. Mind you, I give no promise. I found out for myself who Mr. Clover was, and I hold myself free to do what I think fit. You quite understand?"

Greenacre nodded absently. Then he cleared his throat.

"I quite understand, my dear boy. I should like just to remind you that there's really nothing to be gained, one way or the other, by interfering with Lord Polperro before he has made his plans. The ladies would in no way be benefited, and it's very certain no one else would be. No doubt you'll bear that in mind."

"Of course I shall. You may take it from me, Greenacre, that I'm tolerably wide awake. Can I still address you at the Bilboes?"

"You can," was the grave and dignified reply. "And now, as I happen to have an appointment at the other end of the town, I really must say good-bye. I repeat, Miss Sparkes, you may trust me absolutely. I have your interests and those of my friend Gammon—the same thing now—thoroughly at heart. You will hear from his lordship, Miss Sparkes—no, hang it, Miss Polly. You will very soon have a line from his lordship, who, I may venture to say, is really attached to you. He speaks of you all most touchingly. Good-evening, Miss Polly, not good-bye; we are

o

to meet again very soon. And who knows all the happy changes that are before you. Ta-ta, Gammon. Rely upon me; I never failed a friend yet."

So saying he took his leave with bows and flourishes. Shortly after Polly and Gammon went into the superior room of the tavern and had tea together, talking at a great rate, one as excited as the other. Miss Sparkes being already attired for her evening duties they parted only when they were obliged to do so, agreeing to meet again when Polly left the theatre.

To pass this interval of time Mr. Gammon dropped into a music-hall. He wished to meditate on what had come to his knowledge. Had it not been that Lord Polperro was, in a sense, a public institution, and could not escape him, he would have felt uneasy about the doings of that remarkable fellow Greenacre; as it was, he preferred to muse on the advantages certain to befall Minnie and her mother, and perchance Polly Sparkes. After all, the niece of a lord must benefit substantially by the connexion, and by consequence that young lady's husband. No one could have been freer from secondary motives than he, when he found himself falling in love with Polly; and if it turned out a marriage of unforeseen brilliancy, why, so much the better. Polly had not altered towards him—dear, affectionate girl that she was! He would act honourably; she should have the chance of reconsidering her position; but——

A damsel, sparingly clad, was singing in the serio-comic vein, with a dance after each stanza. As he sipped his whisky, and watched and listened, Gammon felt his heart glow within him. The melody was lulling; it had a refrain of delicious sentiment. The listener's eyes grew moist; there rose a lump in his throat. Dear Polly! Lovely Polly! Would he not cherish her to the day of his death? How could he have fancied that he loved anyone else? Darling Polly!

When the singer withdrew he clapped violently, and thereupon called for another Scotch hot, with lemon.

As a matter of course a friend soon discovered him, a man who declared himself in a whisper "stonebroke," and said, after a glass of the usual beverage, that if the truth must be told he had looked in here this evening to save himself from the torments of despair. Three young children, and the missus just going to have another. Did Gammon know of any opening in the cork line?

"Afraid not," replied the traveller, "but I know a man out Hoxton way who's pushing a new lamp-glass cleaner. You might give him a look in. It goes well, I'm told, in the eastern suburbs."

Presently a coin of substantial value passed from Gammon's pocket into that of his gloomy friend.

"Poor devil!" said the good fellow to himself. "He married a tripe-dresser's daughter, and she nags him. Never had a chance to marry a jolly little girl who turned out to have a lord for her uncle!"

So he drank and applauded, and piped his eye and drank again, till it was time to meet Polly. When he went forth into the cold street never was man more softly amorous, more mirthfully exultant, more kindly disposed to all the dwellers upon earth. Life abounds in such forms of happiness, yet we are told that it is a sad and sorry affair!

CHAPTER XIX.

NOT IN THE SECRET

SINCE his adventure in knight-errantry Christopher Parish had suffered terrible alternations of hope and despair. For fear of offending Miss Sparkes he did not press for an explanation of the errand on which she had sent him; enough that he was again permitted to see her, to entertain her modestly, and to hold her attention whilst he discoursed on the glories of the firm of Swettenham. Every week supplied him with new and astounding Swettenham statistics. He was able to report, as "an absolute fact," that a junior member of the firm —a junior, mind you—was building a house at Eastbourne which would cost him, all told, not one penny less than sixty-five thousand pounds! He would like to see that house; in fact, he must see it. When Easter came round would Miss Sparkes honour him with her company on a day trip to Eastbourne, that they might gaze together on the appalling mansion?

"P'r'aps," replied Polly, "if you're good."

Whereat Mr. Parish perspired with ecstasy, and began at once to plan the details of the outing.

Indeed, Polly was very gracious to him, and presently something happened which enhanced her graciousness—perhaps increased her genuine liking for the amiable young man. Her friend, Miss Waghorn, was about to be married to Mr. Nibby. It was a cheerless time of the year for a wedding, but Mr. Nibby had just come in for a little legacy, on the strength of which he took a house in a south-east suburb, and furnished it on the hire system, with a splendour which caused Miss Waghorn to shriek in delight, and severely tested the magnanimity of Polly's friendship. Polly was to be a bridesmaid, and must needs have a becoming dress; but where was it to come from? Her perfidious uncle had vanished (she knew not yet *who* that uncle really was), and her "tips" of late had been—in Polly's language—measly. In the course of friendly chat she mentioned to Mr. Parish that the wedding was for that day week, and added, with head aside, that she couldn't imagine what she was going to wear.

"I shall patch up some old dress, I s'pose. Lucky it's dark weather."

Christopher became meditative, and seemed to shirk the subject. But on the morrow there arrived for Polly a letter addressed in his handwriting—an envelope rather—which contained two postal orders, each for one pound, but not a word on the paper enfolding them.

"Well now," cried Polly within herself, "if that ain't gentlemanly of him! Who'd a' thought it! And me just going to put my bracelet away!"

By which she meant that she was about to pawn her jewellery to procure a bridesmaid's dress. Gratitude, for the moment, quite overcame her. She sat down and wrote a letter of thanks, so worded that the recipient was beside himself for a whole day. He in turn wrote a letter of three full sheets, wherein, among other lyrical extravagances, he expressed a wish that by dying a death of slow torture he could endow Miss Sparkes with fabulous wealth. How gladly would he perish, knowing that she would come to lay artificial flowers upon his grave, and to the end of her life see that the letters on his tombstone were kept legible!

So Polly made a handsome appearance at the wedding. As a matter of fact, she came near to exciting unpleasantness between bride and bridegroom, so indiscreet was Mr. Nibby in his spoken and silent admiration. After consuming a great deal of indifferent champagne at Mr. Nibby's lodgings the blissful couple departed to spend a week at Bournemouth, and Polly returned to the room in Shaftesbury Avenue, which henceforth she would occupy alone. "And a good riddance!" she said to herself pettishly as she stripped off her wedding garments.

On this very evening she wrote to Mr. Gammon— the letter he was never to read.

Mr. Gammon had received an invitation to the ceremony, but through pressure of business was unable to accept it. He felt, too, that there would have been awkwardness in thus meeting with Polly for the first time since their rupture on the Embankment.

Polly, of course, concluded that he kept away solely because he did not wish to see her. In the mood induced by this reflection, and by the turbid emotions natural to such a day, she penned her farewell to the insulting and perfidious man. Mr. Gammon was informed that never and nowhere would Miss Sparkes demean herself by exchanging another word with him; that he was a low and vulgar and ignorant person, without manners enough for a road-scraper; moreover, that she had long since been the object of *sincere* attentions from someone so vastly his superior that they were not to be named in the same month. This overflow of feeling was some relief, but Polly could not rest until she had also written to Mrs. Clover. She made known to her aunt that Mr. Gammon had of late been guilty of such insolent behaviour to her (the writer) that she had serious thoughts of seeking protection from the police. "As he is such a great friend of yours and Minnie's, I thought I had better warn you. Perhaps you might like to try and teach him better behaviour, though I can't say as you are the person to do it. And you may be pleased to hear that I should not wonder if I am shortly to be married to a *gentleman*, which it won't surprise you after that if I am unable to see anything more of you and your family."

But for a violent storm which broke out after eleven that night, just as she finished these compositions, Polly would have posted them forthwith, and Mr. Gammon would in that case have received his letter by the first post next morning. As it was they remained in Polly's room all night, and only an hour or two after their actual despatch came the fateful telegram which was to make such a revolution in Miss Sparkes' sentiments and prospects. Mrs. Clover duly received her missive, and gave a good deal of thought to it. Being a woman of some self-command she spoke no word of the matter to Minnie, nor, though greatly tempted, did she pen a reply, but in a few days she sent a quiet invitation to Polly's father, desiring the pleasure of his company at tea on Sunday.

Mr. Sparkes came. He was in very low spirits, for during the past week Chaffey's had disgraced itself (if Chaffey's *could* now be disgraced) by supplying a supper at eighteen-pence per head, exclusive of liquors, to certain provincial representatives of the Rag, Bone, and Bottle Dealers' Alliance in town for the purpose of attending a public meeting. He called it 'art-breaking, he did. The long and short of it was, he must prepare himself—and Chaffey's— for the inevitable farewell. Why, it wasn't as if they had supplied the rag-tags with a *good* supper. You should have seen the stuff put before them; every blessed dish a hash-up of leavings and broken meats. No man with a vestige of self-respect could continue to wait at such entertainments. And this amid the gilding and the plush and the marble-topped tables, which sickened one with their surface imitation of real rest'rants.

"Wouldn't you like to retire into private life, Ebenezer?" asked his hostess. "I'm sure you *could*, couldn't you?"

"Well, Louisa," he replied with hesitation, "if it comes to that, I *could*. But I hardly know how I should spend my time."

The conversation turned to the subject of Polly, and, as they were alone together, Mrs. Clover exhibited the letter she had received from that young lady.

"Now what have you to say to that, Ebenezer? Don't you call it shameful?"

Mr. Sparkes sighed deeply.

NOT IN THE SECRET 213

"I've warned her, Louisa, I've warned her solemn. What more can I do?"

"You see how she goes on about Mr. Gammon. Now I'm as sure as I am of anything that it's all lies. I don't believe Mr. Gammon has insulted her. There was something happened before she left Mrs. Bubb's —a bit of unpleasantness there's no need to talk about; but I'm as sure as I sit here, Ebenezer, that Mr. Gammon wouldn't insult any girl in the way Polly says."

"Why don't you ask him?"

Mrs. Clover glanced at the door and betrayed uneasiness.

"To tell you the truth he doesn't come here just now. You won't let it go any further, Ebenezer, but the truth is he began to take a sort of fancy to Minnie, and he told me about it, just as he ought to 'a done, and I had to tell him plain that it wasn't a bit of use. For one thing Minnie was too young, and what's more, she hadn't even given half a thought to him in *that* way; and I wouldn't have the child worried about such things, because, as you know, she's delicate, and it doesn't take much to upset her in her mind, and then she can't sleep at nights. So I told Mr. Gammon plain and straight, and he took it in the right spirit, but he hasn't been here since. And I'm as sure as anything that Polly's letter is a nasty, mean bit of falsehood, though I'm sorry to have to say it to you, Ebenezer."

Mr. Sparkes had the beginning of a cold in the head, which did not tend to make him cheerful. Sitting by the fireside, very upright in his decent suit of Sunday black, he looked more than ever like a clergyman, perchance a curate who is growing old without hope of a benefice. Fortunately there entered about tea-time a young man in much better spirits, evidently a welcome friend of Mrs. Clover's; his name was Nelson. On his arrival Minnie joined the company, and it would have been remarked by anyone with an interest in the affairs of the family that Mrs. Clover was not at all reluctant to see her daughter and this young man amiably conversing. Mr. Nelson had something not unlike the carriage and tone of a gentleman; he talked quietly, though light-heartedly, and from remarks he let fall it appeared that he was somehow connected with the decorative arts. Minnie and he dropped into a discussion of some new ceramic design put forth by Doulton's; they seemed to understand each other, and grew more animated as they exchanged opinions. The hostess, meanwhile, kept glancing at them with a smile of benevolence.

At the tea table Mr. Nelson gratified Mr. Sparkes by an allusion to almost the only topic—apart from Chaffey's—which could draw that grave man into continuous speech. Mr. Sparkes had but one recreation, that of angling; for many years he had devoted such hours of summer leisure as Chaffey's granted him to piscatory excursions, were it only as far as the Welsh Harp. Finding this young man disposed to lend a respectful ear, and to venture intelligent questions, he was presently discoursing at large.

"Chub? Why chub's a kind of carp, don't you see. There's no fish pulls harder than a chub, not in the ordinary way of fishing. A chub he'll pull just like a little pig; he will indeed, if you believe me."

"And a jack, uncle," put in Minnie, who liked to please the old man. "Doesn't a jack pull hard?"

"Well, it's like this, my dear; it depends on the bottom when it's jack. If the bottom's weedy— see?—you must keep your line tight on a jack. Let him run and you're as like as not to lose thirty or forty yards of your line."

"And the lines are expensive, aren't they, uncle?"

"Well, my dear, I give eighteen and six for my preserved jack line—hundred yards. Eighteen and six!"

There followed one of his old stories, of a jack which had been eating up young ducklings on a certain pond; how he had baited for this fellow with a live duckling, the hook through the tips of its wings, got him in twenty minutes, and he turned the scale at four-and-twenty pounds. Roach and perch were afterwards discussed. In Mr. Sparkes' opinion the best bait for these fish was a bit of dough kneaded up with loose wool. Chaffey's —at all events, Chaffey's of to-day—would not have known its head waiter could it have seen and heard him as he thus held forth. The hostess showed a fear lest Mr. Nelson should have more than enough of cockney angling; but he and Minnie were at one in good-natured attentiveness, and in the end Mrs. Clover overcame her uneasiness.

A few days after this Minnie's mother, overcoming a secret scruple and yielding to a long desire, allowed herself to write a letter to Mr. Gammon. It was a very simple, not ill-composed letter; its object to express regret for the ill temper she had shown, now many weeks ago, on her parting with Mr. Gammon in Kennington Road. Would he not look in at the china shop just in the old way? It would please her very much, for indeed she had never meant or dreamt a termination to their friendship. They had known each other so long. Would not Mr. Gammon overlook her foolishness, remembering all she had had to go through? So she signed herself his "friend always the same," and having done so looked at the last line rather timidly, and made haste to close the letter.

An answer arrived without undue delay, and Mrs. Clover went apart to read it, her breath quicker than usual, and her fingers tremulous. Mr. Gammon wrote with unfeigned cordiality, just like himself. He hoped to call very soon, though it might still be a few weeks. There was nothing to forgive on his part; he wasn't such a fool as to be angry with an old friend for a few hasty words. But the truth was he had a lot of business on his hands; he was doing his best to get into a permanency at Quodlings' of Norton Folgate, and he knew Mrs. Clover would be glad to hear that. Let her give his kind regards to Miss Minnie, and believe him when he said that he was just as friendly disposed as ever.

Beneath these words Mrs. Clover naturally enough detected nothing of the strange experiences in which Mr. Gammon was involved. "Kind regards to Minnie." Yes, there was the explanation of his silence. He called her his "old friend," a phrase of double meaning. Mrs. Clover, in spite of her good sense, was vexed, and wished he had not said "old." Why, had she not a year or two the advantage of him in youthfulness?

CHAPTER XX.

THE HUSBAND'S RETURN

GAMMON would gladly have answered in person Mrs. Clover's letter, but he had promised Polly that he would neither visit the china shop nor in any way communicate with her aunt. Polly had made a great point of this, and he thought the reason was not far to seek; she still harboured jealousy of her cousin, and no doubt it would be delightful to make known, just how and when she herself saw fit, her triumph over Minnie. So he kept away from Battersea Park Road, though often wishing to spend an evening there in the old way, with Mrs. Clover's bright face on one side of him and Minnie's modestly bent head on the other.

It would have been so restful after all this excitement, for however he tried to grasp the facts, Mrs. Clover and Minnie still seemed remote from the world of wealth and titles; he could not change their names or see them in any other position than that which was familiar and natural. In talk with Polly he always rose to hilarious anticipations, partly the result of amorous fervour; but this mood did not survive their parting. Alone he was frequently troubled with uneasiness, with misgiving, more so as the days went by without bringing any news from Greenacre. Under the cover of night he visited Lowndes Mansions and hung about there for half an hour, like unto one with sinister intentions; but his trouble profited him nothing. Polly was growing impatient. After the manner of her kind she brooded on suspicions, and hatched numerous more or less wild conjectures. What if Greenacre had spirited Lord Polperro away for some dark purpose of his own? Gammon himself could not help suspecting the mysterious man of deep projects which would tend to the disadvantage of Lord Polperro's forsaken wife and child. At the end of a fortnight he wrote to Greenacre at the Bilboes pressing for information. To his surprise and satisfaction this brought about an interview on the following day. Greenacre seemed radiant with a good conscience.

"All is going well," he declared. "Our noble friend is improving in health, temporarily, at all events. Doubtless it is the result of having his mind more at ease. You can't imagine, Gammon, how that man has been tormented by remorse. I am not yet at liberty to disclose his plans. But I shall certainly be so very soon—very soon. I won't say Christmas, but before New Year's Day I feel confident I shall have got things completely in order. I will only hint to you that his lordship wishes to retire from the world, to live a perfectly quiet and simple domestic life in a locality which will be favourable to his health. You will agree with us, I know, that this is far better than trying to brave the gossip and scandal of society. I may now tell you, in strict confidence, that our friend has already written a letter to his wife, ready to be posted as soon as ever the last details are settled. By-the-bye, Gammon, I hope there can be no doubt as to Lady Polperro's willingness to concur in what her husband proposes?"

"I don't know anything about that," Gammon replied. "I can't answer for her."

"Naturally. Of course not. But I hope there will be no unexpected difficulty on that side. Lord Polperro has his fears, which I have done my best to dispel. We can but hope, put our trust in the forgiving nature of woman."

It now wanted but a very short time to Christmas. As the day drew near Gammon felt that this state of worrying suspense was growing intolerable. Polly's suspicions were louder, her temper became uncertain; once or twice she forgot herself and used language calculated to cause a breach of the peace. On these occasions Gammon found himself doubting whether she really was the girl after his own heart; he could have wished that she had rather less spirit. Overcome by her persistence, he at length definitely engaged to wait no longer than the end of the year. If by that time Greenacre had not put things in order, Polly was to seek her aunt and make known all that they had discovered.

"We won't be 'umbugged!" she exclaimed. "And it begins to look to me jolly like 'umbugging. I don't know what *you* think."

Gammon admitted that the state of things was very unsatisfactory, and must come to an end. The last day of the year—so be it. After that Polly should have her way.

It was the middle of Christmas week. A letter to the Bilboes remained without answer. Gammon and Polly met every day, excited each other, lost their tempers, were stormily reconciled. On the morning of the thirty-first Gammon received four letters begging for pecuniary assistance, but nothing from Greenacre. He had slept badly, his splendid health was beginning to suffer. By jorrocks! there should be an end of this, and that quickly.

As he loitered without appetite over a particularly greasy breakfast, listening to Mrs. Bubb's description of an ailment from which her youngest child was suffering, Moggie came into the kitchen and said that a young man wished to see him. Gammon rushed up to the front door, where, in mist and drizzle, stood a muscular youth whom he did not recognize.

"I'm come from Mrs. Clover's, sir," said this messenger, touching his hat. "She'd be very glad to see you as soon as you could make it convenient to look round."

"Is that all?"

That was all; nothing more could be learnt from the young man, and Gammon promised to come forthwith. Luckily he could absent himself from Quodlings' to-day with no great harm; so after a few words with Mrs. Bubb he pulled on his great coat and set off by the speediest way. Only after starting did he remember his promise to Polly. That could not be helped. The case seemed to be urgent, and he must beg for indulgence. He had an appointment with Polly for six o'clock this evening. In the excitement of decisive action (it being the last day of the year) she would probably overlook this small matter.

He found Mrs. Clover in the shop. She reddened at sight of him, and after a hurried greeting asked him to step into the parlour, where she carefully closed the door.

"Mr. Gammon, have you heard anything about my husband?"

The question disconcerted him; he tried ineffectually to shape a denial.

"You have, I can see you have! It doesn't matter. I don't want you to tell me anything. But he's now in this house."

She was greatly agitated, not angry, but beset by perplexities and distress.

"He came last night about ten o'clock—came to the door wrapped up like a stranger—it was almost too much for me when I heard his voice. He wanted to come in—to stay; and of course I let him. Minnie had to know, poor girl. He's in the spare room. Did you know he meant to come?"

"I? Hadn't an idea of it, Mrs. Clover!"

"But you know something about him. He tells me you do. He wants to see you. There's only one thing I ask—has he been doing wrong? Oh, do tell me that!"

Gammon protested that he knew nothing of the kind, and added that he had only seen the man once, for a minute, now more than a month ago.

"And you kept it from me!" said his friend reproachfully. "I didn't think you'd have done that, Mr. Gammon!"

"There was a reason. I shouldn't have thought of doing it if there hadn't been a good reason."

"Never mind. I won't interfere. I feel as if it had nothing to do with me. Will you go upstairs to him? He looks to me as if he hadn't very long to live, indeed he does. Listen, that's his cough! Oh,

I am so upset. It came so sudden. And to think you'd seen him and never told me! Never mind, go up to him, if you will, and see what he wants with you."

Gammon did her bidding. He ascended lightly and tapped at the door Mrs. Clover indicated. A cough sounded from within; then a voice which the visitor recognized, saying "Come in." On the bed, but fully dressed, lay a tall, meagre man, with a woollen comforter about his neck. The room was in good order, and warmed by a fire, which the sufferer's condition seemed to make very necessary. He fixed his eyes on Gammon, as if trying to smile, but defeated in the effort by pain and misery.

"I'm here, you see," he said hoarsely. "There's no doubt about me now."

"Got a bad cold, eh?" replied the other, as cheerfully as he could.

"Yes, a cold. Always have a cold. Would you mind reaching me the kettle?"

He poured out some brandy from a bottle which stood on the floor, and mixed it with a little hot water. Gammon the while observed him with much curiosity. In five years or a little more he had become an old and feeble man; his thin hair was all but completely grey, his flesh had wasted and discoloured, his hand trembled, his breath came with difficulty. Present illness accounted perhaps for the latter symptoms; but, from that glimpse of him in Norton Folgate, Gammon had known that he was much aged and shaken. Hat, overcoat, and muffler had partly disguised what was now evident. He spoke with the accent of an educated man, and in the tone of one whom nature has endowed with amiable qualities. The bottle beside him seemed to explain certain peculiarities of his manner. When he had drunk thirstily he raised himself to a sitting posture, and nodded to his visitor an invitation to take a chair.

"I'm here, you see, Gammon. Here at last."

"Why did you come?"

"Why?—ah, why indeed!"

Having sighed out this ejaculation he seemed to grow absent, to forget that he was not alone. A violent cough shook him into wakefulness again; he stared at Gammon with red eyes full of pain and fear, and said thickly:

"Are you an honest man—you?"

"Well, I hope so; try to be."

"What's his name? You know him, don't you?"

"Do you mean Greenacre?" asked Gammon, feeling very uncomfortable, for the man before him looked like one who struggles for his last breath.

"Greenacre, yes. What has he told you about me?"

Gammon answered with the simple truth; the situation alarmed him, and he would have nothing more to do with conspiracy in such a case. He could not feel sure that his explanations were followed and understood; now and then the bloodshot eyes turned blankly to him as if in a drunken dream; but in the end he saw a look of satisfaction.

"You're an honest man, aren't you? We used to know each other, you know when. My wife likes you, doesn't she?"

"We've always been friends, of course," Gammon replied.

"Would you mind giving me the kettle?" He mixed another glass of brandy, spilling a great deal in the process. "I don't offer you any, Greenacre, it's medicine; I take it as such. One doesn't offer one's friends a glass of medicine, you know, Greenacre."

"My name is Gammon."

"What am I thinking about! There was something I wanted to ask you. Yes, of course. Does she know?"

"You mean does your wife know who you really are?" said Gammon in a cautious voice. "Haven't you told her?"

"Not yet."

"Then I don't think anyone else has."

The man had fallen back upon the pillow. He began to cough, struggled to raise himself, and became seated on the edge of the bed.

"Well, it's time we were going."

"Where to?" asked Gammon.

The other stared at him in surprise and distress.

"Surely I haven't to tell you all over again! Weren't you listening? You're a man of business, are you not? Surely you ought to have a clear head the first thing in the morning."

"Just tell me again in a word or two. What can I do for you? Do you want to see anybody?"

"Yes, yes, I remember." He laid a hand on his companion's shoulder. "The matter stands thus, Greenacre: I trust you implicitly, once more I assure you of that; but it is absolutely necessary for me to see a solicitor."

"All right. What's his name?"

"I'll tell you, Cuthbertson—Old Jewry Chambers. But first of all let us come to an understanding about that man Quodling. I called upon his brother —why, I told you all that before, didn't I?"

"You had just been there when I met you in Norton Folgate," said Gammon, who felt that before long his own wits would begin to wander.

"To be sure. And now we really must be going."

He stood up staggering, gained his balance, and walked to the window. The prospect thence seemed to recall him to a consciousness of the actual present, and he looked round appealingly, distressfully.

"I tell you what it is," said Gammon. "You ought to get into bed and have a doctor. Shall I help you?"

"No, no; I regret that I came here, Greenacre. I am not welcome; how could I expect to be? If I am going to be ill it mustn't be here."

"Then let me get a cab and take you to your own place, if your wife is willing."

"That would be best. The truth is I feel terribly queer, Greenacre. Suppose I—suppose I died here? Of course, I ought never to have come. Think of the talk there would be; and that's just what I wanted to spare them, the talk and the disgrace. It can all be managed by my solicitor. But I felt that come I must. After all, you see, it's home. You understand that? It's really my home. I've been here often at night, just to see the house. The wonder is that I didn't come in before. Of course, I knew I couldn't be welcome—but one's wife and child, Greenacre. The real wife, whether the other's alive or not."

Gammon started.

"What did you say?" he asked in a whisper.

"Nothing—nothing. You are a good fellow, I am sure, and my wife likes you, that's quite enough. The point is this now, I must destroy that will, and

THE HUSBAND'S RETURN

get Cuthbertson to draw a deed of gift, all in order, you know, but nothing that could get wind and make a scandal. The will would be publicly known, I ought to have remembered that. I repeat, Greenacre, that what I have to do is to provide for them both without causing them any trouble or disgrace."

Catching the listener's eye he became silent and confused for a moment, then added quickly:

"I beg your pardon. I addressed you by the wrong name. Gammon, I meant to say. Gammon, my wife's friend, a thoroughly honest man. Have I made myself clear, Gammon? I—you see how the matter stands?"

Gammon was beginning to see that the matter stood in a perilous position, and that the sooner Mr. Cuthbertson—if such a person existed—could be brought on to the scene the better for everyone concerned. He asked himself whether he ought to summon Mrs. Clover. His glance towards the door must have betrayed his thought, for the sick man spoke as though in reply to it.

"We will say nothing to her yet, if you please. I—I begin to feel a little better. Our long confidential talk has done me good. By-the-bye, Greenacre—I beg your pardon, Gammon—you quite understand that it is all in the strictest confidence. I trust you implicitly as my dear wife's friend; it is all in her interests, as you see. I think now, if you would kindly get a cab—yes, I feel quite equal to it now—we will go to Lowndes Mansions."

The voice was thin, husky, senile; but his tone had more of rationality, and he appeared to have made up his mind to a course of action. Gammon presently went downstairs and told Mrs. Clover that her husband wished to go into town on business. She made no objection, but asked whether Gammon would take the responsibility of looking after him. This he promised. Whether the man would return hither or not was left uncertain.

"If he goes to his own house," said Gammon, "I'll see him safe there and let you know. He lives in the West End. Now don't upset yourself; if he doesn't come back you shall know where he is, and if you want to you shall go and see him. I promise you that. I know all about him, and so shall you; so just keep yourself quiet. He'll have to go to bed and stay there; anyone can see that. If you take my advice you'll let us go out quietly and not speak to him. Just trust to me, Mrs. Clover."

"Do you think he's right in his mind?" she asked.

"Well, he's very shaky, and ought to be kept quiet. What has he told you?"

"Nothing at all; he sat crying for an hour last night, and talked about the old times. When I

THE HUSBAND'S RETURN

asked questions he put me off. And when I went into his room this morning he said nothing except that he wanted to see you, and that he must have some brandy for his cold."

"All right; let us leave the house quietly, and I'll see·you again to-day or to-morrow. Oh, I say, has a man called Greenacre been here at any time?"

"I don't know anyone of that name," answered Mrs. Clover as she turned distressfully away.

A cab was summoned, and Gammon, having helped the sick man to clothe himself warmly in overcoat and muffler, led him from the house. They drove straightway to Lowndes Mansions.

CHAPTER XXI.

HIS LORDSHIP'S WILL

THE movement of the vehicle made Lord Polperro drowsy. In ten minutes he seemed to be asleep, and Gammon had to catch his hat as it was falling forward. When the four-wheeler jolted more than usual he uttered groans; once he shouted loudly, and for a moment stared about him in terror. The man of commerce had never made so unpleasant a journey in his life.

On arriving at their destination it was with much difficulty that Gammon aroused his companion, and with still more that he conveyed him from the cab into the building, a house porter (who smiled significantly) assisting in the job. Lord Polperro, when thoroughly awakened, coughed, groaned, and gasped in a most alarming way. His flat was on the first floor; before reaching it he began to shed tears, and to beg that his medical man might be called immediately. The door was opened by a middle-aged woman dressed as a housekeeper, who viewed his lordship with no great concern. She promised

HIS LORDSHIP'S WILL 233

to send a messenger to the doctor's, and left the two men alone in a room comfortably furnished, but without elegance or expensiveness. Gammon waited upon the invalid, placed him at ease by the fireside, and reached him a cellaret from a cupboard full of various liquors. A few draughts of a restorative enabled Lord Polperro to articulate, and he enquired if any letters had arrived for him.

"Look on the writing table, Greenacre. Anything there?"

There were two letters. The invalid examined them with disappointment and tossed them aside.

"Beggars and blackmailers," he muttered. "Nobody else writes to me."

Of a sudden it occurred to him that he was forgetting the duties of hospitality. He urged his guest to take refreshment; he roused himself, went to the cupboard, brought out half a dozen kinds of beverage.

"And of course you will lunch with me, or will it be dinner? Yes, yes, luncheon of course. Excuse me for one moment, I must give some orders."

He left the room. Gammon, having tossed off a glass of wine, surveyed the objects about him with curiosity. An observer of more education would have glanced with peculiar interest at the books; several volumes lay on the table, one of them a recent work on gipsies, another dealing with the antiquities of Cornwall. For the town traveller these things of course had no significance. But he remarked a painting on the wall, which was probably a portrait of one of Lord Polperro's ancestors—a youngish man (the Trefoyle nose, not to be mistaken) in a strange wild costume, his head bare under a sky blackening to storm, in his hand a sort of hunting knife, and one of his feet resting on a dead wolf. When his host reappeared Gammon asked him whom the picture represented.

"That? That's my father—years before I was born. They tell me that he used to say that in his life he had only done one thing to be proud of. It was in some part of Russia. He killed a wolf at close quarters—only a knife to fight with. He was a fine man, my father. Looks it, don't you think?"

Thirst was upon him again; he drank the first liquor that came to hand, then sat down and was silent.

"You feel better?" said Gammon.

"Better? Oh, thanks, much the same. I shan't be better till things are settled. That won't be long. I expected to hear from Greenacre—I think you said you knew Greenacre?"

"What is he doing for you?" Gammon enquired, thinking he might as well take advantage of this lucid moment, the result, seemingly, of alcoholic stimulation.

"Doing? We'll talk of that presently. Mind you, I have complete confidence in Greenacre. I regret that I didn't know him long ago." He sighed and began to wander. "My best years gone —gone! You remember what I was, Gammon? We don't live like other people, something wrong in our blood; we go down—down. But if I had lived as I was, and let the cursed title alone! That was my mistake, Greenacre. I had found happiness —a good wife. You know my wife? What am I saying? Of course you do. Never an unkind word from her, never one. How many men can say that? The best woman living, Greenacre."

"You keep forgetting who I am," said his guest bluntly.

Lord Polperro gave him a look of surprise, and with effort cleared his thoughts.

"Ah, I called you Greenacre. Excuse me, Gammon, my wife's friend. Be her friend still, a better woman doesn't live, believe me. You will lunch with me, Gammon. We are to have a long talk. And I want you to go with me to my solicitor's. I must settle that to-day. I thought Greenacre would be back. The fact is, you know, I must recover my health. The south of Europe, Greenacre thinks, and I agree with him. A place where we can live quietly, my wife and the little girl, no one to bother us or to gossip. She shall know when we get there, not before. This climate is bad for me, killing me; in fact, I hope to start in a few days, just us three, I and my wife and the little girl. She shall use the title if she likes, if not we'll leave it behind us. Ah, that was my misfortune, you know. It oughtn't to have come to me."

He was seized with a hiccough, which in a few moments became so violent that he had to abandon the attempt to converse. When it had lasted for half an hour Gammon found his position intolerable. He rose, meaning to leave the room and speak to the housekeeper, but just then the door opened to admit Lord Polperro's medical attendant. This gentleman, after a glance at the patient, who was not aware of his presence, put a few questions to Gammon. The latter then withdrew quietly, went out from the flat and down into the street, where the doctor's carriage stood waiting. He was bewildered with novelty of experience, felt thoroughly out of his element, and would have liked to have escaped from these complications by simply taking a cab to Norton Folgate and forgetting all he left behind. But his promise to Mrs. Clover (or Lady Polperro) forbade this. He was very curious as to the proceedings of that mysterious fellow Greenacre, who, as likely as not, had got Lord Polperro into his power for rascally purposes. What was that half-heard allusion to another wife, who might be alive or dead? Nothing to cause astonishment assuredly, but the matter ought to be cleared up.

He crossed the street and walked up and down, keeping his eye on Lowndes Mansions. Before long the doctor came out and drove away. After much indecision Gammon again entered and knocked at the door of his noble friend. The housekeeper said that Lord Polperro was asking for him impatiently. But when he entered the sitting-room there lay his lordship on the sofa fast asleep.

The sleep lasted for a couple of hours, during which Gammon sat in the room, bearing tedium as best he could. He was afraid to go away, lest an opportunity of learning something important should be lost; but never had time passed so slowly. Some neglect of business was involved, but fortunately he had no appointment that could not be postponed. As he said to himself, it was better to "see the thing through," and to make the most of Greenacre's absence.

When Lord Polperro at length awoke he had command of his intellect (such as remained to him), but groaned in severe pain. His first enquiry was whether any letter or telegram had arrived. Assured that there was nothing he tottered about the room for a few minutes, then declared that he must go to bed.

"I always feel better in the evening, Gammon. You'll excuse me, I know; we are old friends. I must see you again to-day; you'll promise to come back? Oh, how ill I am! I don't think this can go on much longer."

"What did the doctor tell you to do?"

"Oh, nothing, nothing," was the irritable reply. "Of course, I must get away as soon as possible. If only I could hear from Greenacre."

Seeing there was no likelihood of the man's leaving home for the next few hours Gammon promised to return in the afternoon, and so took his leave. On the stairs he passed two ladies, who, as he learnt in a moment by the sound of their knock above, were making a call upon the invalid. In the street stood their carriage. He watched it for some time from the other side of the way until the ladies came forth again. It would have soothed Gammon's mind could he have known that they were Lord Polperro's sister and his niece.

Just as the brief daylight was flickering out (the air had begun to nip with a threat of frost) he once more presented himself at Lowndes Mansions. In the meantime he had seen Polly Sparkes, informed her of what was happening, and received her promise that she would take no step until he could communicate with her again. This interview revived his spirits; he felt equal to another effort such as that of the morning—which had taxed him more than the hardest day's work he was ever called upon to do.

Lord Polperro again sat by the fireside with a decanter and glass within his reach. He was evidently more at ease, but seemed to have a difficulty in recognizing his visitor.

"Have you come from Greenacre?" he asked cautiously, peering through the dull light.

"I don't know anything about him."

"No? I cannot understand why I have no news from him. Pray sit down; we were talking about——"

Presently he shook his recollections into order, and when a lamp was brought in he began to talk lucidly.

"Gammon, I feel very uneasy in my mind. This morning I quite intended to have gone and seen Cuthbertson; but I was taken ill, you know. What is the time? I wonder whether Cuthbertson is likely to be at his office still?"

"That's your lawyer, isn't it? Would you like me to go and try to get hold of him? I might bring him here."

"You are very kind, Gammon. For some reason I feel that I really ought to see him to-day. Suppose we go together?"

"But you oughtn't to be out at night, ought you?"

"Oh, I feel much better. Besides, we shall drive, you know—quite comfortable. I really think we will go. Then you shall come back and dine with me. Yes, I think we will go."

Between this decision and the actual step half an hour was wasted in doubts, fresh resolves, moments of forgetfulness, and slow preparation. A messenger had been despatched for a cab, and at length almost by force Gammon succeeded in getting his lordship down the stairs and out into the street. They drove to Old Jewry Chambers. Throughout the journey Lord Polperro kept up a constant babbling, which he meant for impressive talk; much of it was inaudible to his companion, from the noise of the cab, and the sentences that could be distinguished were mere repetitions of what he had said before leaving home—that he felt it absolutely necessary to see Cuthbertson, and that he could not understand Greenacre's silence. They reached the solicitor's office at about half-past five. Lord Polperro entered only to return with a face of disappointment.

"He has gone. No one there but a clerk—no use."

"Couldn't you find him at his private address?" asked Gammon.

"Private address? to be sure! I'll go in again and ask for it."

Mr. Cuthbertson lived at Streatham.

HIS LORDSHIP'S WILL 241

"I tell you what," said Lord Polperro, whose mind seemed to be invigorated by his activity, "we'll go to Streatham, but first of all we must have something to eat. The fact is, I had no lunch; I begin to feel rather faint."

He bade the cabman drive to any restaurant not far away. There the vehicle was dismissed, and they sat down to a meal. Gammon as usual ate heartily. Lord Polperro pretended to do the same, but in reality swallowed only a few mouthfuls, and gave his more serious attention to the wine. Every few minutes he assured his companion in a whisper that he would feel quite at ease when he had seen Cuthbertson.

They looked out the trains to Streatham, and left just in time to catch one. On the journey his lordship dozed. He was growing very husky again, and the cough shook him badly after each effort to talk, so Gammon felt glad to see him resting. By the gaslight in the railway carriage his face appeared to flush and go pale alternately; at moments it looked horribly cadaverous with its half-open eyes, shrivelled lips, and thin, sharp, high-ridged nose. On arriving the man lost all consciousness of where he was and what he purposed; it took many minutes before Gammon could convey him into a cab and extort from him Mr. Cuthbertson's address.

"Greenacre," his lordship kept repeating, "I trust you implicitly. I am convinced you have my interests at heart. When all is settled I shall show myself grateful—believe me."

Between seven and eight o'clock they drove up to a house on Streatham Hill, and without consulting Lord Polperro Gammon went to parley at the door. Ill luck pursued them. Mr. Cuthbertson was dining in town, and could not be home till late. When made to understand this Lord Polperro passed from lethargy to violent agitation.

"We must go back at once!" he exclaimed. "To Lowndes Mansions at once! Greenacre, tell him to drive straight to Sloane Street. You don't know what depends upon it. We must lose not a moment."

The cabman consented, and the return journey began at a good speed. When Gammon, out of regard for the invalid's condition, insisted on having the window of the hansom dropped, Lord Polperro grumbled and lamented. The cool air did him good; he was beginning to breathe more easily than he had done for a long time.

"You are too imperious with me, Greenacre. I have noticed it in you before. You take too much upon yourself."

"I suppose it's no use telling you once more,"

HIS LORDSHIP'S WILL 243

said his companion, "that my name isn't Greenacre."

"Dear me! dear me! I beg your pardon a thousand times. I meant to say Gammon. I can't tell you, Gammon, how much I feel your kindness. But for you I should never have managed all this in my state of health. You don't mind coming home with me?"

"Of course not. What are you going to do when you get there?"

"I told you, my dear Gammon, it shall be done this very night, whether I have news or not. I shall see Cuthbertson the first thing to-morrow, and get him to draw the deed of gift. That settles everything; no gossip, no scandal, if anything should happen. Life is so uncertain, and as you see I am in anything but robust health. Yes, it shall be done this very night."

Tired of futile questioning Gammon resolved to wait and see what was done, though it seemed to him more than likely that nothing at all would come of these vehement expressions. At all events Lord Polperro was now wide awake, and seemed in no danger of relapsing into the semi-comatose or semi-delirious condition. He no longer addressed his companion by the name of Greenacre; his talk was marked with a rational reserve; he watched the course of their drive along the highways of South

London, and showed satisfaction as they approached his own district.

The cabman was paid with careless liberality, and Lord Polperro ran up the stairs to his flat. More strictly speaking, he ran for a few yards, when breath failed him, and it was all he could do to stagger with loud pantings up the rest of the ascent. Arrived in his sitting-room he sank exhausted on to the nearest chair. Gammon saw that he pointed feebly to the drink cupboard, and heard a gasp that sounded like "brandy."

"Better not," replied the clear-headed man. "I wouldn't if I were you."

But his lordship insisted, looking reproachfully, and the brandy was produced. It did him good; that is to say, it brought colour to his face, and enabled him to sit upright. No sooner was he thus recovered than his eyes fell upon the envelope of a telegram which lay on his writing-table.

"There it is, at last!"

He tore the paper, all but sobbing with agony of impatience.

"Good God, I can't see it! I've gone half blind all at once. Read it for me, Gammon."

"*Hope see you to-night. Important news. If not, in morning.*—Greenacre."

"Where did he send it from?"

HIS LORDSHIP'S WILL 245

"Euston, six o'clock."

"Then he came by the Irish day-mail. Why didn't I think of that and meet the train? What does he mean by to-night or to-morrow morning? What does he *mean?*"

"How can I tell?" replied Gammon. "Perhaps he has called here while you were away."

Lord Polperro rang the bell, only to find that no one had asked for him. He was in a state of pitiable agitation, kept shuffling about the room with coughs and gasps, demanding ceaselessly why Greenacre left the hour of his appearance uncertain. Gammon, scarcely less excited in his own way, shouted assurances that the fellow might turn up at any moment. It was not yet ten o'clock. Why not sit down and wait quietly?

"I will," said the other. "I will; thank you, Gammon. I will sit down and wait. But I cannot conceive why he didn't come straight here from Euston. I may as well tell you he has been to Ireland for me on business of the gravest importance. I am not impatient without cause. I trust Greenacre implicitly. He had a gentleman's education. I am convinced he could not deceive me."

More brandy helped him to surmount this crisis, then he was silent for a few minutes. Gammon thought he had begun to doze again, but of a sudden he spoke distinctly and earnestly.

"I am forgetting. You remember what I had decided to do. It shall be done at once, Gammon. I know it will relieve my mind."

He rose, went to the writing-table, unlocked a drawer, and took out a large sealed envelope, on which something was written.

"Gammon, you are witness of what I now do. This is my will, executed about a year ago. I have reasons for wishing to dispose of my property in another way. Cuthbertson will see to that for me to-morrow. A will becomes public. I did not think of that at the time. There!"

He threw the sealed packet into the fire, where it was quickly caught by the flames and consumed.

"Now I feel easier in mind, much easier."

He drank from the replenished glass, smiling and nodding.

CHAPTER XXII.

NEW YEAR'S EVE

GAMMON had the strangest sensation. He felt as though he were acting in a melodrama; he stood in a constrained position, as if the eyes of the house were upon him; he suffered from a sort of stage fright. Much more of this kind of thing would assuredly unsettle his wits. To recover tone he helped himself to a stiff glass of whisky.

"That's right," said his host encouragingly. "Make yourself comfortable. Greenacre may drop in at any moment. You can't think how much better I feel, Gammon. So clear in the mind, you know—why, it has only just occurred to me, this is New Year's Eve."

"So it is. Here's to your health and happiness, Lord Polperro!"

"Thank you, my dear Gammon. I heartily wish you the same. To-morrow, or at all events in a few days, a new life begins for me, as you know. In the climate of the south of Europe, with my wife and the little girl—ah, but for this idiotic title!—I was saying———"

He began to wander unintelligibly, then complained of physical sufferings, then coughed until he sank in exhaustion.

Time went on. Gammon began to ask himself how long he should wait. At half-past ten he made a suggestion that his lordship might do worse than go to bed, but this was ill received.

"By no means. Greenacre may be here at any moment. He will certainly come to-night. If he doesn't come, do you know what occurs to me? Why shouldn't we drive into the City and ask whether he has returned?"

"Ask where?"

"He lives at a place—a sort of hotel—which he calls the Bilboes. Greenacre is eccentric, but thoroughly trustworthy. He had a gentleman's education."

"He lives there, does he?" exclaimed Gammon.

"Finds it convenient, I suppose. Yes, we will go and enquire, we certainly will."

Gammon's objections were unheeded. No one could take any harm, said Lord Polperro, from driving in a closed cab to the City and back. He would leave directions that if Greenacre called during their absence he should be asked to wait. So they made ready and went forth, and once more a hansom bore them through the dark, cold night.

Lord Polperro talked unceasingly, and from his

rambling hints it was not difficult to conjecture the business on which Greenacre had been despatched to Ireland. Someone had to be discovered : a doubt as to whether some person was alive or dead had to be set at rest. Gammon ventured a few questions, which were answered evasively, but the nature of his companion's anxiety was by this time clear enough to him. He felt quite as desirous of meeting Greenacre as Lord Polperro himself. Every hour spent in this way added to his responsibility, and he had made up his mind that at the earliest possible moment to-morrow he would himself see Mr. Cuthbertson, and confide to him everything that had happened during this extraordinary day.

As the cab ascended Ludgate Hill it passed through crowds of people moving in the same direction. Gammon was for a moment surprised, then he called to mind again that it was New Year's Eve ; the people were thronging to hear St. Paul's strike the hour of midnight. Last year he had himself joined in this celebration. He remembered with a smile that he reached home by circuitous routes, and after one or two short intervals of repose on convenient doorsteps. What was more, on that very night he had first made Greenacre's acquaintance at a bar ; they swore eternal brotherhood, and Greenacre borrowed half a sovereign, never repaid.

With Gammon's help the cabman found his way to the Bilboes.

"Don't get out," he said to his companion. "I'll ask if he has come."

Lord Polperro suddenly aroused himself and tumbled out of the vehicle; but for Gammon's attention he would have fallen full length. They entered together, and by a confused process of enquiry learnt that Greenacre was still absent.

"Does he live here?" Gammon asked of a waiter whom he had drawn aside.

"He has a bedroom, sir."

Lord Polperro said that he felt a sudden faintness and must take refreshment. Having drunk, he began to talk in a loud voice about his private affairs, addressing a stranger who sat by him and whom he took for Gammon.

"I shall stay here. I shall certainly wait here for Greenacre. I can't run the risk of missing him to-night."

Gammon caught him by the arm and persuaded him to come out into the passage; but the only result of this was that Lord Polperro dismissed the cab, repeating obstinately that he would wait Greenacre's arrival.

"But ten to one he's waiting for us down yonder," urged Gammon.

"He won't wait very long, and we shall pass him

on the road if we go back now. I tell you it is my pleasure to remain here! You forget yourself, Gammon. I know we are old friends, but you forget our positions."

The man of commerce laughed contemptuously.

"Look here," he said the next moment. "Let's walk as far as St. Paul's and have a look at the crowd."

"The crowd? What crowd?"

When he had heard the explanation his lordship readily assented. Certainly they would stroll as far as St. Paul's and back again, by that time Greenacre might have come. It seemed probable that when they had gone a little distance Lord Polperro would feel shaky and consent to take a cab. Drink, however, had invigorated the man; he reeled a little and talked very huskily, but declared that the walk was enjoyable.

"Let's go into the crowd, Gammon. I like a crowd. What are those bells ringing for? Yes, yes, of course, I remember—New Year's Eve. I had no idea that people came here to see the New Year in. I shall come again. I shall come every year; it's most enjoyable."

They entered the Churchyard and were soon amid a noisy, hustling throng, an assembly composed of clerks and countermen, roughs and pickpockets, with a sprinkling of well-to-do rowdies, and numerous girls
R

or women, whose shrieks, screams, and yelps sounded above the deeper notes of masculine uproar. Gammon, holding tight to his companion's arm, endeavoured to pilot him in a direction where the crowd was thinnest, still moving westward; but Lord Polperro caught the contagion of the tumult and began pressing vehemently into the surging mass.

"This does me good, Gammon. It's a long time since I've mixed with people. I always enjoyed a crowd. Hollo—o—o!"

His excited shout made him cough terribly; none the less he pushed on.

"You'll come to harm," said the other. "Don't be a fool; get out of this."

A struggle began between them; but by this time they were so thickly encompassed that Gammon had small chance of forcing his companion away. Lord Polperro did not resent the tugs at his arm; he took it for genial horseplay, and only shouted louder.

"On we go! This makes one feel alive, eh? Splendid idea to come and see this. Hollo—o—o!"

Blackguards in front of him were bellowing a filthy song; his lordship tried to join in the melody. A girl who was jammed against him shot liquid into his ear out of a squirt, and another of her kind knocked his hat off; he struggled to recover it, but someone was beforehand with him and sent the silky headgear flying skyward, after which it was tossed from hand to hand and then trampled under foot.

"Now you'll catch your bloomin' death of cold," said Gammon. "Stick on to me and get out of this."

"I'm all right! Leave me alone, can't you! How often have I a damned chance of enjoying myself?"

It was the first syllable of bad language that Gammon had heard from Polperro's lips. Struck with the fact, and all the more conscious of his duty to this high-born madman, he hit on a device for rescuing him from the crowd.

"Look!" he cried suddenly, "there's Greenacre!"

"Where?" replied the other, all eagerness.

"Just in front; don't you see him? This way; come along, or we shall lose him."

Flecks of dim white had for some minutes been visible above their heads; it was beginning to snow. Gammon shouldered his way steadily, careful not to come into quarrelsome conflict. Polperro hung on behind, shouting Greenacre's name. This clamour and the loss of his hat drew attention upon him; he was a mark for squirts and missiles, to say nothing of verbal insult. St. Paul's struck the first note of twelve, and from all the bestial mob arose a howl and roar. Polperro happened to press against a drunken woman; she caught him by his disordered hair and tugged at it, yelling into his face. To release himself he bent forward, pushing the woman away; the result was a violent blow from her fist, after which she raised a shriek as if of pain and terror. Instantly a man sprang forward to her defence, and he, too, planted his fist between the eyes of the hapless peer. Gammon saw at once that they were involved in a serious row, the very thing he had been trying to avoid. He would not desert his friend, and was too plucky to see him ill-used without reprisals. The rough's blows were answered with no less vigour by the man of commerce.

"Hook it!" shouted Gammon to the tottering Polperro. "Get out of it!"

The clock was still striking; the crowd kept up its brutal blare, aided by shrill instruments of noise. Only a few people heard Polperro's shout defying the enemy.

"Let him come on! Let him come on like a man! Take that, you ruffian, and that!"

Gammon, knowing the conflict grossly unequal, did not scruple to fight his own way. Polperro, wildly thrashing about him with both fists, excited wrath in every direction. There was a general scrimmage; shouts of rage mingled with wild laughter; the throng crushed this way and that. Grappling in his own defence with a big brute who had clutched his throat, Gammon saw Polperro

NEW YEAR'S EVE

go down. It was his last glimpse of the unfortunate man. Fighting savagely he found himself borne far away by an irresistible rush, and when he had lost sight of his foe he tried vainly to return to the place where Polperro had fallen. The police were now interfering, the crowd swayed more violently than ever, and began to scatter itself in off-streets.

From church towers of east and west chimes rang merrily for the New Year. Softly fell the snow from a black sky, and was forthwith trodden into slush.

Though he was badly mauled and felt sick Gammon would not abandon the hope of discovering his friend. After resting for a few minutes against the front of a shop he moved again into the crowd, now much thinner, and soon to be altogether dispersed. The helmets of policemen drew him in a certain direction; two constables were clearing the way, and he addressed them, asking whether they had seen a bareheaded man recently damaged in a fight.

"There's been a disturbance over yonder," one replied, carelessly pointing to a spot where other helmets could be discerned.

Thither Gammon made his way. He found police and public gathered thickly about some person invisible; a vigorous effort and he got near enough to see a recumbent body, quite still, on which the flakes of snow were falling.

"Let me look at him," he requested of a constable who would have pushed him away. "It's a friend of mine, I believe."

Yes, it was Lord Polperro, unconscious, and with blood about his mouth.

The police were waiting as a matter of professional routine to see whether he recovered his senses; they had, of course, classed him as "drunk and incapable."

"I say," Gammon whispered to one of them, "let me tell you who that is."

The conference led to the summoning of a cab, which by police direction was driven to the nearest hospital, St. Bartholomew's. Here Gammon soon learnt that the case was considered serious, so serious that the patient had been put to bed and must there remain.

Utterly done up Gammon threw himself into the cab to be driven to Kennington Road. When he reached Mrs. Bubb's he was fast asleep, but there a voice addressed him which restored his consciousness very quickly indeed.

CHAPTER XXIII.

HIS LORDSHIP RETIRES

IT was the voice of Greenacre, unsteady with wrath, stripped utterly of its bland intonations.

"So here you are! What have you been up to, Gammon? Are you drunk?"

Just as the cab drove up Greenacre was turning reluctantly from the house door, where he had held a warm parley with Mrs. Bubb; the landlady irritable at being disturbed in her first sleep, the untimely visitor much ruffled in temper by various causes.

"Drunk!" echoed Gammon, as he leapt to the pavement and clutched at Greenacre's arm. "Drunk yourself, more likely! Where have you been since you sent that telegram? Hold on a minute." He paid the cabman. "Now then, give an account of yourself."

"What the devil do you mean?" cried the other. "What account do I owe to you?"

"Well, I might answer that question," said Gammon with a grin, "if I took time to calculate."

"We can't talk in the street at this time of night, with snow coming down. Suppose we go up to your room?"

"As you please. But I advise you to talk quietly; the walls and the floors are not over thick."

The latch-key admitted them, and they went as softly as possible up the stairs, only one involuntary kick from Greenacre on sounding wood causing his host to mutter a malediction. By a light in the bedroom they viewed each other, and Greenacre showed astonishment.

"So you *are* drunk, or have been! You've got a black eye, and your clothes are all pulled about. You've been in a row."

"You're not far wrong. Tell me what you've been doing, and you shall hear where the row was and who was with me."

"Gammon, you've been behaving like a cad—a scoundrel. I didn't think it of you. You went to that place in Sloane Street. No use lying; I've been told you were there. You must have found out I was going away, and you've played old Harry. I didn't think you were a fellow of that sort; I had more faith in you."

Upon mutual recrimination followed an exchange of narratives. Greenacre's came first. He was the victim, he declared, of such ill luck as rarely befell

HIS LORDSHIP RETIRES 259

a man. Arriving at Euston by the Irish mail, and hastening to get a cab, whom should he encounter on the very platform but a base-minded ruffian who nursed a spite against him; a low fellow who had taken advantage of his good nature, and who—in short, a man from whom it was impossible to escape, for several good reasons, until they had spent some hours together. He got off a telegram to Lord Polperro, and could do no more till nearly eleven o'clock at night. Arriving headlong at Lowndes Mansions, he learnt with disgust what had gone on there in his absence. And now, what defence had Gammon to offer? What was his game?

"I guess pretty well what yours is, my boy," answered the listener. "And I'm not sorry I've spoilt it."

Thereupon he related the singular train of events between breakfast time this (or rather yesterday) morning and the ringing out of the old year. When it came to a description of Lord Polperro's accident Greenacre lost all control of himself.

"Ass! blockhead! You know no better than to let such a man in his state of health get mixed up in a crowd of roughs at midnight? Good God! He may die!"

"I shouldn't wonder a bit," returned Gammon coolly. "If he does it may be awkward for you, eh?"

From his story he had omitted one detail, thinking it better to keep silence about the burning of the will until he learnt more than Greenacre had as yet avowed to him.

"Fool!" blustered the other. "Idiot!"

"You'd better stop that, Greenacre, or I shan't be the only man with a black eye. Do you want to be kicked downstairs? or would you prefer to drop out of the window? Keep a civil tongue in your head."

At this moment both were startled into silence by a violent thumping at the wall.

It came from the room which used to be occupied by Polly Sparkes, and was accompanied by angry verbal remonstrance from a lodger disturbed in his slumbers.

"Didn't I tell you?" muttered Gammon. "You'd better get home and go to bed; the walk will cool you down. It's all up with your little game for the present. Look here," he added in a friendly whisper, "you may as well tell me. Has he another wife?"

"Find out," was Greenacre's surly answer; "and go to the devil!"

A rush, a scuffling, a crash somewhere which shook the house. The disturbed lodger flung open his door and shouted objurgations. From below sounded the shrill alarm of Mrs. Bubb, from else-

HIS LORDSHIP RETIRES

where the anxious outcries of Mrs. Cheeseman and her husband.

Amid all this Greenacre and his quondam friend somehow reached the foot of the stairs, where the darkness that enveloped their struggle was all at once dispersed by a candle in the hand of Mrs. Bubb.

"Don't alarm yourself," shouted Gammon cheerily, "I'm only kicking this fellow out. No one hurt."

"Well, Mr. Gammon, I do think——"

But the landlady's protest was cut short by a loud slamming of the house-door.

"It's nothing," said the man of commerce, breathing hard. "Very sorry to have disturbed you all. It shan't happen again. Good-night, Mrs. Bubb."

He ran up to his room, laughed a good deal as he undressed, and was asleep five minutes afterwards. Before closing his eyes he said to himself that he must rise at seven; business claimed him to-morrow, and he felt it necessary to see Mrs. Clover (or Lady Polperro) with the least possible delay. However tired, Gammon could always wake at the hour he appointed. The dark, snowy morning found him little disposed to turn out; he had something of a headache, and a very bad taste in the mouth; for all that he faced duty with his accustomed vigour. Of course he had to leave the house without breakfast, but a cup of tea at the nearest eating-house supplied his immediate wants, and straightway he betook himself to the china shop near Battersea Park Road.

That was not a pleasant meeting with his friend Mrs. Clover. To describe all that had happened yesterday would have taxed his powers at any time; at eight-thirty a.m. on the first of January, his head aching and his stomach ill at ease, he was not likely to achieve much in the way of lucid narrative. Mrs. Clover regarded him with a severe look. His manifest black eye, and an unwonted slovenliness of appearance, could not but suggest that he had taken leave of the bygone year in a too fervid spirit. His explanations she found difficulty in believing, but the upshot of it all—the fact that her husband lay at St. Bartholomew's Hospital—seemed beyond doubt, and this it was that mainly concerned her.

"I shall go at once," she said in a hard tone, turning her face from him.

"But there's something else I must tell you," pursued Gammon, with much awkwardness. "You don't know—who to ask for."

The woman's eyes, even now not in their depths unkindly, searched him with a startled expression.

"I suppose I shall ask for Mr. Clover?"

"They wouldn't know who you meant. That isn't his real name."

A cry escaped her; she turned pale.

"Not his real name? I thought it—I was afraid of that! Who am I, then? What—what have I a right to call myself?"

With a glance to the door of the sitting-room, nervousness bringing the sweat to his forehead, Gammon told what he knew, all except the burning of the will, and the fact of Greenacre's mission to Ireland. The listener was at first sight utterly bewildered, looked incredulous, and only when certain details had been repeated and emphasized began to grasp the reality of what she heard.

"Oh!" she exclaimed at length in profound agitation, "that explains so many things! I never thought of this, but I've often wondered. I understand now."

She paused, struggling to control herself. Then, not without dignity, in the tone and with the face that are natural at such moments only to a woman here and there, the nobler of her sex, she added:

"I can't go to the hospital. Someone else must tell me about him. I can't go."

"I shall have time to call on my way," said Gammon, "and I could send you a wire."

"Will you? I can't go."

She sobbed, but quietly, hiding her face in her hands. Gammon, more distressed by her emotion than he had ever felt at the sight of a woman weeping, did his clumsy best to solace her. He would call at the hospital straight away and telegraph the news as soon as possible. And anything else he could learn about Lord Polperro should be made known to her without delay. He wrote on a piece of paper the address in Sloane Street, and that of the house in Stanhope Gardens. On the point of departure something occurred to him that it was wise to say.

"I shouldn't do anything just yet." He looked at her impressively. "In your position I should just wait a little. I'm sure it would be better, and I may be able to give you a reason before long."

She nodded.

"I shall do nothing—nothing."

"That's best, I assure you. You're not angry with me? You'll shake hands?"

She gave him her hand; withdrew it quickly; turned to hide her face again. And Gammon hastened Citywards.

A telegram came from him in little more than an hour. It reported that the patient was still unconscious and dangerously ill.

When, later in the afternoon, Gammon went to the hospital to make another enquiry he learnt that Lord Polperro was dead.

Turning away, debating whether to send the widow a telegram or to break the news by word

HIS LORDSHIP RETIRES 265

of mouth, he saw a cab drive up, out of which jumped Mr. Greenacre. Their eyes met, but they exchanged no sign of recognition. Scarcely, however, had Gammon walked a dozen yards when a quick step sounded behind him, and he was addressed in tones of the most conciliatory politeness.

"Gammon, may I beg one word? I owe you an apology. My behaviour last night was quite unjustifiable. I can only explain it by the fact that I had undergone a severe trial to the nerves. I was not myself. May I hope, my dear Gammon, to be forgiven? I apologise most humbly—believe me."

"Oh, that's all right," replied the other with a grin; "I hope I didn't hurt you?"

"My dear fellow, it would have served me right. But no—just a few trifling bruises. By-the-bye, our friend has departed."

"Dead—yes!"

"Do you know, Gammon, I think we ought to have a quiet talk. You and I have common interests in this matter. There will be an inquest, you know, and the fact is I think"—he spoke very confidentially—"it might be as well for us both if we came to some sort of mutual understanding. As things have turned out we are victims of circumstances. Might I suggest with all deference that we should dine together very quietly? I know a very suitable place. It's early for dinner, but, to tell the truth, I have had no particular appetite to-day; in fact, have hardly touched food."

Gammon accepted this invitation and decided to send a telegram to the china shop.

Their conference—tentative on both sides for the first half hour—led eventually to a frank disclosure of all that was in their minds with regard to Lord Polperro. Each possessed of knowledge that made him formidable to the other, should their attitude be one of mutual hostility, they agreed, in Greenacre's phrase, to "pool" all information and then see how they stood. Herein Gammon had the advantage; he learnt much more than it was in his power to communicate, for, whilst Greenacre had been playing a deliberate game, the man of commerce had become possessed of secrets only by chance, which his friend naturally could not believe.

Greenacre had been to Ireland on the track of a woman whom Lord Polperro had lost sight of for some five-and-twenty years; he had obtained satisfactory evidence that this woman was dead - a matter of some moment, seeing that, if still alive, she would have been his lordship's wife. The date of her death was seven years and a few months ago.

"By jorrocks!" cried the listener at this point,

greatly disturbed. "Then Mrs. Clover—as we call her—wasn't really his wife at all?"

"I regret to say that she was not," replied Greenacre with proper solemnity. "I grieve to tell you that our deceased friend committed bigamy. Our deceased friend was a most peculiar man; I can't say that I approve of his life, viewed as a whole."

Then came Gammon's disclosure about the burning of the will and about Lord Polperro's intention to see his solicitor.

Greenacre smiled grimly.

"If I may make a personal remark, Gammon," he said in measured tones, "I will confess that I should never have allowed the destruction of that document. You, my friend, if I am not mistaken, had a still greater interest in preventing it. That will provided very handsomely for Mrs. Clover, for Miss Clover, and—I may say liberally—for a young lady named Miss Sparkes."

He smiled more grimly than ever.

Gammon drew in his breath and refrained from speech.

"Of course, I understand his motives," pursued Greenacre. "They were prudent, no doubt, and well meaning. He did not foresee that there would be no opportunity for that interview with his solicitor."

s

"Look here, Greenacre, I want to know how you found out first of all that he'd married twice."

"Very simply; I took it for granted that he had. I am a student, as you know, of genealogy, also of human nature in general. In my first interview with Lord Polperro I let fall a word or two which obviously alarmed him. That was quite enough. In his singular state of mind he jumped to the conclusion that—as they say on the stage—I knew everything; and, of course, I very soon did; as much, that is to say, as he himself knew. He married at two-and-twenty a young girl whom he met in Ireland; married her in his right name—Trefoyle (not Clover)—and they travelled together for a year or two. Then somehow they parted, and never saw or heard of each other again. No, there was no child. I had little difficulty in persuading his lordship to let me investigate this matter for him; I did it with complete success. The girl belonged to a peasant family, I may tell you; she led, on the whole, a decidedly adventurous life, and died suddenly on a ship in which she was returning to the old country from America. I gather that she never knew her husband's aristocratic connexion. Of course, I was discretion itself whilst making these enquiries, and I feel pretty sure that no claim will ever be made from that quarter—the peasant family—on our friend's estate."

HIS LORDSHIP RETIRES 269

"Why, then," exclaimed Gammon, "what is to prevent Mrs. Clover from coming forward? She knows nothing; she needn't ever hear a word."

"Gammon, you surprise me. Clearly you haven't the legal mind. How could you reconcile yourself to stand by whilst the law of your country was so grossly defeated?"

"Humbug! Don't use such long words, old chap. But perhaps Polperro's family knew of the marriage?"

"They did not, I can assure you. Our friend was the kind of man who doesn't like the class in which he was born; he preferred a humbler station. He was never on very good terms with his relatives."

"Well, then," Gammon persisted, "who is to let them know that Mrs. Clover wasn't the real wife? Hanged if I see why she shouldn't come forward!"

"My friend," replied Greenacre, smiling gently, "it will be my privilege to make known all the facts of this case to the Honourable Miss Trefoyle, his lordship's sister and nearest surviving relative."

"What?"

"I regard it as a simple duty. I cannot even argue the subject, Gammon; if *you* have no conscience, *I* have."

Gammon sat pondering until light began to break

upon him. The other, meanwhile, watched his countenance.

"I see," he said at length bluntly. "You think it'll do you more good to take that side. I see."

"Gammon, my leanings are aristocratic. They always were. It puts me at a disadvantage sometimes in our democratic society. But I disregard that. You may call it prejudice. I, for my part, prefer to call it principle. I take my stand always on the side of birth and position. When you have thought about it I am sure you will forgive this weakness in me. It need not affect our friendship."

"Wait a bit. There's another question I want to ask. What had Lord Polperro to do with the Quodlings?"

"The Quodlings? Ah! I grieve to tell you that Francis Quodling, an illegitimate half-brother of our friend, had of late given trouble to his lordship. Francis Quodling has long been in Queer Street; he seemed to think that he had a claim—a natural claim, I might say—on Lord Polperro. When you first met his lordship he had been seeing the other Quodling on this matter. Pure kindness of heart—he was very kind-hearted. He wanted to heal a breach between the brothers, and, if possible, to get Francis a partnership in the firm—your firm. I fear he exerted himself vainly."

HIS LORDSHIP RETIRES

"Greenacre!" exclaimed the man of commerce, thumping the table. "It's beastly hard lines that that woman and her daughter shouldn't have a penny!"

"I agree with you. By-the-bye, you have told her?"

"Yes, this morning."

"Gammon, you are so impulsive. Still, I suppose she had to know. Yes, I suppose it was inevitable. Will she molest his relatives do you think?"

"She?" Gammon reflected. "I can't quite see her doing it. She may be a bit angry, but—no, I don't think she'll bother anybody. I can't see her doing it."

And still he meditated.

"You reserve to yourself, I presume, the duty of acquainting her with these painful facts?"

"Me tell her? Why, I suppose I must if it comes to that. But—I'm hanged if I shall enjoy it. Who else knows? Jorrocks! there's Polly. I'd forgotten Polly!"

Gammon grew perplexed in mind and shadowed in countenance. Of a truth Polly Sparkes had not once entered his mind since he saw her yesterday. But he must see her again, and that to-night. Whew! He would now have given a substantial sum to deprive Polly of the knowledge he had so recklessly confided to her.

"You are impulsive, my friend," remarked the other, quietly amused. "Impulsive and lacking in foresight."

"And you——! Never mind; I won't say it. Still, you used to be a puzzle to me, Greenacre; now I feel as if I was beginning to understand you a bit."

The man of foresight—he was remarkably well-dressed this evening—watched the smoke from his cigarette and smiled.

CHAPTER XXIV.

THE TRAVELLER'S FICKLENESS AND FRAUD

IN due course a coroner and his jury sat on the body of Lord Polperro; in the order of things this inquest was publicly reported.

Readers of newspapers learnt that the eccentric nobleman, though in a weak state of health, had the indiscretion to mingle with a crowd on New Year's Eve; that he either accidentally fell or was knocked down by some person unknown in the rough-and-tumble of the hour; in short, that his death might fairly be accounted for by misadventure. The results of the autopsy were not made known in detail, but a professional whisper went about that among the causes contributory to Lord Polperro's death were congestion of the lungs, softening of the brain, chronic inflammation of the stomach, drunkard's liver, and Bright's disease of the kidneys.

The unprofessional persons who came forward were Mr. Gammon, Lord Polperro's housekeeper, and Miss Trefoyle. The name of Greenacre was not so much as mentioned; the existence of a lady named Mrs. Clover remained unknown to court and public.

On the following day Mr. Gammon had a private interview with Miss Trefoyle. He was aware that this privilege had already been sought by and granted to Mr. Greenacre, and as his one great object was to avert shame and sorrow from his friends at Battersea Park, Gammon acquitted himself with entire discretion; that is to say, he did not allow Miss Trefoyle to suspect that there had been anything between him and her brother except a sort of boon companionship. In behaving thus he knew that he was acting as Mrs. Clover most earnestly desired. Not many hours before he had discharged what he felt to be his duty, had made known to Mrs. Clover the facts of her position, and had heard the unforgettable accent of her voice as she entreated him to keep this secret. That there might be no doubt as to the truth of Greenacre's assertions he had accompanied that gentleman to Somerset House, and had perused certain entries in the registers of marriage and of death indicated to him by his friend's forefinger; clearly then, if he and Greenacre kept silence, it would never become known, even to Polperro's kinsfolk, that his lordship had been guilty of bigamy.

Stay! one other person knew the true name of Mrs. Clover's husband—Polly Sparkes.

FICKLENESS AND FRAUD

"Polly be hanged," muttered Gammon.

"When is the wedding?" Greenacre enquired casually in one of their conversations.

"Wedding? Whose wedding?"

"Why, yours."

Gammon's face darkened. A change had come about in his emotions. He was afraid of Polly, he was weary of Polly, he heartily wished he had never seen Polly's face. For self-scrutiny Gammon had little inclination and less aptitude; he could not have explained the origin and progress of his nearer relations with Miss Sparkes. Going straight to the point, like a man of business, he merely knew that he had made a condemnable mistake, and the question was how to put things right.

"There's one bit of luck," he remarked, instead of answering the enquiry, "she isn't on speaking terms with her aunt."

"I'm rather glad to hear that. But do you think she'll hold out against her curiosity?"

"In any case she won't learn anything from Mrs. Clover. I'm pretty sure of that."

"I can only hope you're right about Mrs. Clover," said Greenacre musingly. "If so, she must be a rather uncommon sort of woman, especially—if you will excuse the remark—in that class."

"She is," replied Gammon with noteworthy emphasis. "I don't know a woman like her—no one like her. I wouldn't mind betting all I have that she'll never speak a word as long as she lives about that man. She'll never tell her daughter. Minnie will suppose that her father turned up somehow just for a few hours and then went off again for good and all."

"Remarkable woman," murmured Greenacre. "It saves trouble, of course."

Possibly he was reflecting whether it might be to his advantage or not to reveal this little matter in Stanhope Gardens. Perhaps it seemed to him on the whole that he had done wisely in making known to Miss Trefoyle only the one marriage (which she might publish or not as her conscience dictated), and that his store of private knowledge was the richer by a detail he might or might not some day utilise. For Mr. Greenacre had a delicacy of his own. He did not merely aim at sordid profits. In avowing his weakness for aristocratic companionship he told a truth which explained many singularities in what would otherwise have been a career of commonplace dishonesty.

"I suppose she must be told," said Gammon with bent head. "Polly, I mean."

"Miss Sparkes is a young lady of an enquiring spirit. She will want to know why she does not benefit by Lord Polperro's death."

"You told her yourself about the will, remember."

"I did. As things turn out it was a pity. By-the-bye, I should like to have seen that document. As Cuthbertson has no knowledge of it, our deceased friend no doubt drafted it himself. More likely than not it would have been both amusing and profitable to the lawyers, like his father's in the days of our youth. I wonder whether he called Mrs. Clover his wife? We shall never solve all these interesting doubts."

"I had better not let Polly know he burnt it," remarked Gammon.

"Why, no; I shouldn't advise that," said the other with a smile. "But I have heard that married men——"

"Shut up! I'm not going to marry her."

Driven to this bold declaration, Gammon at once felt such great relief that he dared everything.

"Then there'll be the devil to pay," said Greenacre.

"Wait a bit. Of course I shall take my time about breaking off."

"Gammon, I am surprised and shocked—not for the first time—at your utter want of principle."

Each caught the other's eye. The muscles of their faces relaxed, and they joined in a mirthful peal.

It was a long and exciting week for the town traveller. Greenacre, always on the look out for romance in common life, was never surprised when he discovered it, but to Gammon it came with such a sense of novelty that he had much ado to keep a clear head for every-day affairs. He drove about London as usual, but beset with fantastic visions and desires. Not only was Polly quite dismissed from his thoughts (in the tender sense), but he found himself constantly occupied with the image of Mrs. Clover, heretofore seldom in his mind, notwithstanding her brightness and comeliness and the friendship they had so long felt for each other. Minnie he had forgotten; the mother came before him in such a new light that he could hardly believe his former wish to call her mother-in-law. This strange emotion was very disturbing. As if he had not worry enough already!

Delicacy kept him away from the china shop. He knew how hard it must be for the poor woman to disguise her feelings before Minnie and other people. Minnie, to be sure, would understand signs of distress as a result of her father's brief reappearance, but Mrs. Clover's position was no less lamentable. He wished to be at her side endeavouring to console her. Yet, as likely as not, all he said would give her more pain than comfort.

Ah, but there was a woman! Was he likely ever to meet another who had pluck and goodness and self-respect like hers? Minnie? Some day, perhaps,

FICKLENESS AND FRAUD

being her mother's daughter. But Minnie after all was little more than a child. And he could no longer think of her in the old way, it made him uncomfortable if he tried to do so.

Polly? Ah, Polly! Polly be hanged!

He had an appointment with her for this evening —not at the theatre door, for Polly no longer went to the theatre. Change in the management had put an end to her pleasant and lucrative evenings; she had tried in vain to get like employment at other places. In a letter received this morning she remarked significantly that of course it was not worth while to take up any other pursuit again.

It could not be called a delightful letter from any point of view. Polly had grown tired of uniform sweetness, and indulged herself in phrases of an acid flavour.

"Haven't you got anything yet to tell me about the will? If I don't hear anything from you before long I shall jolly well go and ask somebody else. I believe you know more than you want to tell, which I call it shameful. Mind you bring some news to-night."

They met at six o'clock in the Lowther Arcade; it was raining, cold, and generally comfortless. By way of cheery beginning Gammon declared that he was hungry, and invited Miss Sparkes to eat with him.

They transferred themselves to a restaurant large enough to allow of their conversing as they chose under cover of many noises. Gammon had by this time made up his mind to a very bold step, a stratagem so audacious that assuredly it deserved to succeed. Only despair could have supplied him with such a suggestion and with the nerve requisite for carrying it out.

"What about that will?" asked Polly, as soon as they were seated and the order had been given.

"There is no will."

This answer, and the carelessness with which it was uttered, took away Polly's breath. She glared, and unconsciously handled a table knife in an alarming way.

"What d'you mean? Who are you kidding?"

"He's left no will. And what's more, if he had, your name wouldn't have been in it, old girl."

"Oh, indeed! We'll soon see about that! I'll go straight from 'ere to that 'ouse, see if I don't! I'll see his sister for myself this very night, so there!"

"Go it, Polly, you're welcome, my dear. You'll wake 'em up in Stanhope Gardens."

The waiter interrupted their colloquy. Gammon began to eat; Polly, heeding not the savoury dish, kept fierce eyes upon him.

"What d'you mean? Don't go stuffing like a

pig, but listen to me, and tell me what you're up to."

"You're talking about Lord P., ain't you?" asked Gammon in a lower voice.

"Course I am."

"And you think he was your uncle? So did I till a few days ago. Well, Polly, he wasn't. Lord P. didn't know you from Adam, nor your aunt either."

He chuckled, and ate voraciously. The artifice seemed to him better and better, enjoyment of it gave him a prodigious appetite.

"If you'll get on with your eating I'll tell you about it. Do you remember what I told you about the fellow Quodling in the City? Well, listen to this. Lord P. had another brother knocking about —you understand, a brother—like Quodling, who had no name of his own. And this brother, Polly, is your uncle Clover."

Miss Sparkes did not fail to understand, but she at once and utterly declined to credit the statement.

"You mean to say it wasn't Lord P. at all as I met —as I saw at the theatre?"

"You saw his illegitimate brother, your uncle, and never Lord P. at all. Now just listen. This fellow who called himself Clover is a precious rascal. We don't know as much about him as we'd like to, but I daresay we shall find out more. How did he come to be sitting with those ladies in the theatre, you're wanting to ask? Simple enough. Knowing his likeness to the family of Lord Polperro he palmed himself off on them as a distant relative, just come back from the colonies; they were silly enough to make things soft for him. He seems to have got money, no end of it, out of Lord P. No doubt he was jolly frightened when you spotted him, and you know how he met you once or twice and tipped you. That's the story of your uncle Clover, Polly."

The girl was impressed. She could believe anything ill of Mrs. Clover's husband. Her astonishment at learning that he was a lord had never wholly subsided. That he should be a cunning rascal seemed vastly more probable.

"But what about that letter you sent—eh?" pursued Gammon with an artful look. "Didn't you address it to Lord P. himself? So you did, Polly. But listen to this. By that time Lord P. and his people had found out Clover's little game; never mind *how*, but they had. You remember that he wouldn't come again to meet you at Lincoln's Inn. Good reason, old girl; he had had to make himself scarce. Lord P. had set a useful friend of his—that's Greenacre—to look into Clover's history. Greenacre, you must know, is a private detective." He nodded solemnly. "Well now, when your letter came to Lord P. he showed it to Greenacre, and they saw at once that it couldn't be meant for him,

FICKLENESS AND FRAUD

but no doubt was meant for Clover. 'I'll see to this,' said Greenacre. And so he came to meet us that night."

"But it was *you* told me he was Lord P.," came from the listener.

"I did, Polly. Not to deceive you, my dear, but because I was taken in myself. I'd found what they call a mare's nest. I was on the wrong scent. I take all the blame to myself."

"But why did Greenacre go on with us like that? Why didn't he say at once that it wasn't Lord P. as had met me?"

"Why? Because private detectives are cautious chaps. Greenacre wanted to catch Clover, and didn't care to go talking about the story to everybody. He deceived me, Polly, just as much as you."

She had begun to eat, swallowing a mouthful now and then mechanically, the look of resentful suspicion still on her face.

"And what do you think?" pursued her companion, after a delicious draught of lager beer. "Would you believe that only a day or two before Lord P.'s death the fellow Clover went to your aunt's house, to the china shop, and stayed overnight there! What do you think of that, eh? He did. Ask Mrs. Clover. He went there to hide, and to get money from his wife."

This detail evidently had a powerful effect. Polly

ate and drank and ruminated, one eye on the speaker.

"I got to know of that," went on the wily Gammon. "And I told Greenacre. And Greenacre made me tell it to Lord P. himself. And that's how I came to be with Lord P. on New Year's Eve! Now you've got it all."

"Why didn't you tell me?" asked Polly with ferocity.

"Ah, why? I was ashamed to, my dear. I couldn't own up that I'd made a fool of myself and you too."

"How did you know that he'd been at my aunt's?"

"She sent for me, Polly; sent for me and told me, because I was an old friend. And I was so riled at the fellow coming and going in that way that I spoke to Greenacre about it. And then Greenacre told me how things were. I felt a fool, I can tell you. But the fact is, I never saw two men so like in the face as Clover and Lord P."

"When you was there—at my aunt's—did you talk about me?" asked the girl with a peculiar awkwardness.

"Not a word, I swear! We were too much taken up with the other business."

For a minute or two neither spoke.

"And you mean to say," burst at length from

FICKLENESS AND FRAUD

Polly, "that my uncle's still alive and going about?"

"All alive and kicking, not a doubt of it, and Lord P. buried at Kensal Green; no will left behind him, and all his property going to the next of kin, of course. Now listen here, Polly. I want to tell you that I shouldn't wonder if you have a letter from Greenacre. He may be asking you to meet him."

"What for?"

"Just to have a talk about Clover—see? He's still after Clover, and he thinks you might be of use to him. I leave it to you—understand? You can meet him if you like; there's no harm. He'll tell you all the story if you ask him nicely."

On this idea, which had occurred to him in the course of his glowing mendacity, Gammon acted as soon as he and Polly had said good-bye. He discovered Greenacre, who no longer slept at the Bilboes, but in a house of like cosiness and obscurity a little further west; told him of the brilliant ingenuity with which he had escaped from a galling complication, and received his promise of assistance in strengthening the plot. Greenacre wrote to Polly that very night, and on the morrow conversed with her, emphasizing by many devices the secrecy and importance of their interview. Would Polly engage to give him the benefit of her shrewdness, her knowledge of life, in his search for the man Clover?

His air of professional eagerness, his nods, winks, and flattery so wrought upon the girl that she ceased to harbour suspicion. Her primitive mind, much fed on penny fiction, accepted all she was told, and in the consciousness of secret knowledge affecting lords and ladies she gave up without a sigh the air-drawn vision of being herself actually a member of an aristocratic family.

At the same time she thought of Gammon with disappointment, with vague irritation, and began all but to wish that she had never weakly pardoned him for his insulting violence at Mrs. Bubb's.

CHAPTER XXV.

THE MISSING WORD

JUST at this time the inhabitants of England—
one might say of the British Isles—but more
especially those privileged to dwell in London and
its suburbs, submitted to one of the waves of
intellectual excitement which, as is well known,
are wont at intervals to pass over this fervidly
imaginative people. Some representative person—
ingenious, philosophic, and ardent for the public
good — had conceived in a bright moment a
thought destined to stir with zeal the pensive
leisure of millions. This genius owned, or edited,
a weekly paper already dear to the populace,
and one day he announced in its columns a
species of lottery—ignoble word dignified by the
use here made of it. Readers of adequate culture
were invited to exercise their learning and their
wit in the conjectural completion of a sentence
— no quotation, but an original apophthegm —
whereof one word was represented by a blank.
Each competitor sent, together with the fruit of

his eager brain, a small sum of money, and the brilliant enthusiast who at the earliest moment declared the missing word reaped as guerdon the total of these numerous remittances. It was an amusement worthy of our time; it appealed alike to the villa and the humble lodging, encouraged the habit of literary and logical discussion, gave an impulse to the sale of dictionaries. High and low, far and wide, a spirit of noble emulation took hold upon the users of the English tongue. "The missing word"—from every lip fell the phrase which had at first sounded so mysteriously; its vogue exceeded that, in an earlier time, of "the missing link." The demand for postage stamps to be used in transmitting the entrance fee threatened to disorganise that branch of the public service; sorting clerks and letter carriers, though themselves contributory, grew dismayed at the additional labour imposed upon them.

Naturally the infection was caught by most of the lively little group of Londoners in whose fortunes we are interested. Mr. Gammon threw himself with mirthful ardour into a competition which might prove so lucrative. Mr. Greenacre gave part of his supple mind to this new branch of detective energy. The newly-wedded pair, Mr. and Mrs. Nibby, ceased from the wrangling that follows upon a honeymoon, and incited each other

THE MISSING WORD 289

to a more profitable contest. The Parish household devoted every possible moment with native earnestness to the choice and the weighing of vocables. Polly Sparkes, unable to get upon the track of her missing uncle, abandoned her fiery intelligence to the missing word. The Cheeseman couple, Mrs. Bubb, nay, even Moggie the general, dared verbal conjecture and risked postage stamps. Only in a certain china shop near Battersea Park Road was the tumult unregarded, for Mrs. Clover had fallen from her wonted health, her happy temper, and Minnie in good truth cared neither for the recreation nor the dangled prize.

When Gammon and Polly met they talked no longer of Lord Polperro or Uncle Clover, but of words.

"I've got it this time, Polly! I swear I've got it! 'Undeserved misfortune is often a —— to the noble mind.' Why, it's *stimulus*, of course!"

"I never heard the word," declared Polly. "I'm sending in *stroke*."

"*Stroke?* What do you mean by that?"

"What do I mean by it? Why, what they want to say is, that 'Undeserved misfortune is often a *blow* to the noble mind,' don't they? But *blow* can't be the word, 'cause everybody'd get it. The dictionary gives *stroke* for *blow*, and I'm sure that's it."

"Rot! they don't mean to say that at all! It ain't a *blow* to the noble mind, it's just the opposite; that's what *they* mean."

"How can it be the opposyte?" shrilled Polly. "Ain't it a knock-down if you get what you don't deserve?"

"I tell you *they* don't mean that. Can't you understand? Why, it's as plain as the nose on your face."

"Is it?" retorted Polly with indignation. "If I've got a plain nose, why didn't you tell me so before? If that's your way of talking to a lady——"

"Don't be a fool, Polly! It's a saying, ain't it?"

And they parted as usual, in dudgeon on both sides, which was not soothed when both found themselves wrong in the literary contest; for the missing word this week, discovered by an East-end licensed victualler, was *pick-me-up*.

Public opinion found fault with this editorial English. There rose a general murmur; the loftier spirits demanded a purer vocabulary, the multitude wanted to know whether that licensed victualler really existed. All looked for an easy word next week; easy it must be this time, or the game would begin to lose its zest. When the new number went forth in its myriads of copies, and was snatched

THE MISSING WORD

from street vendors, stalls, shops, general expectation seemed to be justified.

"As nations grow civilized they give more and more attention to——"

Every man, every woman, had a word ready. Mr. Greenacre said nothing, but hastily wrote down *genealogy*. Gammon, before consulting with Polly Sparkes, sent off his postage stamps and *commerce*. Mr. and Mrs. Parish declared in one shout that the word could only be *hyjene*.

"Nonsense!" said Christopher, who was in the room. "That's just because you're always thinking of it."

For all that, as he went to business the word hummed in his head. It might be the solution after all; his objection originated only in scorn of a word so familiar, and therefore, he had thought at first, so improbable. But, really, the more he thought of it——

In his pocket he carried an envelope, already addressed, and a blank sheet of paper enfolding stamps. Should he once more enter the lottery—risk the price of a luncheon? He had resolved not to do so, but every moment the temptation gained upon him. "Hyjene." By-the-bye, how did one spell the word? *H-y*—he grew uncertain at the third letter. Mis-spelling, he knew, would invalidate his chance; on the other hand, he must post as soon as possible; already thousands of answers were on their way to the office of the editor.

He was sitting in a London Bridge tram-car. At its next stoppage there entered a staid old gentleman, with whom he had made the Cityward journey for years; they always nodded to each other. This morning the grave senior chanced to take a place at his side, and a greeting passed between them. Christopher felt a sudden impulse, upon which he acted before timidity and other obstacles could interfere.

"Would you tell me, sir," he whispered, "the c'rect spelling of *hyjene;* meaning 'ealthiness, you know?"

"Why, what a queer thing!" answered his neighbour with all friendliness. "I've just been reading the word in the paper. Here it is."

He folded the sheet conveniently for Christopher's inspection, and pointed—

"*H-y-g-i-e-n-e.*"

Mr. Parish read eagerly, his eyes close to the print, dreading lest he should forget.

"Thanks very much, sir. I—a friend of mine told me I was wrong. I knew I wasn't—thanks awfully!"

The white-haired man smiled approval, and returned to his study of the news. Christopher kept spelling the word in silence, and though the weather was very cold, soon perspired under the dread that he had got a letter wrong. At St. George's Church agitation quite overcame him; he hurried from the car, ran into a by-street, and with his pocket pencil wrote on the blank sheet of paper "Hygiene." Yes, he had it right. It looked right. Now for the nearest letter-box.

But his faith in "Hygiene" had risen to such fervour that he dreaded the delay of postal delivery. Why not carry the letter himself to the editorial office, which was at no very great distance? He would, even though it made him late at Swettenham's. And he began to run.

Panting, but exultant, he delivered his answer in the national competition, thus gaining a march upon the unhappy multitudes who dwelt far away, and whose resource and energy fell short of his. Then he looked at the time and was frightened; he would be dreadfully unpunctual at business; Swettenham's might meet him with stern rebuke. There was nothing for it, he hailed a cab.

Only in the middle of the morning did he remember that he had in his pocket a love-letter to Polly Sparkes, which he had meant to post early. He had seen Polly a few days ago, and suspected that she was in some sort of trouble and difficulty, possibly—though she denied it—caused by her want of employment. Polly declared that she had resources which enabled her to take a holiday. Not very long ago such a statement would have racked Christopher with jealous suspicions; suspicious he was, and a little uneasy, but not to the point of mental torture. The letter in his pocket declared that he could never cease to love Polly, and that he groaned over the poverty which condemned him to idle hopes; for all that, he thought much less of her just now than of the missing word. And when, in the luncheon hour, he posted his amorous missive, it was with almost a careless hand.

On this same day it happened that Mr. Gammon, speeding about his business in Messrs. Quodling's neat little trap, found he could conveniently stop for a mid-day meal somewhere near Battersea Park Road. The boy who accompanied him took the horse to bait, and Mr. Gammon presently directed his steps to the little china shop.

Mrs. Clover had just finished dinner; her female assistant had returned into the shop, and by her Gammon sent a request for a moment's private conversation. He soon entered the sitting-room.

"It's strange you have looked in to-day," said Mrs. Clover, with the dull air of one who has a headache. "I wanted to see you."

"I'm very glad."

He sat down at a distance from her and observed her face. This was a new habit of his; he saw more, much more, than he had been wont to see

THE MISSING WORD

in the healthy, sweet-tempered, and still young countenance; its present languor disturbed him.

"What was it, Mrs. Clover?" he asked in a voice not quite like his own.

"Well, I wanted to speak about Polly. Her father has been here asking questions."

Gammon set his lips almost angrily.

"What's wrong?"

"I don't know as anything is. But—have you heard anything about her going to be married?"

"Has she told her father that?" he asked, with a shuffle of his feet.

"Not in plain words. But she's doing nothing—except roam about the streets—and she won't give any straightforward account of herself. Now would you mind telling me, Mr. Gammon, whether"—her eyes fell—"I mean, if you've done anything since that night, you know, to make her offended with you?"

"Offended? Not that I know of," was his prompt answer with genuine surprise.

Mrs. Clover watched him, and seemed not dissatisfied.

"I'll tell you why I ask. Some time ago she wrote me a queer letter. It said she *was* going to be married—or thought about it; and there was something I couldn't understand about *you*. I shall show you that letter. I think it's only right."

She withdrew for a moment and returned with Polly's abusive epistle, which she handed to her visitor.

Gammon first read it, then looked for a date, but none was discernible.

"When did you get this?" he asked.

Mrs. Clover could mention the very day, and on reflecting Gammon felt sure that Polly must have written this just before the exciting events which threw him and her into each other's arms. In the same moment he recalled Polly's eagerness to become possessed of a letter she had posted to him—the letter he was not to open.

"You may well say it's queer." He laughed and laughed again. "She gives me a nice character, eh? And you've been wondering what I'd done? All I've got to say is, that it's a blessed lie from beginning to end. But perhaps you won't believe me?"

"I will believe you if you tell me plain and straight that you hadn't done anything wrong—nothing to be ashamed of."

"Well, then, I do tell you that. I never gave her the least cause to speak of me in that way. It's all lies."

"I more than half thought it was."

Mrs. Clover heaved a sigh and looked more cheerful.

"And what," she added, "does she mean about marrying a gentleman?"

"That's more than I can tell you."

Again he laughed, laughed like a man enjoying sudden relief of mind.

"More than I can tell you, Mrs. Clover. But I'll see if I can't find out; indeed I will. Her friends, the Nibbys, may be able to tell me something. Have you asked her to come and see you?"

"No. For one thing I don't know the address, and after a letter like this——"

"Quite right. Leave it to me." He bent his head, hesitated, and added quietly, "I may have something to tell you."

Thereupon they parted, and Mrs. Clover felt her head so much better that she was able to attend to business.

CHAPTER XXVI.

A DOUBLE EVENT

WITH clang and twang the orchestra (a music-hall orchestra) summoned to hilarity an audience of the first half-hour; stragglers at various prices, but all alike in their manifest subdual by a cold atmosphere, a dull illumination, empty seats, and inferior singers put on for the early "turns." A striking of matches to kindle pipe or cigar, a thudding of heavy boots, clink of glass or pewter, and a waiter's spiritless refrain—"Any orders, gents?" Things would be better presently. In the meantime Mr. Gammon was content to have found a place where he could talk with Polly, sheltered from the January night, at small expense. He sipped thoughtfully from a tumbler of rich Scotch; he glanced cautiously at his companion, who seemed very much under the influence of the hour. Polly, in fact, had hardly spoken. Her winter costume could not compare in freshness and splendour with that which had soothed her soul through the bygone sunny season; to tell the truth,

A DOUBLE EVENT

she was all but shabby. But Gammon had no eye for this. He was trying to read Polly's thoughts, and wondering how she could take what he had made up his mind to tell her.

"I saw your aunt yesterday."

"You did?"

"Yes, I did. She was telling me about a letter she had from you some time ago, the last letter you wrote her."

Their eyes met. Miss Sparkes was defiant—on her guard, but not wholly courageous; Gammon twinkled a mocking smile, and held himself ready for whatever might come.

"She shows you people's letters, does she?" said Polly with a sneer.

"This one she did. Good reason. It was funny reading, old girl. That's your opinion of me, is it? Do you mind telling me who the gentleman is—the *real* gentleman—you think of taking up with?"

Gammon could not strike a really ungenerous note. He had meant to be severe, but did not get beyond sly banter.

"She's a cat for showing it to you!" replied Miss Sparkes. "That was wrote before we—you know what. It was after you'd took your 'ook that Sunday on the Embankment. I didn't mean it. I was a bit cross. I'll pay her out some day for this, see if I don't."

U

Much more did Polly say, the gist of it all being an evident desire to soothe her companion's feelings. Gammon found himself in an unexpected and awkward position. He had taken for granted an outbreak of violence, he had counted upon the opportunity of mutual invective, he wished to tell Polly to go further. In the face of such singular mildness he was at a loss for weapons. Mere brutality would soon have settled the matter, but of that Mr. Gammon was incapable. At this juncture too, as if in support of Polly's claim to indulgence, a strain, irresistible by heart of man, preluded a song of the affections. Gammon began to understand what a mistake it was to have brought Polly to a music-hall for the purpose of breaking with her. Under cover of the languishing lyric Miss Sparkes put her head nearer to him.

"What am I to do, eh?"

"To do?"

"I cawn't go on like this. Do you want me to get another job somewhere? I sh'd think you might see I cawn't wear this jacket much longer."

The crisis was dreadful. Gammon clutched at the only possible method of appeasing his conscience, and postponing decisive words he took Polly's hand — poorly gloved — and secretly pressed the palm with a coin, which Polly in less than a clock-tick ascertained to be one pound sterling. She smiled.

"What's that for?"

"For—for the present."

And in this way another evening went by, leaving things as before.

"I'd never have believed I was such a fool," said Gammon to himself at a late hour. He meant, of course, that experience was teaching him for the first time the force of a moral obligation, which, as theorist, he had always held mere matter for joke. He by no means prided himself on this newly-acquired perception; he saw it only as an obstacle to business-like behaviour. But it was there, and —by jorrocks! the outlook began to alarm him.

Meanwhile Mr. Greenacre was pursuing a laudable object. Greatly pleased at the dexterity with which Miss Sparkes had been hoodwinked in the matter of Lord Polperro and her uncle Clover, he determined to set all at rest in that direction by making Polly believe that Mr. Clover, her uncle himself as distinct from Lord Polperro, was also dead and gone and done for. Gammon knew of the design and strongly favoured it, for he was annoyed by Mrs. Clover's false position; he wished her to be proclaimed a widow, without the necessity of disagreeable revelations.

An exciting post-card brought about one more interview between Miss Sparkes and the so-called private detective. They met in a spot chosen for its impressiveness, the City office of a great line of ocean steamers. When Polly had with some difficulty discovered the place and entered shyly she was met by Greenacre, who at once drew her aside and began talking in a whisper with much show of worry and perturbation. In his hand rustled a printed form, with a few words in pencil.

"It's all over, Miss Sparkes. We have no more hope. This last cable settles it. Don't let me agitate you. But I thought it best that you should come here and see the cable for yourself." Sinking his voice and with his lips at her ear he added, "Your uncle is dead."

Polly was not overcome.

"Is it *reely* him this time?"

"Clover—not a doubt of it. I got on his track, but too late, he was off to South Africa. Here is a cable from the Cape. He died at sea—some obscure disease, probably an affection of the heart —and was buried off the West Coast. Read it for yourself. 'Clover, second cabin passenger, died and buried 23·4 S., 8·2 W.; effects await instructions.' There he lies at the bottom of the sea, poor fellow. This is only a confirmatory cable; I have spent lots of money in learning particulars. Perhaps you would like to see one of the officials about it, Miss Sparkes? Unfortunately they can only repeat what I have told you."

A DOUBLE EVENT 303

Polly had no desire to hold converse with these gentlemen; she was thoroughly awed and convinced by Greenacre's tones and the atmosphere of the office.

"I have already communicated with your aunt. I daresay you would like to go and see her."

But neither for this had Polly any present inclination. She wanted to be alone and to reflect. Having made sure that she was not likely to visit Mrs. Clover forthwith, Greenacre took his leave, blending a decent melancholy with the air of importance and hurry proper to a man involved in so much business.

This week she had not entered for the missing word competition; and as few things interested Polly in which she had no personal concern, the morning on which the result was published found her in her ordinary frame of mind. She was thinking of Gammon, determined to hold him to his engagement, but more out of obstinacy than in obedience to the dictates of her heart, which had of late grown decidedly less fervid. Gammon could keep her respectably; he would make a very presentable husband; she did not fear ill treatment from him. On the other hand, she felt only too certain that he would be the stronger. When it came to a struggle (the inevitable result of marriage in Polly's mind) Gammon was not the man to give in. She remembered the battle at Mrs. Bubb's. All very well, that kind of thing, in days of courtship, but after marriage—no! Some girls might be willing to find their master. Polly had always meant to rule, and that undisputedly.

Breakfasting in her bedroom at ten o'clock, she was surprised by the receipt of a telegram. It came from Christopher Parish and ran thus:—

"*Great news. Do meet me at entrance to Liverpool Street Station one o'clock. Wonderful news.*"

What this news could be puzzled her for a moment; then she remembered that Mr. Parish had spoke of a possible "rise" at Swettenham's early in the New Year. That must be it. He had got an increase of salary; perhaps five shillings a week more; no doubt.

Would that make any difference? Was it "good enough"? So her thoughts phrased the anxious question.

Regarding Christopher one thing was certain—he would be her very humble slave. She imagined herself his wife, she pictured him inclining to revolt, she saw the results of that feeble insubordination, and laughed aloud. Christopher was respectable; he would undoubtedly continue to rise at Swettenham's, he would take a pride in the magnificence of her costume. When her temper called for natural relief she could quarrel with him by the hour without the least apprehension, and in the end would graciously forgive him. Yes, there was much to be said for Christopher.

A little before one o'clock she was at Liverpool Street, sheltered from a drizzle that brought down all the smoke of myriad chimneys. A slim figure in overcoat and shining hat rushed through the puddles towards her, waving an umbrella to the peril of other people speeding only less frantically.

"Polly! I've got it!"

He could gasp no more; he seized her arm as if for support.

"How much is it?" she asked calmly.

"Five hundred and fifty pounds! *Hyjene!*"

"What—five hundred and fifty a year?"

Christopher stared at her.

"You don't understand. The missing word. I've got it this week. Cheque for five hundred and fifty pounds! *Hyjene!*"

"*Reely!*"

"Look here—here's the cheque! *Hyjene!*"

Polly fingered the paper, studied the inscription. All the time she was thinking that this sum of money would furnish a house in a style vastly superior to that of Mrs. Nibby's. Mrs. Nibby would go black in the face with envy, hatred, and malice. As she reflected Christopher talked, drawing her to the least-frequented part of the huge roaring railway station.

"Will you, Polly? Why don't you speak? Do, Polly, do!"

She all but spoke, would have done but for an ear-rending whistle from an engine.

"I shall have a rise, too, Polly. I'm feeling my feet at Swettenham's. Who knows what I may get to? Polly, I might—I might some day have a big business of my own, and build a house at Eastbourne. It's all on the cards, Polly. Others have done it before me. Swettenham began as a clerk—he did. Think, Polly, five hundred and fifty pounds—*Hyjene!*"

She met his eye; she nodded.

"You *will?*"

"Don't mind if I do."

"Hooray! *Hyjene* for ever! Hooray-ay-ay!"

CHAPTER XXVII.

THE TRAVELLER AT REST

TWO or three days after this Gammon heard unexpectedly from Mrs. Clover, who enclosed for his perusal a letter she had just received from Polly Sparkes. What, she asked, could be the meaning of Polly's reference to her deceased uncle? Was there never to be an end of mysteries and miseries in relation to that unhappy man?

Turning to Polly's scrawl (which contrasted so strongly with Mrs. Clover's neat, clear hand), Gammon discovered the passage which had disturbed his correspondent. "You mustn't expect me to go into black for your husband, for uncle I won't call him. I heard about him coming to you for money and then taking his hook because detectives was after him. A nice sort of man. It's a pity he had to be buried at the bottom of the sea, where you can't put up a monniment to him, as I'm sure you would like to do. So this is all I have to say, and I shall not trouble you again."

Here was no puzzle for Gammon, who had approved Greenacre's scheme for finally getting rid of Mr. Clover. But Polly's letter began with an announcement which occasioned him the greatest surprise he had known since the identification of Clover with Lord Polperro. So completely did it engross and confuse his mind that not until some quarter of an hour elapsed could he think about the passage quoted above. "I write to inform you," began Miss Sparkes, without any introductory phrase, "that I am going to be married to a gentleman who has a high place at Swettenham's, the big tea merchants, and his name is Mr. Parish. He has won the missing word, which is five hundred and fifty pounds, and which, every penny of it, he will spend on furniture at one of the best places. You shall have one of our cards when we send them out, though I cannot say you have behaved accordingly. The reason I do not invite you to the wedding is because Mr. Parish's friends are very particular."

After reading these remarkable lines again and again Mr. Gammon was much disposed to shout; but something restrained him. He felt, perhaps, that shouting would be inadequate or even inappropriate. When his first emotions subsided he went quietly forth from the house (it was evening) and took a walk about the adjacent streets, stopping at a stationer's to purchase note-paper. Returned to his room he gently whistled an old-fashioned melody; his face passed from grave thoughtfulness to a merry smile. Before going to bed he meant to write a letter, but there was no hurry; two hours had to pass before the midnight collection.

The letter was brief, lucid, sensible. He explained to Mrs. Clover that the painfulness and difficulty of her situation since Lord Polperro's death had impelled him to a strange, but harmless and justifiable, expedient for putting her affairs in order. He made known the nature of the artifice, which, "for several reasons," he had tried in the first instance upon Polly Sparkes, with complete success. If Mrs. Clover took his advice she would straightway go into moderate mourning and let it be known that her husband was dead. Reserve as to details would seem strange to no one; ordinary acquaintances might be told that Mr. Clover had died abroad, friends and relatives that he had died at sea. He hoped she would not be offended by what he had done, as it relieved her from a wretched burden of secrecy, and greatly improved the position of her daughter, Miss Minnie. She need not reply to this letter unless she liked, and he would make an opportunity of calling upon her before very long.

A week passed without reply.

By discreet enquiry Gammon learnt that Mrs.

Clover had assumed the garb of widowhood, and this was quite enough.

"There," he said to himself, "there's an end of lies!" And he shook his shoulders as if to get quite clear of the unpleasant entanglement; for Mr. Gammon, though ingenious at a pinch, had no natural bent towards falsehood. To be rid at almost the same moment of Mr. Clover and Polly Sparkes seemed to him marvellous good luck; and in these bitter sodden days of the early year he was lighter hearted than for many months.

He had heard from Polly.

"DEAR MR. GAMMON,

"I don't think we are suited to each other, which is better for both parties. I shall send you a wedding-card in a few days, and I'm sure I wish you all happiness. And so I remain with my best respects,

"Yours truly,
"MISS SPARKES."

This time Mr. Gammon felt no restraint upon his mirth. He threw his head back and roared joyously. That same day he went to a jeweller's and purchased—for more than he could afford—a suitable trinket, and sent it with a well-meaning note to Polly's address.

Winter brightened into spring, spring bloomed into summer. Gammon had paid several visits to

THE TRAVELLER AT REST

the china shop, where all was going very well indeed. Minnie Clover now spent her evenings almost invariably with the young man interested in ceramic art, but it never disturbed Gammon to have ocular evidence of the fact. With Mrs. Clover he conversed in the respectfully familiar tone of an old friend, now and then reporting little matters which concerned his own welfare, such as his growing conviction that at Quodlings' he had found a "permanency," and his decision to go no more to Dulwich, to sell all his bow-wows, to find another employment for leisure hours.

But he was not wholly at ease. Time after time he had purposed making a confession to Mrs. Clover, time after time he "funked it"—his own mental phrase—and put it off.

He grew discontented with his room at Mrs. Bubb's. In getting up these bright mornings he looked with entirely new distaste upon the prospect from his window at the back. Beneath lay parallel strips of ground, divided from each other by low walls. These were called the "gardens" of the houses in Kennington Road, but no blade of grass ever showed upon the black, hard-trodden soil. Lank fowls ran about among discarded furniture and indescribable rubbish, or children—few as well-tended as Mrs. Bubb's—played and squabbled under the dropping soot. Beyond rose a huge block of tenements, each storey entered from an external platform, the levels connected by flights of iron steps; the lofty roof, used as a drying ground by the female population, was surrounded with iron railings. Gammon had hitherto seen nothing disagreeable in this outlook, nor had the shrieks and curses which at night too frequently sounded from the huge building ever troubled his repose. But he was growing fastidious. He thought constantly of a clean little street not far from Battersea Park—of a gleaming china shop—of a little parlour which seemed to him the perfection of comfort and elegance.

Courage and opportunity came together. He sat alone with Mrs. Clover one Sunday evening, and she told him that Minnie was to be married in six months' time. Gammon bore the announcement very well indeed; he seemed really glad to hear it. Then his countenance became troubled, he dropped awkward sentences; with a burst of honest feeling, which made him very red, he at length plunged into his confession. Not a little astonished, Mrs. Clover learnt all that had passed between him and Polly Sparkes, now Polly Parish. Nothing did he extenuate, but he wronged neither Polly nor himself.

"There, I've got it out. You had to know. Thank goodness it's over!"

"Why did you tell me?" asked Mrs. Clover, a

flush on her comely face, which could not yet smile, though she asked the question with a suggestion of slyness.

"It seemed only right—to make things square, don't you see. I shall know next time I come how you've taken it. And perhaps the next time after that——"

Mrs. Clover was now smiling, and so gently, so modestly, that Gammon forgot all about his scheme for a gradual approach. He began to talk excitedly, and talked for such a long time that his hostess, who wished him to disappear before Minnie's return, had at length to drive him away.

"I shall certainly keep on the shop," were her last words before the door opened. "I've got used to it, and—it'll keep me out of mischief."

Her merry little laugh echoed in Gammon's ears all the way home, and for hours after. And when, as he rose next morning, he looked out on to the strips of back-yard and the towering tenements, they had lost all their ugliness.

"By jorrocks!" he ejaculated, after gashing his chin with the razor, "I'll send Polly a handsome present next Christmas."

THE END

PLYMOUTH:
WILLIAM BRENDON AND SON,
PRINTERS.

A CATALOGUE OF BOOKS AND ANNOUNCEMENTS OF METHUEN AND COMPANY PUBLISHERS : LONDON 36 ESSEX STREET W.C.

CONTENTS

	PAGE
FORTHCOMING BOOKS,	2
POETRY,	8
BELLES LETTRES,	9
ILLUSTRATED BOOKS,	11
HISTORY,	12
BIOGRAPHY,	14
TRAVEL, ADVENTURE AND TOPOGRAPHY,	15
NAVAL AND MILITARY,	17
GENERAL LITERATURE,	18
SCIENCE,	19
TECHNOLOGY,	20
PHILOSOPHY,	20
THEOLOGY,	21
FICTION,	23
BOOKS FOR BOYS AND GIRLS,	34
THE PEACOCK LIBRARY,	34
UNIVERSITY EXTENSION SERIES,	35
SOCIAL QUESTIONS OF TO-DAY	36
CLASSICAL TRANSLATIONS	37
EDUCATIONAL BOOKS,	37

APRIL 1898

APRIL 1898.

MESSRS. METHUEN'S
ANNOUNCEMENTS

Poetry

THE POEMS OF WILLIAM SHAKESPEARE. Edited with an Introduction and Notes by GEORGE WYNDHAM, M.P. *Demy 8vo. Buckram, gilt top.* 10s. 6d.

This edition contains the 'Venus,' 'Lucrece' and Sonnets, and is prefaced with an elaborate introduction of over 140 pp. The text is founded on the first quartos, with an endeavour to retain the original reading. A set of notes deals with the problems of Date, The Rival Poets, Typography, and Punctuation; and the editor has commented on obscure passages in the light of contemporary works. The publishers believe that no such complete edition has ever been published.

Travel and Adventure

THREE YEARS IN SAVAGE AFRICA. By LIONEL DECLE. With an Introduction by H. M. STANLEY, M.P. With 100 Illustrations and 5 Maps. *Demy 8vo.* 21s.

Few Europeans have had the same opportunity of studying the barbarous parts of Africa as Mr. Decle. Starting from the Cape, he visited in succession Bechuanaland, the Zambesi, Matabeleland and Mashonaland, the Portuguese settlement on the Zambesi, Nyasaland, Ujiji, the headquarters of the Arabs, German East Africa, Uganda (where he saw fighting in company with the late Major 'Roddy' Owen), and British East Africa. In his book he relates his experiences, his minute observations of native habits and customs, and his views as to the work done in Africa by the various European Governments, whose operations he was able to study. The whole journey extended over 7000 miles, and occupied exactly three years.

EXPLORATION AND HUNTING IN CENTRAL AFRICA. By Major A. ST. H. GIBBONS, F.R.G.S. With 8 full-page Illustrations by C. WHYMPER, photographs and Map. *Demy 8vo.* 15s.

This is an account of travel and adventure among the Marotse and contiguous tribes, with a description of their customs, characteristics, and history, together with the author's experiences in hunting big game. The illustrations are by Mr. Charles Whymper, and from photographs. There is a map by the author of the hitherto unexplored regions lying between the Zambezi and Kafukwi rivers and from 18° to 15° S. lat.

WITH THE MOUNTED INFANTRY AND MASHONALAND FIELD FORCE, 1896. By Lieut.-Colonel ALDERSON. With numerous Illustrations and Plans. *Demy 8vo.* 10s. 6d.

This is an account of the military operations in Mashonaland by the officer who commanded the troops in that district during the late rebellion. Besides its interest as a story of warfare, it will have a peculiar value as an account of the services of mounted infantry by one of the chief authorities on the subject.

CAMPAIGNING ON THE UPPER NILE AND NIGER.
By Lieut. SEYMOUR VANDELEUR. With an Introduction by Sir G.
GOLDIE. With four Maps, Illustrations and Plans. *Large Cr. 8vo.*
10s. 6d.

A narrative of service (1) in the Equatorial Lakes and on the Upper Nile in 1895 and 1896; and (2) under Sir George Goldie in the Niger campaign of January 1897, describing the capture of Bida and Ilorin, and the French occupation of Boussa. The book thus deals with the two districts of Africa where now the French and English stand face to face.

THE NIGER SOURCES. By Colonel J. TROTTER, R.A.
With a Map and Illustrations. *Crown 8vo.* 5s.

A book which at the present time should be of considerable interest, being an account of a Commission appointed for frontier delimitation.

LIFE AND PROGRESS IN AUSTRALASIA. By MICHAEL
DAVITT, M.P. With two Maps. *Crown 8vo.* 6s.

This book, the outcome of a recent journey through the seven Australasian colonies, is an attempt to give to English readers a more intimate knowledge of a continent colonised by their own race. The author sketches the general life, resources, politics, parties, progress, prospects, and scenery of each colony. He made a careful examination of the West Australian goldfields, and he has paid special attention to the development of practical politics in the colonies. The book is full of anecdotes and picturesque description.

History and Biography

A HISTORY OF THE ART OF WAR. By C. W. OMAN,
M.A., Fellow of All Souls', Oxford. Vol. II. MEDIÆVAL WAR-
FARE. *Demy 8vo Illustrated.* 21s.

Mr. Oman is engaged on a History of the Art of War, of which the above, though covering the middle period from the fall of the Roman Empire to the general use of gunpowder in Western Europe, is the first instalment. The first battle dealt with will be Adrianople (378) and the last Navarette (1367). There will appear later a volume dealing with the Art of War among the Ancients, and another covering the 15th, 16th, and 17th centuries.
The book will deal mainly with tactics and strategy, fortifications and siegecraft, but subsidiary chapters will give some account of the development of arms and armour, and of the various forms of military organization known to the Middle Ages.

RELIGION AND CONSCIENCE IN ANCIENT EGYPT.
By W. M. FLINDERS PETRIE, D.C.L., LL.D. *Fully Illustrated.*
Crown 8vo. 2s. 6d.

This volume deals mainly with the historical growth of the Egyptian religion, and the arrangement of all the moral sayings into something like a handbook. But far larger interests are also discussed as the origin of intolerance, the fusion of religions, the nature of conscience, and the experimental illustration of British conscience.

SYRIA AND EGYPT FROM THE TELL EL AMARNA
TABLETS. By W. M. FLINDERS PETRIE, D.C.L., LL.D. *Crown 8vo.* 2s. 6d.

This book describes the results of recent researches and discoveries and the light thereby thrown on Egyptian history.

MESSRS. METHUEN'S ANNOUNCEMENTS

THE DECLINE AND FALL OF THE ROMAN EMPIRE. By EDWARD GIBBON. A New Edition, edited with Notes, Appendices, and Maps by J. B. BURY, M.A., Fellow of Trinity College, Dublin. *In Seven Volumes. Demy 8vo, gilt top.* 8s. 6d. each. *Crown 8vo.* 6s. each. *Vol. V.*

THE EASTERN QUESTION IN THE EIGHTEENTH CENTURY. By ALBERT SOREL of the French Academy. Translated by F. C. BRAMWELL, M.A., with an Introduction by R. C. L. FLETCHER, Fellow of Magdalen College, Oxford. With a Map. *Crown 8vo.* 4s. 6d.

This book is a study of the political conditions which led up to and governed the first partition of Poland, and the Russo-Turkish war of 1768-1774. It is probably the best existing examination of Eastern European politics in the eighteenth century, and is an early work of one of the ablest of living historians.

THE LETTERS OF VICTOR HUGO. Translated from the French by F. CLARKE, M.A. *In Two Volumes. Demy 8vo.* 10s. 6d. each. *Vol. II.* 1815-35.

A HISTORY OF THE GREAT NORTHERN RAILWAY, 1845-95. By C. H. GRINLING. With Maps and many Illustrations. *Demy 8vo.* 10s. 6d.

A record of Railway enterprise and development in Northern England, containing much matter hitherto unpublished. It appeals both to the general reader and to those specially interested in railway construction and management.

ANARCHISM. By E. V. ZENKER. *Demy 8vo.* 7s. 6d.

A critical study and history, as well as trenchant criticism of the Anarchist movement in Europe. The book has aroused considerable attention on the Continent.

THOMAS CRANMER. By A. J. MASON, D.D., Canon of Canterbury. With a Portrait. *Crown 8vo.* 3s. 6d.

[*Leaders of Religion.*

Theology

THE MINISTRY OF DEACONESSES. By CECILIA ROBINSON, Deaconess. With an Introduction by the LORD BISHOP OF WINCHESTER, and an Appendix by Professor ARMITAGE ROBINSON. *Crown 8vo.* 3s. 6d.

This book is a review of the history and theory of the office and work of a Deaconess and it may be regarded as authoritative.

DISCIPLINE AND LAW. By H. HENSLEY HENSON, B.D., Fellow of All Soul's, Oxford; Incumbent of St. Mary's Hospital, Ilford; Chaplain to the Bishop of St. Albans. *Fcap. 8vo.* 2s. 6d.

This volume of devotional addresses, suitable for Lent, is concerned with the value, method, and reward of Discipline; and with Law—family, social and individual.

REASONABLE CHRISTIANITY. By HASTINGS RASHDALL, M.A., Fellow and Tutor of New College, Oxford. *Crown 8vo.* 6s.

This volume consists of twenty sermons, preached chiefly before the University of Oxford. They are an attempt to translate into the language of modern thought some of the leading ideas of Christian theology and ethics.

MESSRS. METHUEN'S ANNOUNCEMENTS 5

THE HOLY SACRIFICE. By F. WESTON, M.A., Curate of St. Matthew's, Westminster. *Pott 8vo. 6d. net.*

A small volume of devotions at the Holy Communion, especially adapted to the needs of servers and of those who do not communicate.

The Churchman's Library.

Edited by J. H. BURN, B.D.

A series of books by competent scholars on Church History, Institutions, and Doctrine, for the use of clerical and lay readers.

THE BEGINNINGS OF ENGLISH CHRISTIANITY. By W. E. COLLINS, M.A., Professor of Ecclesiastical History at King's College, London. With Map. *Crown 8vo. 3s. 6d.*

An investigation in detail, based upon original authorities, of the beginnings of the English Church, with a careful account of earlier Celtic Christianity. The larger aspects of the continental movement are described, and some very full appendices treat of a number of special subjects.

SOME NEW TESTAMENT PROBLEMS. By ARTHUR WRIGHT, Fellow and Tutor of Queen's College, Cambridge. *Crown 8vo. 6s.*

This book deals with a number of important problems from the standpoint of the 'Higher Criticism,' and is written in the hope of advancing the historico-critical study of the Synoptic Gospels and of the Acts.

The Library of Devotion.

Messrs. METHUEN have arranged to publish under the above title a number of the older masterpieces of devotional literature. It is their intention to entrust each volume of the series to an editor who will not only attempt to bring out the spiritual importance of the book, but who will lavish such scholarly care upon it as is generally expended only on editions of the ancient classics.

The books will be furnished with such Introductions and Notes as may be necessary to explain the standpoint of the author, and to comment on such difficulties as the ordinary reader may find, without unnecessary intrusion between the author and reader.

Mr. Laurence Housman has designed a title-page and a cover design. *Pott 8vo. 2s.; leather 3s.*

THE CONFESSIONS OF ST. AUGUSTINE. Newly Translated, with an Introduction and Notes, by C. BIGG, D.D., late Student of Christ Church.

This volume contains the nine books of the 'Confessions' which are suitable for devotional purposes.

THE CHRISTIAN YEAR. By JOHN KEBLE. With Introduction and Notes, by WALTER LOCK, D.D., Warden of Keble College, Ireland Professor at Oxford.

Messrs. Methuen's Announcements

THE IMITATION OF CHRIST. A Revised Translation with an Introduction, by C. BIGG, D.D., late Student of Christ Church.

Dr. Bigg has made a practically new translation of this book, which the reader will have, almost for the first time, exactly in the shape in which it left the hands of the author.

A BOOK OF DEVOTIONS. By J. W. STANBRIDGE, M.A., Rector of Bainton, Canon of York, and sometime Fellow of St. John's College, Oxford. *Pott 8vo.*

This book contains devotions, Eucharistic, daily and occasional, for the use of members of the English Church, sufficiently diversified for those who possess other works of the kind. It is intended to be a companion in private and public worship, and is in harmony with the thoughts of the best Devotional writers.

General Literature

THE GOLFING PILGRIM. By HORACE G. HUTCHINSON. *Crown 8vo. 6s.*

This book, by a famous golfer, contains the following sketches lightly and humorously written:—The Prologue—The Pilgrim at the Shrine—Mecca out of Season—The Pilgrim at Home—The Pilgrim Abroad—The Life of the Links—A Tragedy by the Way—Scraps from the Scrip—The Golfer in Art—Early Pilgrims in the West —An Interesting Relic.

WORKHOUSES AND PAUPERISM. By LOUISA TWINING. *Crown 8vo. 2s. 6d.* [*Social Questions Series.*

Educational

THE ODES AND EPODES OF HORACE. Translated by A. D. GODLEY, M.A., Fellow of Magdalen College, Oxford. *Crown 8vo. 2s.* [*Classical Translations.*

PASSAGES FOR UNSEEN TRANSLATION. By E. C. MARCHANT, M.A., Fellow of Peterhouse, Cambridge; and A. M. COOK, M.A., late Scholar of Wadham College, Oxford: Assistant Masters at St. Paul's School. *Crown 8vo. 3s. 6d.*

This book contains Two Hundred Latin and Two Hundred Greek Passages, and has been very carefully compiled to meet the wants of V. and VI. Form Boys at Public Schools. It is also well adapted for the use of Honour men at the Universities.

EASY LATIN EXERCISES ON THE SYNTAX OF THE SHORTER AND REVISED LATIN PRIMER. By A. M. M. STEDMAN, M.A. With Vocabulary. *Seventh and Cheaper Edition. Crown 8vo. 1s. 6d.* Issued with the consent of Dr. Kennedy.

A new and cheaper edition, thoroughly revised by Mr. C. G. Botting, of St. Paul's School.

TEST CARDS IN EUCLID AND ALGEBRA. By D. S. CALDERWOOD, Headmaster of the Normal School, Edinburgh. In a Packet of 40, with Answers. 1s.

A set of cards for advanced pupils in elementary schools.

MESSRS. METHUEN'S ANNOUNCEMENTS   7

Byzantine Texts
Edited by J. B. BURY, M.A., Professor of Modern History at Trinity College, Dublin.

EVAGRIUS. Edited by PROFESSOR LÉON PARMENTIER of Liége and M. BIDEZ of Gand. *Demy 8vo.*
PSELLUS (HISTORIA). Edited by C. SATHAS. *Demy 8vo.*

Fiction

THE STANDARDBEARER. By S. R. CROCKETT, Author of 'The Raiders,' Lochinvar,' etc. *Large crown 8vo.* 6s.

SIMON DALE. By ANTHONY HOPE. Illustrated by W. ST. J. HARPER. *Crown 8vo.* 6s.
A romance of the reign of Charles II., and Mr. Anthony Hope's first historical novel.

TRAITS AND CONFIDENCES. By The Hon. EMILY LAWLESS, Author of ' Hurrish,' ' Maelcho,' etc. *Crown 8vo.* 6s.

THE VINTAGE. By E. F. BENSON, Author of 'Dodo.' Illustrated by G. P. JACOMB-HOOD. *Crown 8vo.* 6s.
A romance of the Greek War of Independence.

A VOYAGE OF CONSOLATION. By SARA JEANETTE DUNCAN. Author of 'An American Girl in London.' Illustrated by ROBERT SAUBER. *Crown 8vo.* 6s.
The adventures of an American girl in Europe.

THE CROOK OF THE BOUGH. By MÉNIE MURIEL DOWIE, Author of 'Gallia.' *Crown 8vo.* 6s.

ACROSS THE SALT SEAS. By J. BLOUNDELLE-BURTON. *Crown 8vo.* 6s.

SONS OF ADVERSITY. By L. COPE CORNFORD, Author of 'Captain Jacobus.' *Crown 8vo.* 6s.
A romance of Queen Elizabeth's time.

MISS ERIN. By M. E. FRANCIS, Author of 'In a Northern Village.' *Crown 8vo.* 6s.

WILLOWBRAKE. By R. MURRAY GILCHRIST. *Crown 8vo.* 6s.

THE KLOOF BRIDE. By ERNEST GLANVILLE, Author of ' The Fossicker.' Illustrated. *Crown 8vo.* 3s. 6d.
A story of South African Adventure.

BIJLI THE DANCER. By JAMES BLYTHE PATTON. Illustrated. *Crown 8vo.* 6s.
A Romance of India.

JOSIAH'S WIFE. By NORMA LORIMER. *Crown 8vo.* 6s.

BETWEEN SUN AND SAND. By W. C. SCULLY, Author of ' The White Hecatomb.' *Crown 8vo.* 6s.

CROSS TRAILS. By VICTOR WAITE. Illustrated. *Crown 8vo.* 6s.
A romance of adventure in America and Australia.

THE PHILANTHROPIST. By LUCY MAYNARD. *Crown 8vo.* 6s.

VAUSSORE. By FRANCIS BRUNE. *Crown 8vo.* 6s.

A LIST OF

Messrs. Methuen's
Publications

Poetry

RUDYARD KIPLING'S NEW POEMS

Rudyard Kipling. THE SEVEN SEAS. By RUDYARD KIPLING. *Third Edition. Crown 8vo. Buckram, gilt top. 6s.*
'The new poems of Mr. Rudyard Kipling have all the spirit and swing of their predecessors. Patriotism is the solid concrete foundation on which Mr. Kipling has built the whole of his work.'—*Times.*
'The Empire has found a singer; it is no depreciation of the songs to say that statesmen may have, one way or other, to take account of them.'—*Manchester Guardian.*
'Animated through and through with indubitable genius.'—*Daily Telegraph.*
'Packed with inspiration, with humour, with pathos.'—*Daily Chronicle.*
'All the pride of empire, all the intoxication of power, all the ardour, the energy, the masterful strength and the wonderful endurance and death-scorning pluck which are the very bone and fibre and marrow of the British character are here.'—*Daily Mail.*

Rudyard Kipling. BARRACK-ROOM BALLADS. By RUDYARD KIPLING. *Thirteenth Edition. Crown 8vo. 6s.*
'Mr. Kipling's verse is strong, vivid, full of character. . . . Unmistakable genius rings in every line.'—*Times.*
'The ballads teem with imagination, they palpitate with emotion. We read them with laughter and tears; the metres throb in our pulses, the cunningly ordered words tingle with life; and if this be not poetry, what is?'—*Pall Mall Gazette.*

"Q." POEMS AND BALLADS. By "Q." *Crown 8vo. 3s. 6d.*
'This work has just the faint, ineffable touch and glow that make poetry.'—*Speaker.*

"Q." GREEN BAYS: Verses and Parodies. By "Q.," Author of 'Dead Man's Rock,' etc. *Second Edition. Crown 8vo. 3s. 6d.*

E. Mackay. A SONG OF THE SEA. By ERIC MACKAY, *Second Edition. Fcap. 8vo. 5s.*
'Everywhere Mr. Mackay displays himself the master of a style marked by all the characteristics of the best rhetoric.'—*Globe.*

Ibsen. BRAND. A Drama by HENRIK IBSEN. Translated by WILLIAM WILSON. *Second Edition. Crown 8vo. 3s. 6d.*
'The greatest world-poem of the nineteenth century next to "Faust." It is in the same set with "Agamemnon," with "Lear," with the literature that we now instinctively regard as high and holy.'—*Daily Chronicle.*

MESSRS. METHUEN'S LIST 9

"A. G." VERSES TO ORDER. By "A. G." *Cr. 8vo.* 2*s.* 6*d.* net.

A capital specimen of light academic poetry. These verses are very bright and engaging, easy and sufficiently witty.'—*St. James's Gazette.*

Cordery. THE ODYSSEY OF HOMER. A Translation by J. G. CORDERY. *Crown 8vo.* 7*s.* 6*d.*

'This new version of the Odyssey fairly deserves a place of honour among its many rivals. Perhaps there is none from which a more accurate knowledge of the original can be gathered with greater pleasure, at least of those that are in metre.' —*Manchester Guardian.*

Belles Lettres, Anthologies, etc.

R. L. Stevenson. VAILIMA LETTERS. By ROBERT LOUIS STEVENSON. With an Etched Portrait by WILLIAM STRANG, and other Illustrations. *Second Edition. Crown 8vo. Buckram.* 7*s.* 6*d.*

'Few publications have in our time been more eagerly awaited than these "Vailima Letters," giving the first fruits of the correspondence of Robert Louis Stevenson. But, high as the tide of expectation has run, no reader can possibly be disappointed in the result.'—*St. James's Gazette.*

Henley. ENGLISH LYRICS. Selected and Edited by W. E. HENLEY. *Crown 8vo. Buckram gilt top.* 6*s.*

'It is a body of choice and lovely poetry.'—*Birmingham Gazette.*
'Mr. Henley's notes, in their brevity and their fulness, their information and their suggestiveness, seem to us a model of what notes should be.'—*Manchester Guardian.*

Henley and Whibley. A BOOK OF ENGLISH PROSE. Collected by W. E. HENLEY and CHARLES WHIBLEY. *Crown 8vo. Buckram gilt top.* 6*s.*

'A unique volume of extracts—an art gallery of early prose.'—*Birmingham Post.*
'An admirable companion to Mr. Henley's "Lyra Heroica."'—*Saturday Review.*
'Quite delightful. A greater treat for those not well acquainted with pre-Restoration prose could not be imagined.'—*Athenæum.*

H. C. Beeching. LYRA SACRA : An Anthology of Sacred Verse. Edited by H. C. BEECHING, M.A. *Crown 8vo. Buckram.* 6*s.*

'A charming selection, which maintains a lofty standard of excellence.'—*Times.*

"Q." THE GOLDEN POMP : A Procession of English Lyrics from Surrey to Shirley, arranged by A. T. QUILLER COUCH. *Crown 8vo. Buckram.* 6*s.*

'A delightful volume : a really golden "Pomp."'—*Spectator.*

W. B. Yeats. AN ANTHOLOGY OF IRISH VERSE. Edited by W. B. YEATS. *Crown 8vo.* 3*s.* 6*d.*

'An attractive and catholic selection.'—*Times.*

G. W. Steevens. MONOLOGUES OF THE DEAD. By G. W. STEEVENS. *Foolscap 8vo.* 3s. 6d.

A series of Soliloquies in which famous men of antiquity—Julius Cæsar, Nero, Alcibiades, etc., attempt to express themselves in the modes of thought and language of to-day.

'The effect is sometimes splendid, sometimes bizarre, but always amazingly clever.' —*Pall Mall Gazette.*

Victor Hugo. THE LETTERS OF VICTOR HUGO. Translated from the French by F. CLARKE, M.A. *In Two Volumes. Demy 8vo.* 10s. 6d. each. *Vol. I.* 1815-35.

C. H. Pearson. ESSAYS AND CRITICAL REVIEWS. By C. H. PEARSON, M.A., Author of 'National Life and Character.' With a Portrait. *Demy 8vo.* 10s. 6d.

W. M. Dixon. A PRIMER OF TENNYSON. By W. M. DIXON, M.A., Professor of English Literature at Mason College. *Crown 8vo.* 2s. 6d.

'Much sound and well-expressed criticism and acute literary judgments. The bibliography is a boon.'—*Speaker.*

W. A. Craigie. A PRIMER OF BURNS. By W. A. CRAIGIE. *Crown 8vo.* 2s. 6d.

'A valuable addition to the literature of the poet.'—*Times.*
'An admirable introduction.'—*Globe.*

Magnus. A PRIMER OF WORDSWORTH. By LAURIE MAGNUS. *Crown 8vo.* 2s. 6d.

'A valuable contribution to Wordsworthian literature.'—*Literature.*
'A well-made primer, thoughtful and informing.'—*Manchester Guardian.*

Sterne. THE LIFE AND OPINIONS OF TRISTRAM SHANDY. By LAWRENCE STERNE. With an Introduction by CHARLES WHIBLEY, and a Portrait. *2 vols.* 7s.

'Very dainty volumes are these; the paper, type, and light-green binding are all very agreeable to the eye. *Simplex munditiis* is the phrase that might be applied to them.'—*Globe.*

Congreve. THE COMEDIES OF WILLIAM CONGREVE. With an Introduction by G. S. STREET, and a Portrait. *2 vols.* 7s.

Morier. THE ADVENTURES OF HAJJI BABA OF ISPAHAN. By JAMES MORIER. With an Introduction by E. G. BROWNE, M.A., and a Portrait. *2 vols.* 7s.

Walton. THE LIVES OF DONNE, WOTTON, HOOKER, HERBERT, AND SANDERSON. By IZAAK WALTON. With an Introduction by VERNON BLACKBURN, and a Portrait. 3s. 6d.

Johnson. THE LIVES OF THE ENGLISH POETS. By SAMUEL JOHNSON, LL.D. With an Introduction by J. H. MILLAR, and a Portrait. *3 vols.* 10s. 6d.

MESSRS. METHUEN'S LIST 11

Burns. THE POEMS OF ROBERT BURNS. Edited by ANDREW LANG and W. A. CRAIGIE. With Portrait. *Demy 8vo, gilt top.* 6s.

This edition contains a carefully collated Text, numerous Notes, critical and textual, a critical and biographical Introduction, and a Glossary.
'Among the editions in one volume, Mr. Andrew Lang's will take the place of authority.'—*Times.*

F. Langbridge. BALLADS OF THE BRAVE: Poems of Chivalry, Enterprise, Courage, and Constancy. Edited by Rev. F. LANGBRIDGE. *Crown 8vo.* 3s. 6d. *School Edition.* 2s. 6d.

'A very happy conception happily carried out. These "Ballads of the Brave" are intended to suit the real tastes of boys, and will suit the taste of the great majority.' —*Spectator.* 'The book is full of splendid things.'—*World.*

Illustrated Books

Bedford. NURSERY RHYMES. With many Coloured Pictures. By F. D. BEDFORD. *Super Royal 8vo.* 5s.

'An excellent selection of the best known rhymes, with beautifully coloured pictures exquisitely printed.'—*Pall Mall Gazette.*
'The art is of the newest, with well harmonised colouring.'—*Spectator.*

S. Baring Gould. A BOOK OF FAIRY TALES retold by S. BARING GOULD. With numerous illustrations and initial letters by ARTHUR J. GASKIN. *Second Edition. Crown 8vo. Buckram.* 6s.

'Mr. Baring Gould is deserving of gratitude, in re-writing in honest, simple style the old stories that delighted the childhood of "our fathers and grandfathers."'—*Saturday Review.*

S. Baring Gould. OLD ENGLISH FAIRY TALES. Collected and edited by S. BARING GOULD. With Numerous Illustrations by F. D. BEDFORD. *Second Edition. Crown 8vo. Buckram.* 6s.

'A charming volume. The stories have been selected with great ingenuity from various old ballads and folk-tales, and now stand forth, clothed in Mr. Baring Gould's delightful English, to enchant youthful readers.'—*Guardian.*

S. Baring Gould. A BOOK OF NURSERY SONGS AND RHYMES. Edited by S. BARING GOULD, and Illustrated by the Birmingham Art School. *Buckram, gilt top. Crown 8vo.* 6s.

'The volume is very complete in its way, as it contains nursery songs to the number of 77, game-rhymes, and jingles. To the student we commend the sensible introduction, and the explanatory notes.'—*Birmingham Gazette.*

H. C. Beeching. A BOOK OF CHRISTMAS VERSE. Edited by H. C. BEECHING, M.A., and Illustrated by WALTER CRANE. *Crown 8vo, gilt top.* 5s.

A collection of the best verse inspired by the birth of Christ from the Middle Ages to the present day.
'An anthology which, from its unity of aim and high poetic excellence, has a better right to exist than most of its fellows.'—*Guardian.*

History

Gibbon. THE DECLINE AND FALL OF THE ROMAN EMPIRE. By EDWARD GIBBON. A New Edition, Edited with Notes, Appendices, and Maps, by J. B. BURY, M.A., Fellow of Trinity College, Dublin. *In Seven Volumes. Demy 8vo. Gilt top. 6s. 6d. each. Also crown 8vo. 6s. each. Vols. I., II., III., and IV.*

'The time has certainly arrived for a new edition of Gibbon's great work.... Professor Bury is the right man to undertake this task. His learning is amazing, both in extent and accuracy. The book is issued in a handy form, and at a moderate price, and it is admirably printed.'—*Times*.

'This edition, so far as one may judge from the first instalment, is a marvel of erudition and critical skill, and it is the very minimum of praise to predict that the seven volumes of it will supersede Dean Milman's as the standard edition of our great historical classic.'—*Glasgow Herald*.

'The beau-ideal Gibbon has arrived at last.'—*Sketch*.

'At last there is an adequate modern edition of Gibbon. . . . The best edition the nineteenth century could produce.'—*Manchester Guardian*.

Flinders Petrie. A HISTORY OF EGYPT, FROM THE EARLIEST TIMES TO THE PRESENT DAY. Edited by W. M. FLINDERS PETRIE, D.C.L., LL.D., Professor of Egyptology at University College. *Fully Illustrated. In Six Volumes. Crown 8vo. 6s. each.*

Vol. I. PREHISTORIC TIMES TO XVITH. DYNASTY. W. M. F. Petrie. *Third Edition*.

Vol. II. THE XVIITH AND XVIIITH DYNASTIES. W. M. F. Petrie. *Second Edition*.

'A history written in the spirit of scientific precision so worthily represented by Dr. Petrie and his school cannot but promote sound and accurate study, and supply a vacant place in the English literature of Egyptology.'—*Times*.

Flinders Petrie. EGYPTIAN TALES. Edited by W. M. FLINDERS PETRIE. Illustrated by TRISTRAM ELLIS. *In Two Volumes. Crown 8vo. 3s. 6d. each.*

'A valuable addition to the literature of comparative folk-lore. The drawings are really illustrations in the literal sense of the word.'—*Globe*.

'It has a scientific value to the student of history and archæology. —*Scotsman*.

'Invaluable as a picture of life in Palestine and Egypt.'—*Daily News*.

Flinders Petrie. EGYPTIAN DECORATIVE ART. By W. M. FLINDERS PETRIE. With 120 Illustrations. *Cr. 8vo. 3s. 6d.*

'Professor Flinders Petrie is not only a profound Egyptologist, but an accomplished student of comparative archæology. In these lectures he displays both qualifications with rare skill in elucidating the development of decorative art in Egypt, and in tracing its influence on the art of other countries.'—*Times*.

S. Baring Gould. THE TRAGEDY OF THE CÆSARS. With numerous Illustrations from Busts, Gems, Cameos, etc. By S. BARING GOULD. *Fourth Edition. Royal 8vo. 15s.*

'A most splendid and fascinating book on a subject of undying interest. The great feature of the book is the use the author has made of the existing portraits of the Cæsars, and the admirable critical subtlety he has exhibited in dealing with this line of research. It is brilliantly written, and the illustrations are supplied on a scale of profuse magnificence.'—*Daily Chronicle*.

MESSRS. METHUEN'S LIST 13

H. de B. Gibbins. INDUSTRY IN ENGLAND: HISTORICAL OUTLINES. By H. DE B. GIBBINS, M.A., D.Litt. With 5 Maps. *Second Edition. Demy 8vo.* 10s. 6d.

This book is written with the view of affording a clear view of the main facts of English Social and Industrial History placed in due perspective.

H. E. Egerton. A HISTORY OF BRITISH COLONIAL POLICY. By H. E. EGERTON, M.A. *Demy 8vo.* 12s. 6d.

This book deals with British Colonial policy historically from the beginnings of English colonisation down to the present day. The subject has been treated by itself, and it has thus been possible within a reasonable compass to deal with a mass of authority which must otherwise be sought in the State papers. The volume is divided into five parts:—(1) The Period of Beginnings, 1497-1650; (2) Trade Ascendancy, 1651-1830; (3) The Granting of Responsible Government, 1831-1860; (4) *Laissez Aller*, 1861-1885; (5) Greater Britain.

'The whole story of the growth and administration of our colonial empire is comprehensive and well arranged, and is set forth with marked ability.'—*Daily Mail.*
'It is a good book, distinguished by accuracy in detail, clear arrangement of facts, and a broad grasp of principles'—*Manchester Guardian.*
'Able, impartial, clear. . . . A most valuable volume.'—*Athenæum.*

A. Clark. THE COLLEGES OF OXFORD: Their History and their Traditions. By Members of the University. Edited by A. CLARK, M.A., Fellow and Tutor of Lincoln College. *8vo.* 12s. 6d.

'A work which will certainly be appealed to for many years as the standard book on the Colleges of Oxford.'—*Athenæum.*

Perrens. THE HISTORY OF FLORENCE FROM 1434 TO 1492. By F. T. PERRENS. *8vo.* 12s. 6d.

A history of Florence under the domination of Cosimo, Piero, and Lorenzo de Medicis.

J. Wells. A SHORT HISTORY OF ROME. By J. WELLS, M.A., Fellow and Tutor of Wadham Coll., Oxford. With 4 Maps. *Crown 8vo.* 3s. 6d.

This book is intended for the Middle and Upper Forms of Public Schools and for Pass Students at the Universities. It contains copious Tables, etc.
'An original work written on an original plan, and with uncommon freshness and vigour.'—*Speaker.*

O. Browning. A SHORT HISTORY OF MEDIÆVAL ITALY, A.D. 1250-1530. By OSCAR BROWNING, Fellow and Tutor of King's College, Cambridge. *Second Edition. In Two Volumes. Crown 8vo.* 5s. each.

VOL. I. 1250-1409.—Guelphs and Ghibellines.
VOL. II. 1409-1530.—The Age of the Condottieri.

'Mr. Browning is to be congratulated on the production of a work of immense labour and learning.'—*Westminster Gazette.*

O'Grady. THE STORY OF IRELAND. By STANDISH O'GRADY, Author of 'Finn and his Companions.' *Cr. 8vo.* 2s. 6d.

Most delightful, most stimulating. Its racy humour, its original imaginings, make it one of the freshest, breeziest volumes.'—*Methodist Times.*

Biography

S. Baring Gould. THE LIFE OF NAPOLEON BONAPARTE. By S. BARING GOULD. With over 450 Illustrations in the Text and 12 Photogravure Plates. *Large quarto. Gilt top.* 36s.

'The best biography of Napoleon in our tongue, nor have the French as good a biographer of their hero. A book very nearly as good as Southey's "Life of Nelson."'—*Manchester Guardian.*
'The main feature of this gorgeous volume is its great wealth of beautiful photogravures and finely-executed wood engravings, constituting a complete pictorial chronicle of Napoleon I.'s personal history from the days of his early childhood at Ajaccio to the date of his second interment under the dome of the Invalides in Paris.'—*Daily Telegraph.*
'Particular notice is due to the vast collection of contemporary illustrations.'—*Guardian.*
'Nearly all the illustrations are real contributions to history.'—*Westminster Gazette.*

Morris Fuller. THE LIFE AND WRITINGS OF JOHN DAVENANT, D.D. (1571-1641), Bishop of Salisbury. By MORRIS FULLER, B.D. *Demy 8vo.* 10s. 6d.
'A valuable contribution to ecclesiastical history.'—*Birmingham Gazette.*

J. M. Rigg. ST. ANSELM OF CANTERBURY: A CHAPTER IN THE HISTORY OF RELIGION. By J. M. RIGG. *Demy 8vo.* 7s. 6d.
'Mr. Rigg has told the story of the great Primate's life with scholarly ability, and has thereby contributed an interesting chapter to the history of the Norman period.'—*Daily Chronicle.*

F. W. Joyce. THE LIFE OF SIR FREDERICK GORE OUSELEY. By F. W. JOYCE, M.A. With Portraits and Illustrations. *Crown 8vo.* 7s. 6d.
'This book has been undertaken in quite the right spirit, and written with sympathy, insight, and considerable literary skill.'—*Times.*

W. G. Collingwood. THE LIFE OF JOHN RUSKIN. By W. G. COLLINGWOOD, M.A. With Portraits, and 13 Drawings by Mr. Ruskin. *Second Edition.* 2 vols. *8vo.* 32s.
'No more magnificent volumes have been published for a long time.'—*Times.*
'It is long since we had a biography with such delights of substance and of form. Such a book is a pleasure for the day, and a joy for ever.'—*Daily Chronicle.*

C. Waldstein. JOHN RUSKIN: a Study. By CHARLES WALDSTEIN, M.A., Fellow of King's College, Cambridge. With a Photogravure Portrait after Professor HERKOMER. *Post 8vo.* 5s.
'A thoughtful, impartial, well-written criticism of Ruskin's teaching, intended to separate what the author regards as valuable and permanent from what is transient and erroneous in the great master's writing.'—*Daily Chronicle.*

Darmesteter. THE LIFE OF ERNEST RENAN. By MADAME DARMESTETER. With Portrait. *Second Edition. Cr. 8vo. 6s.*
A biography of Renan by one of his most intimate friends.
'A polished gem of biography, superior in its kind to any attempt that has been made of recent years in England. Madame Darmesteter has indeed written for English readers "*The* Life of Ernest Renan."'—*Athenæum.*
'It is a fascinating and biographical and critical study, and an admirably finished work of literary art.'—*Scotsman.*
'It is interpenetrated with the dignity and charm, the mild, bright, classical grace of form and treatment that Renan himself so loved; and it fulfils to the uttermost the delicate and difficult achievement it sets out to accomplish.'—*Academy.*

W. H. Hutton. THE LIFE OF SIR THOMAS MORE. By W. H. HUTTON, M.A. *With Portraits. Crown 8vo. 5s.*
'The book lays good claim to high rank among our biographies. It is excellently, even lovingly, written.'—*Scotsman.*   'An excellent monograph.'—*Times.*

Travel, Adventure and Topography

Johnston. BRITISH CENTRAL AFRICA. By Sir H. H. JOHNSTON, K.C.B. With nearly Two Hundred Illustrations, and Six Maps. *Second Edition. Crown 4to. 30s. net.*
'A fascinating book, written with equal skill and charm—the work at once of a literary artist and of a man of action who is singularly wise, brave, and experienced. It abounds in admirable sketches from pencil.'—*Westminster Gazette.*
'A delightful book . . . collecting within the covers of a single volume all that is known of this part of our African domains. The voluminous appendices are of extreme value.'—*Manchester Guardian.*
'The book takes front rank as a standard work by the one man competent to write it.'—*Daily Chronicle.*
'The book is crowded with important information, and written in a most attractive style; it is worthy, in short, of the author's established reputation.'—*Standard.*

Prince Henri of Orleans. FROM TONKIN TO INDIA. By PRINCE HENRI OF ORLEANS. Translated by HAMLEY BENT, M.A. With 100 Illustrations and a Map. *Second Edition. Crown 4to, gilt top. 25s.*
The travels of Prince Henri in 1895 from China to the valley of the Bramaputra covered a distance of 2100 miles, of which 1600 was through absolutely unexplored country. No fewer than seventeen ranges of mountains were crossed at altitudes of from 11,000 to 13,000 feet. The journey was made memorable by the discovery of the sources of the Irrawaddy.

'A welcome contribution to our knowledge. The narrative is full and interesting, and the appendices give the work a substantial value.'—*Times.*
'The Prince's travels are of real importance . . . his services to geography have been considerable. The volume is beautifully illustrated.'—*Athenæum.*
'The story is instructive and fascinating, and will certainly make one of the books of 1898. The book attracts by its delightful print and fine illustrations. A nearly model book of travel.'—*Pall Mall Gazette.*
'An entertaining record of pluck and travel in important regions.'—*Daily Chronicle.*
'The illustrations are admirable and quite beyond praise.'—*Glasgow Herald.*
'The Prince's story is charmingly told, and presented with an attractiveness which will make it, in more than one sense, an outstanding book of the season.'—*Birmingham Post.*
'An attractive book which will prove of considerable interest and no little value. A narrative of a remarkable journey.'—*Literature.*
'China is the country of the hour. All eyes are turned towards her, and Messrs. Methuen have opportunely selected the moment to launch Prince Henri's work.'—*Liverpool Daily Post.*

R. S. S. Baden-Powell. THE DOWNFALL OF PREMPEH.
A Diary of Life in Ashanti, 1895. By Colonel BADEN-POWELL.
With 21 Illustrations and a Map. *Demy 8vo.* 10s. 6d.
'A compact, faithful, most readable record of the campaign.'—*Daily News.*

R. S. S. Baden-Powell. THE MATABELE CAMPAIGN 1896.
By Colonel BADEN-POWELL. With nearly 100 Illustrations. *Second Edition. Demy 8vo.* 15s.
'As a straightforward account of a great deal of plucky work unpretentiously done, this book is well worth reading. The simplicity of the narrative is all in its favour, and accords in a peculiarly English fashion with the nature of the subject.' *Times.*

Captain Hinde. THE FALL OF THE CONGO ARABS.
By L. HINDE. With Plans, etc. *Demy 8vo.* 12s. 6d.
The book is full of good things, and of sustained interest.'—*St. James's Gazette.*
'A graphic sketch of one of the most exciting and important episodes in the struggle for supremacy in Central Africa between the Arabs and their European rivals. Apart from the story of the campaign, Captain Hinde's book is mainly remarkable for the fulness with which he discusses the question of cannibalism. It is, indeed, the only connected narrative—in English, at any rate—which has been published of this particular episode in African history.'—*Times.*

W. Crooke. THE NORTH-WESTERN PROVINCES OF INDIA : THEIR ETHNOLOGY AND ADMINISTRATION. By W. CROOKE. With Maps and Illustrations. *Demy 8vo.* 10s. 6d.
'A carefully and well-written account of one of the most important provinces of the Empire. In seven chapters Mr. Crooke deals successively with the land in its physical aspect, the province under Hindoo and Mussulman rule, the province under British rule, the ethnology and sociology of the province, the religious and social life of the people, the land and its settlement, and the native peasant in his relation to the land. The illustrations are good and well selected, and the map is excellent.'—*Manchester Guardian.*

A. Boisragon. THE BENIN MASSACRE. By CAPTAIN BOISRAGON. With Portrait and Map. *Second Edition. Crown 8vo.* 3s. 6d.
'If the story had been written four hundred years ago it would be read to-day as an English classic.'—*Scotsman.*
'If anything could enhance the horror and the pathos of this remarkable book it is the simple style of the author, who writes as he would talk, unconscious of his own heroism, with an artlessness which is the highest art.'—*Pall Mall Gazette.*

H. S. Cowper. THE HILL OF THE GRACES : OR, THE GREAT STONE TEMPLES OF TRIPOLI. By H. S. COWPER, F.S.A. With Maps, Plans, and 75 Illustrations. *Demy 8vo.* 10s. 6d.
'The book has the interest of all first-hand work, directed by an intelligent man towards a worthy object, and it forms a valuable chapter of what has now become quite a large and important branch of antiquarian research.'—*Times.*

Kinnaird Rose. WITH THE GREEKS IN THESSALY.
By W. KINNAIRD ROSE, Reuter's Correspondent. With Plans and 23 Illustrations. *Crown 8vo.* 6s.

W. B. Worsfold. SOUTH AFRICA. By W. B. WORSFOLD, M.A. *With a Map. Second Edition. Crown 8vo.* 6s.
'A monumental work compressed into a very moderate compass.'—*World.*

Naval and Military

G. W. Steevens. NAVAL POLICY: By. G. W. STEEVENS. *Demy 8vo. 6s.*

This book is a description of the British and other more important navies of the world, with a sketch of the lines on which our naval policy might possibly be developed.
'An extremely able and interesting work.'—*Daily Chronicle.*

D. Hannay. A SHORT HISTORY OF THE ROYAL NAVY, FROM EARLY TIMES TO THE PRESENT DAY. By DAVID HANNAY. Illustrated. 2 *Vols. Demy 8vo. 7s. 6d. each.* Vol. I., 1200-1688.

'We read it from cover to cover at a sitting, and those who go to it for a lively and brisk picture of the past, with all its faults and its grandeur, will not be disappointed. The historian is competent, and he is endowed with literary skill and style.'—*Standard.*
'We can warmly recommend Mr. Hannay's volume to any intelligent student of naval history. Great as is the merit of Mr. Hannay's historical narrative, the merit of his strategic exposition is even greater.'—*Times.*
'His book is brisk and pleasant reading, for he is gifted with a most agreeable style. His reflections are philosophical, and he has seized and emphasised just those points which are of interest.'—*Graphic.*

Cooper King. THE STORY OF THE BRITISH ARMY. By Lieut.-Colonel COOPER KING, of the Staff College, Camberley. Illustrated. *Demy 8vo. 7s. 6d.*

'An authoritative and accurate story of England's military progress.'—*Daily Mail.*
'This handy volume contains, in a compendious form, a brief but adequate sketch of the story of the British army.'—*Daily News.*

R. Southey. ENGLISH SEAMEN (Howard, Clifford, Hawkins, Drake, Cavendish). By ROBERT SOUTHEY. Edited, with an Introduction, by DAVID HANNAY. *Second Edition. Crown 8vo. 6s.*

'Admirable and well-told stories of our naval history.'—*Army and Navy Gazette.*
'A brave, inspiriting book.'—*Black and White.*

W. Clark Russell. THE LIFE OF ADMIRAL LORD COLLINGWOOD. By W. CLARK RUSSELL, With Illustrations by F. BRANGWYN. *Third Edition. Crown 8vo. 6s.*

'A book which we should like to see in the hands of every boy in the country.'—*St. James's Gazette.* 'A really good book.'—*Saturday Review.*

E. L. S. Horsburgh. THE CAMPAIGN OF WATERLOO. By E. L. S. HORSBURGH, B.A. *With Plans. Crown 8vo. 5s.*

'A brilliant essay—simple, sound, and thorough.'—*Daily Chronicle.*

H. B. George. BATTLES OF ENGLISH HISTORY. By H. B. GEORGE, M.A., Fellow of New College, Oxford. *With numerous Plans. Third Edition. Crown 8vo. 6s.*

'Mr. George has undertaken a very useful task—that of making military affairs intelligible and instructive to non-military readers—and has executed it with laudable intelligence and industry, and with a large measure of success.'—*Times.*

General Literature

S. Baring Gould. OLD COUNTRY LIFE. By S. BARING GOULD. With Sixty-seven Illustrations. *Large Crown 8vo. Fifth Edition.* 6s.

'"Old Country Life," as healthy wholesome reading, full of breezy life and movement, full of quaint stories vigorously told, will not be excelled by any book to be published throughout the year. Sound, hearty, and English to the core.'—*World.*

S. Baring Gould. HISTORIC ODDITIES AND STRANGE EVENTS. By S. BARING GOULD. *Fourth Edition. Crown 8vo.* 6s.

'A collection of exciting and entertaining chapters. The whole volume is delightful reading.'—*Times.*

S. Baring Gould. FREAKS OF FANATICISM. By S. BARING GOULD. *Third Edition. Crown 8vo.* 6s.

'Mr. Baring Gould has a keen eye for colour and effect, and the subjects he has chosen give ample scope to his descriptive and analytic faculties. A perfectly fascinating book.'—*Scottish Leader.*

S Baring Gould. A GARLAND OF COUNTRY SONG: English Folk Songs with their Traditional Melodies. Collected and arranged by S. BARING GOULD and H. F. SHEPPARD. *Demy 4to.* 6s.

S. Baring Gould. SONGS OF THE WEST: Traditional Ballads and Songs of the West of England, with their Traditional Melodies. Collected by S. BARING GOULD, M.A., and H. F. SHEPPARD, M.A. Arranged for Voice and Piano. In 4 Parts Parts I., II., III., 3s. each. Part IV., 5s. In one Vol., French morocco, 15s.

'A rich collection of humour, pathos, grace, and poetic fancy.'—*Saturday Review.*

S. Baring Gould. YORKSHIRE ODDITIES AND STRANGE EVENTS. *Fourth Edition. Crown 8vo.* 6s.

S. Baring Gould. STRANGE SURVIVALS AND SUPERSTITIONS. With Illustrations. By S. BARING GOULD. *Crown 8vo. Second Edition.* 6s.

S. Baring Gould. THE DESERTS OF SOUTHERN FRANCE. By S. BARING-GOULD. 2 vols. *Demy 8vo.* 32s.

Cotton Minchin. OLD HARROW DAYS. By J. G. COTTON MINCHIN. *Crown 8vo. Second Edition.* 5s.

'This book is an admirable record.'—*Daily Chronicle.*

'Mr. Cotton Minchin's bright and breezy reminiscences of 'Old Harrow Days' will delight all Harrovians, old and young, and may go far to explain the abiding enthusiasm of old Harrovians for their school to readers who have not been privileged to be their schoolfellows.'—*Times.*

W. E. Gladstone. THE SPEECHES OF THE RT. HON. W. E. GLADSTONE, M.P. Edited by A. W. HUTTON, M.A., and H. J. COHEN, M.A. With Portraits. *8vo. Vols. IX. and X.* 12s. 6d. each.

J. Wells. OXFORD AND OXFORD LIFE. By Members of the University. Edited by J. WELLS, M.A., Fellow and Tutor of Wadham College. *Crown 8vo.* 3s. 6d.
  'We congratulate Mr. Wells on the production of a readable and intelligent account of Oxford as it is at the present time, written by persons who are possessed of a close acquaintance with the system and life of the University.'—*Athenæum.*

J. Wells. OXFORD AND ITS COLLEGES. By J. WELLS, M.A., Fellow and Tutor of Wadham College. Illustrated by E. H. NEW. *Second Edition. Fcap. 8vo.* 3s. *Leather.* 4s.
  This is a guide—chiefly historical—to the Colleges of Oxford. It contains numerous illustrations.
  'An admirable and accurate little treatise, attractively illustrated.'—*World.*
  'A luminous and tasteful little volume.'—*Daily Chronicle.*
  'Exactly what the intelligent visitor wants.'—*Glasgow Herald.*

C. G. Robertson. VOCES ACADEMICÆ. By C. GRANT ROBERTSON, M.A., Fellow of All Souls', Oxford. *With a Frontispiece. Pott. 8vo.* 3s. 6d.
  'Decidedly clever and amusing.'—*Athenæum.*
  'The dialogues are abundantly smart and amusing.'—*Glasgow Herald.*
  'A clever and entertaining little book.'—*Pall Mall Gazette.*

L. Whibley. GREEK OLIGARCHIES: THEIR ORGANISATION AND CHARACTER. By L. WHIBLEY, M.A., Fellow of Pembroke College, Cambridge. *Crown 8vo.* 6s.
  'An exceedingly useful handbook: a careful and well-arranged study.'—*Times.*

L. L. Price. ECONOMIC SCIENCE AND PRACTICE. By L. L. PRICE, M.A., Fellow of Oriel College, Oxford. *Crown 8vo.* 6s.
  'The book is well written, giving evidence of considerable literary ability, and clear mental grasp of the subject under consideration.'—*Western Morning News.*

J. S. Shedlock. THE PIANOFORTE SONATA: Its Origin and Development. By J. S. SHEDLOCK. *Crown 8vo.* 5s.
  'This work should be in the possession of every musician and amateur. A concise and lucid history of the origin of one of the most important forms of musical composition. A very valuable work for reference.'—*Athenæum.*

E. M. Bowden. THE EXAMPLE OF BUDDHA: Being Quotations from Buddhist Literature for each Day in the Year. Compiled by E. M. BOWDEN. *Third Edition.* 16mo. 2s. 6d.

Morgan-Browne. SPORTING AND ATHLETIC RECORDS. By H. MORGAN-BROWNE. *Crown 8vo.* 1s. *paper;* 2s. *cloth.*
  'Should meet a very wide demand.'—*Daily Mail.*
  'A very careful collection, and the first one of its kind.'—*Manchester Guardian.*
  'Certainly the most valuable of all books of its kind.'—*Birmingham Gazette.*

Science

Freudenreich. DAIRY BACTERIOLOGY. A Short Manual for the Use of Students. By Dr. ED. VON FREUDENREICH. Translated by J. R. AINSWORTH DAVIS, B.A. *Crown 8vo.* 2s. 6d.

Chalmers Mitchell. OUTLINES OF BIOLOGY. By P. CHALMERS MITCHELL, M.A., *Illustrated. Crown 8vo. 6s.*

A text-book designed to cover the new Schedule issued by the Royal College of Physicians and Surgeons.

G. Massee. A MONOGRAPH OF THE MYXOGASTRES. By GEORGE MASSEE. With 12 Coloured Plates. *Royal 8vo. 18s. net.*

'A work much in advance of any book in the language treating of this group of organisms. Indispensable to every student of the Myxogastres.'—*Nature.*

Technology

Stephenson and Suddards. ORNAMENTAL DESIGN FOR WOVEN FABRICS. By C. STEPHENSON, of The Technical College, Bradford, and F. SUDDARDS, of The Yorkshire College, Leeds. With 65 full-page plates, and numerous designs and diagrams in the text. *Demy 8vo. 7s. 6d.*

'The book is very ably done, displaying an intimate knowledge of principles, good taste, and the faculty of clear exposition.'—*Yorkshire Post.*

HANDBOOKS OF TECHNOLOGY.
Edited by PROFESSORS GARNETT and WERTHEIMER.

HOW TO MAKE A DRESS. By J. A. E. WOOD. *Illustrated. Crown 8vo. 1s. 6d.*

A text-book for students preparing for the City and Guilds examination, based on the syllabus. The diagrams are numerous.

'Though primarily intended for students, Miss Wood's dainty little manual may be consulted with advantage by any girls who want to make their own frocks. The directions are simple and clear, and the diagrams very helpful.'—*Literature.*

'A splendid little book.'—*Evening News.*

Philosophy

L. T. Hobhouse. THE THEORY OF KNOWLEDGE. By L. T. HOBHOUSE, Fellow of C.C.C, Oxford. *Demy 8vo. 21s.*

'The most important contribution to English philosophy since the publication of Mr. Bradley's "Appearance and Reality." Full of brilliant criticism and of positive theories which are models of lucid statement.'—*Glasgow Herald.*

'A brilliantly written volume.'—*Times.*

W H. Fairbrother. THE PHILOSOPHY OF T. H. GREEN. By W. H. FAIRBROTHER, M.A. *Crown 8vo. 3s. 6d.*

'In every way an admirable book.'—*Glasgow Herald.*

F. W. Bussell. THE SCHOOL OF PLATO : its Origin and its Revival under the Roman Empire. By F. W. BUSSELL, D.D., Fellow and Tutor of Brasenose College, Oxford. *Demy 8vo. 10s. 6d.*

'A highly valuable contribution to the history of ancient thought.'—*Glasgow Herald.*

'A clever and stimulating book, provocative of thought and deserving careful reading.'—*Manchester Guardian.*

F. S. Granger. THE WORSHIP OF THE ROMANS. By F. S. GRANGER, M.A., Litt.D., Professor of Philosophy at University College, Nottingham. *Crown 8vo.* 6s.

'A scholarly analysis of the religious ceremonies, beliefs, and superstitions of ancient Rome, conducted in the new light of comparative anthropology.'—*Times.*

Theology

HANDBOOKS OF THEOLOGY.
General Editor, A. ROBERTSON, D.D., Principal of King's College, London.

THE XXXIX. ARTICLES OF THE CHURCH OF ENGLAND. Edited with an Introduction by E. C. S. GIBSON, D.D., Vicar of Leeds, late Principal of Wells Theological College. *Second and Cheaper Edition in One Volume. Demy 8vo.* 12s. 6d.

'Dr. Gibson is a master of clear and orderly exposition, and he has enlisted in his service all the mechanism of variety of type which so greatly helps to elucidate a complicated subject. And he has in a high degree a quality very necessary, but rarely found, in commentators on this topic, that of absolute fairness. His book is pre-eminently honest.'—*Times.*

'After a survey of the whole book, we can bear witness to the transparent honesty of purpose, evident industry, and clearness of style which mark its contents. They maintain throughout a very high level of doctrine and tone.'—*Guardian.*

'An elaborate and learned book, excellently adapted to its purpose.'—*Speaker.*

'The most convenient and most acceptable commentary.'—*Expository Times.*

AN INTRODUCTION TO THE HISTORY OF RELIGION. By F. B. JEVONS, M.A., Litt.D., Principal of Bishop Hatfield's Hall. *Demy 8vo.* 10s. 6d.

'Dr. Jevons has written a notable work, which we can strongly recommend to the serious attention of theologians and anthropologists.'—*Manchester Guardian.*

'The merit of this book lies in the penetration, the singular acuteness and force of the author's judgment. He is at once critical and luminous, at once just and suggestive. A comprehensive and thorough book.'—*Birmingham Post.*

THE DOCTRINE OF THE INCARNATION. By R. L. OTTLEY, M.A., late fellow of Magdalen College, Oxon., and Principal of Pusey House. *In Two Volumes. Demy 8vo.* 15s.

'Learned and reverent: lucid and well arranged.'—*Record.*
'Accurate, well ordered, and judicious.'—*National Observer.*
'A clear and remarkably full account of the main currents of speculation. Scholarly precision . . . genuine tolerance . . . intense interest in his subject—are Mr. Ottley's merits.'—*Guardian.*

C. F. Andrews. CHRISTIANITY AND THE LABOUR QUESTION. By C. F. ANDREWS, B.A. *Crown 8vo.* 2s. 6d.

S. R. Driver. SERMONS ON SUBJECTS CONNECTED WITH THE OLD TESTAMENT. By S. R. DRIVER, D.D., Canon of Christ Church, Regius Professor of Hebrew in the University of Oxford. *Crown 8vo.* 6s.

'A welcome companion to the author's famous 'Introduction.' No man can read these discourses without feeling that Dr. Driver is fully alive to the deeper teaching of the Old Testament.'—*Guardian.*

T. K. Cheyne. FOUNDERS OF OLD TESTAMENT CRITICISM. By T. K. CHEYNE, D.D., Oriel Professor at Oxford. *Large crown 8vo.* 7s. 6d.

This book is a historical sketch of O. T. Criticism in the form of biographical studies from the days of Eichhorn to those of Driver and Robertson Smith.
'A very learned and instructive work.'—*Times.*

H. H. Henson. LIGHT AND LEAVEN : HISTORICAL AND SOCIAL SERMONS. By the Rev. H. HENSLEY HENSON, M.A., Fellow of All Souls', Incumbent of St. Mary's Hospital, Ilford. *Crown 8vo.* 6s.

'They are always reasonable as well as vigorous, and they are none the less impressive because they regard the needs of a life on this side of a hereafter.'—*Scotsman.*

W. H. Bennett. A PRIMER OF THE BIBLE. By Prof. W. H. BENNETT. *Second Edition. Crown 8vo.* 2s. 6d.

'The work of an honest, fearless, and sound critic, and an excellent guide in a small compass to the books of the Bible.'—*Manchester Guardian.*
'A unique primer. Mr. Bennett has collected and condensed a very extensive and diversified amount of material, and no one can consult his pages and fail to acknowledge indebtedness to his undertaking.'—*English Churchman.*

C. H. Prior. CAMBRIDGE SERMONS. Edited by C. H. PRIOR, M.A., Fellow and Tutor of Pembroke College. *Crown 8vo.* 6s.

A volume of sermons preached before the University of Cambridge by various preachers, including the late Archbishop of Canterbury and Bishop Westcott.

E. B. Layard. RELIGION IN BOYHOOD. Notes on the Religious Training of Boys. By E. B. LAYARD, M.A. *18mo.* 1s.

W. Yorke Faussett. THE *DE CATECHIZANDIS RUDIBUS* OF ST. AUGUSTINE. Edited, with Introduction, Notes, etc., by W. YORKE FAUSSETT, M.A., late Scholar of Balliol Coll. *Crown 8vo.* 3s. 6d.

An edition of a Treatise on the Essentials of Christian Doctrine, and the best methods of impressing them on candidates for baptism.

À Kempis. THE IMITATION OF CHRIST. By THOMAS À KEMPIS. With an Introduction by DEAN FARRAR. Illustrated by C. M. GERE, and printed in black and red. *Second Edition. Fcap. 8vo. Buckram.* 3s. 6d. *Padded morocco*, 5s.

'Amongst all the innumerable English editions of the "Imitation," there can have been few which were prettier than this one, printed in strong and handsome type, with all the glory of red initials.'—*Glasgow Herald.*

J. Keble. THE CHRISTIAN YEAR. By JOHN KEBLE. With an Introduction and Notes by W. LOCK, D.D., Warden of Keble College, Ireland Professor at Oxford. Illustrated by R. ANNING BELL. *Second Edition. Fcap. 8vo. Buckram.* 3s. 6d. *Padded morocco*, 5s.

'The present edition is annotated with all the care and insight to be expected from Mr. Lock. The progress and circumstances of its composition are detailed in the Introduction. There is an interesting Appendix on the MSS. of the "Christian Year," and another giving the order in which the poems were written. A "Short Analysis of the Thought" is prefixed to each, and any difficulty in the text is explained in a note.'—*Guardian.*

Leaders of Religion

Edited by H. C. BEECHING, M.A. *With Portraits, crown 8vo.*

A series of short biographies of the most prominent leaders of religious life and thought of all ages and countries.

The following are ready—

CARDINAL NEWMAN. By R. H. HUTTON.
JOHN WESLEY. By J. H. OVERTON, M.A.
BISHOP WILBERFORCE. By G. W. DANIEL, M.A.
CARDINAL MANNING. By A. W. HUTTON, M.A.
CHARLES SIMEON. By H. C. G. MOULE, M.A.
JOHN KEBLE. By WALTER LOCK, D.D.
THOMAS CHALMERS. By Mrs. OLIPHANT.
LANCELOT ANDREWES. By R. L. OTTLEY, M.A.
AUGUSTINE OF CANTERBURY. By E. L. CUTTS, D.D.
WILLIAM LAUD. By W. H. HUTTON, B.D.
JOHN KNOX. By F. M'CUNN.
JOHN HOWE. By R. F. HORTON, D.D.
BISHOP KEN. By F. A. CLARKE, M.A.
GEORGE FOX, THE QUAKER. By T. HODGKIN, D.C.L.
JOHN DONNE. By AUGUSTUS JESSOPP, D.D.

Other volumes will be announced in due course.

Fiction

SIX SHILLING NOVELS

Marie Corelli's Novels

Crown 8vo. 6s. each.

A ROMANCE OF TWO WORLDS. *Seventeenth Edition.*
VENDETTA. *Thirteenth Edition.*
THELMA. *Eighteenth Edition.*
ARDATH. *Eleventh Edition.*
THE SOUL OF LILITH *Ninth Edition.*
WORMWOOD. *Eighth Edition.*
BARABBAS: A DREAM OF THE WORLD'S TRAGEDY. *Thirty-first Edition.*

> 'The tender reverence of the treatment and the imaginative beauty of the writing have reconciled us to the daring of the conception, and the conviction is forced on us that even so exalted a subject cannot be made too familiar to us, provided it be presented in the true spirit of Christian faith. The amplifications of the Scripture narrative are often conceived with high poetic insight, and this "Dream of the World's Tragedy" is, despite some trifling incongruities, a lofty and not inadequate paraphrase of the supreme climax of the inspired narrative.'—*Dublin Review.*

THE SORROWS OF SATAN. *Thirty-seventh Edition.*
'A very powerful piece of work. . . . The conception is magnificent, and is likely to win an abiding place within the memory of man. . . . The author has immense command of language, and a limitless audacity. . . . This interesting and remarkable romance will live long after much of the ephemeral literature of the day is forgotten. . . . A literary phenomenon . . . novel, and even sublime.'—W. T. STEAD in the *Review of Reviews.*

Anthony Hope's Novels
Crown 8vo. 6s. each.

THE GOD IN THE CAR. *Seventh Edition.*
'A very remarkable book, deserving of critical analysis impossible within our limit; brilliant, but not superficial; well considered, but not elaborated; constructed with the proverbial art that conceals, but yet allows itself to be enjoyed by readers to whom fine literary method is a keen pleasure.'—*The World.*

A CHANGE OF AIR. *Fourth Edition.*
'A graceful, vivacious comedy, true to human nature. The characters are traced with a masterly hand.'—*Times.*

A MAN OF MARK. *Fourth Edition.*
'Of all Mr. Hope's books, "A Man of Mark" is the one which best compares with "The Prisoner of Zenda."'—*National Observer.*

THE CHRONICLES OF COUNT ANTONIO. *Third Edition.*
'It is a perfectly enchanting story of love and chivalry, and pure romance. The Count is the most constant, desperate, and modest and tender of lovers, a peerless gentleman, an intrepid fighter, a faithful friend, and a magnanimous foe.'—*Guardian.*

PHROSO. Illustrated by H. R. MILLAR. *Third Edition.*
'The tale is thoroughly fresh, quick with vitality, stirring the blood, and humorously, dashingly told.'—*St. James's Gazette.*
'A story of adventure, every page of which is palpitating with action.'—*Speaker.*
'From cover to cover "Phroso" not only engages the attention, but carries the reader in little whirls of delight from adventure to adventure.'—*Academy.*

S. Baring Gould's Novels
Crown 8vo. 6s. each.

'To say that a book is by the author of "Mehalah" is to imply that it contains a story cast on strong lines, containing dramatic possibilities, vivid and sympathetic descriptions of Nature, and a wealth of ingenious imagery.'—*Speaker.*
'That whatever Mr. Baring Gould writes is well worth reading, is a conclusion that may be very generally accepted. His views of life are fresh and vigorous, his language pointed and characteristic, the incidents of which he makes use are striking and original, his characters are life-like, and though somewhat exceptional people, are drawn and coloured with artistic force. Add to this that his descriptions of scenes and scenery are painted with the loving eyes and skilled hands of a master of his art, that he is always fresh and never dull, and under such conditions it is no wonder that readers have gained confidence both in his power of amusing and satisfying them, and that year by year his popularity widens.'—*Court Circular.*

ARMINELL: A Social Romance. *Fourth Edition.*

URITH: A Story of Dartmoor. *Fifth Edition.*
'The author is at his best.'—*Times.*

MESSRS. METHUEN'S LIST 25

IN THE ROAR OF THE SEA *Sixth Edition.*
'One of the best imagined and most enthralling stories the author has produced.' —*Saturday Review.*

MRS. CURGENVEN OF CURGENVEN. *Fourth Edition.*
'The swing of the narrative is splendid.'—*Sussex Daily News.*

CHEAP JACK ZITA. *Fourth Edition.*
'A powerful drama of human passion.'—*Westminster Gazette.*
'A story worthy the author.'—*National Observer.*

THE QUEEN OF LOVE. *Fourth Edition.*
'Can be heartily recommended to all who care for cleanly, energetic, and interesting fiction.'—*Sussex Daily News.*

KITTY ALONE. *Fourth Edition.*
'A strong and original story, teeming with graphic description, stirring incident, and, above all, with vivid and enthralling human interest.'—*Daily Telegraph.*

NOÉMI : A Romance of the Cave-Dwellers. Illustrated by R. CATON WOODVILLE. *Third Edition.*
'A powerful story, full of strong lights and shadows.'—*Standard.*

THE BROOM-SQUIRE. Illustrated by FRANK DADD. *Fourth Edition.*
'A strain of tenderness is woven through the web of his tragic tale, and its atmosphere is sweetened by the nobility and sweetness of the heroine's character.'—*Daily News.*

THE PENNYCOMEQUICKS. *Third Edition.*

DARTMOOR IDYLLS.
'A book to read, and keep and read again; for the genuine fun and pathos of it will not early lose their effect.'—*Vanity Fair.*

GUAVAS THE TINNER. Illustrated by FRANK DADD. *Second Edition.*
'There is a kind of flavour about this book which alone elevates it above the ordinary novel. The story itself has a grandeur in harmony with the wild and rugged scenery which is its setting.'—*Athenæum.*

BLADYS. *Second Edition.*
'A story of thrilling interest.'—*Scotsman.*
'A sombre but powerful story.'—*Daily Mail.*

Gilbert Parker's Novels
Crown 8vo. 6s. each.

PIERRE AND HIS PEOPLE. *Fourth Edition.*
'Stories happily conceived and finely executed. There is strength and genius in Mr. Parker's style.'—*Daily Telegraph.*

MRS. FALCHION. *Fourth Edition.*
'A splendid study of character.'—*Athenæum.*
'But little behind anything that has been done by any writer of our time.'—*Pall Mall Gazette.* 'A very striking and admirable novel.'—*St. James's Gazette.*

THE TRANSLATION OF A SAVAGE.
'The plot is original and one difficult to work out; but Mr. Parker has done it with great skill and delicacy. The reader who is not interested in this original, fresh, and well-told tale must be a dull person indeed.'—*Daily Chronicle.*

THE TRAIL OF THE SWORD. *Fifth Edition. Illustrated.*
'A rousing and dramatic tale. A book like this, in which swords flash, great surprises are undertaken, and daring deeds done, in which men and women live and love in the old passionate way, is a joy inexpressible.'—*Daily Chronicle.*

WHEN VALMOND CAME TO PONTIAC: The Story of a Lost Napoleon. *Fourth Edition.*
'Here we find romance—real, breathing, living romance. The character of Valmond is drawn unerringly. The book must be read, we may say re-read, for any one thoroughly to appreciate Mr. Parker's delicate touch and innate sympathy with humanity.'—*Pall Mall Gazette.*

AN ADVENTURER OF THE NORTH: The Last Adventures of 'Pretty Pierre.' *Second Edition.*
'The present book is full of fine and moving stories of the great North, and it will add to Mr. Parker's already high reputation.'—*Glasgow Herald.*

THE SEATS OF THE MIGHTY. *Illustrated. Ninth Edition.*
'The best thing he has done; one of the best things that any one has done lately.'—*St. James's Gazette.*
'Mr. Parker seems to become stronger and easier with every serious novel that he attempts. He shows the matured power which his former novels have led us to expect, and has produced a really fine historical novel. The finest novel he has yet written.'—*Athenæum.*
'A great book.'—*Black and White.*
'One of the strongest stories of historical interest and adventure that we have read for many a day.... A notable and successful book.'—*Speaker.*

THE POMP OF THE LAVILETTES. *Second Edition.* 3s. 6d.
'Living, breathing romance, genuine and unforced pathos, and a deeper and more subtle knowledge of human nature than Mr. Parker has ever displayed before. It is, in a word, the work of a true artist.'—*Pall Mall Gazette.*

Conan Doyle. ROUND THE RED LAMP. By A. CONAN DOYLE, Author of 'The White Company,' 'The Adventures of Sherlock Holmes,' etc. *Fifth Edition. Crown 8vo. 6s.*
'The book is, indeed, composed of leaves from life, and is far and away the best view that has been vouchsafed us behind the scenes of the consulting-room. It is very superior to "The Diary of a late Physician."'—*Illustrated London News.*

Stanley Weyman. UNDER THE RED ROBE. By STANLEY WEYMAN, Author of 'A Gentleman of France.' With Twelve Illustrations by R. Caton Woodville. *Twelfth Edition. Crown 8vo. 6s.*
'A book of which we have read every word for the sheer pleasure of reading, and which we put down with a pang that we cannot forget it all and start again.'—*Westminster Gazette.*
'Every one who reads books at all must read this thrilling romance, from the first page of which to the last the breathless reader is haled along. An inspiration of manliness and courage.'—*Daily Chronicle.*

Lucas Malet. THE WAGES OF SIN. By LUCAS MALET. *Thirteenth Edition. Crown 8vo. 6s.*

Lucas Malet. THE CARISSIMA. By LUCAS MALET, Author of 'The Wages of Sin,' etc. *Third Edition. Crown 8vo. 6s.*

S. R. Crockett. LOCHINVAR. By S. R. CROCKETT, Author of 'The Raiders,' etc. Illustrated. *Second Edition. Crown 8vo. 6s.*

'Full of gallantry and pathos, of the clash of arms, and brightened by episodes of humour and love. . . . Mr. Crockett has never written a stronger or better book. An engrossing and fascinating story. The love story alone is enough to make the book delightful.'—*Westminster Gazette.*

Arthur Morrison. TALES OF MEAN STREETS. By ARTHUR MORRISON. *Fourth Edition. Crown 8vo. 6s.*

'Told with consummate art and extraordinary detail. In the true humanity of the book lies its justification, the permanence of its interest, and its indubitable triumph.'—*Athenæum.*
'A great book. The author's method is amazingly effective, and produces a thrilling sense of reality. The writer lays upon us a master hand. The book is simply appalling and irresistible in its interest. It is humorous also; without humour it would not make the mark it is certain to make.'—*World.*

Arthur Morrison. A CHILD OF THE JAGO. By ARTHUR MORRISON. *Third Edition. Crown 8vo. 6s.*

'The book is a masterpiece.'—*Pall Mall Gazette.*
'Told with great vigour and powerful simplicity.'—*Athenæum.*

Mrs. Clifford. A FLASH OF SUMMER. By Mrs. W. K. CLIFFORD, Author of 'Aunt Anne,' etc. *Second Edition. Crown 8vo. 6s.*

'The story is a very sad and a very beautiful one, exquisitely told, and enriched with many subtle touches of wise and tender insight.'—*Speaker.*

Emily Lawless. HURRISH. By the Honble. EMILY LAWLESS, Author of 'Maelcho,' etc. *Fifth Edition. Crown 8vo. 6s.*

A reissue of Miss Lawless' most popular novel, uniform with 'Maelcho.'

Emily Lawless. MAELCHO: a Sixteenth Century Romance. By the Honble. EMILY LAWLESS. *Second Edition. Crown 8vo. 6s.*

'A really great book.'—*Spectator.*
'There is no keener pleasure in life than the recognition of genius. A piece of work of the first order, which we do not hesitate to describe as one of the most remarkable literary achievements of this generation.'—*Manchester Guardian.*

Jane Barlow. A CREEL OF IRISH STORIES. By JANE BARLOW, Author of 'Irish Idylls.' *Second Edition. Crown 8vo. 6s.*

'Vivid and singularly real.'—*Scotsman.*
'Genuinely and naturally Irish.'—*Scotsman.*
'The sincerity of her sentiments, the distinction of her style, and the freshness of her themes, combine to lift her work far above the average level of contemporary fiction.'—*Manchester Guardian.*

J. H. Findlater. THE GREEN GRAVES OF BALGOWRIE. By JANE H. FINDLATER. *Fourth Edition. Crown 8vo. 6s.*

'A powerful and vivid story.'—*Standard.*
'A beautiful story, sad and strange as truth itself.'—*Vanity Fair.*
'A work of remarkable interest and originality.'—*National Observer.*
'A very charming and pathetic tale.'—*Pall Mall Gazette.*
'A singularly original, clever, and beautiful story.'—*Guardian.*
'Reveals to us a new writer of undoubted faculty and reserve force.'—*Spectator.*
'An exquisite idyll, delicate, affecting, and beautiful.'—*Black and White.*

J. H. Findlater. A DAUGHTER OF STRIFE. By JANE HELEN FINDLATER, Author of 'The Green Graves of Balgowrie.' *Crown 8vo.* 6s.

'A story of strong human interest.'—*Scotsman.*
'It has a sweet flavour of olden days delicately conveyed.'—*Manchester Guardian.*
'Her thought has solidity and maturity.'—*Daily Mail.*

Mary Findlater. OVER THE HILLS. By MARY FINDLATER. *Second Edition. Crown 8vo.* 6s.

'A strong and fascinating piece of work.'—*Scotsman.*
'A charming romance, and full of incident. The book is fresh and strong.'—*Speaker.*
'There is quiet force and beautiful simplicity in this book which will make the author's name loved in many a household.'—*Literary World.*
'Admirably fresh and broad in treatment. The novel is markedly original and excellently written.'—*Daily Chronicle.*
'A strong and wise book of deep insight and unflinching truth.'—*Birmingham Post.*
'Miss Mary Findlater combines originality with strength.'—*Daily Mail.*

H. G. Wells. THE STOLEN BACILLUS, and other Stories. By H. G. WELLS. *Second Edition. Crown 8vo.* 6s.

'The ordinary reader of fiction may be glad to know that these stories are eminently readable from one cover to the other, but they are more than that; they are the impressions of a very striking imagination, which, it would seem, has a great deal within its reach.'—*Saturday Review.*

H. G. Wells. THE PLATTNER STORY AND OTHERS. By H. G. WELLS. *Second Edition. Crown 8vo.* 6s.

'Weird and mysterious, they seem to hold the reader as by a magic spell.'—*Scotsman.*
'No volume has appeared for a long time so likely to give equal pleasure to the simplest reader and to the most fastidious critic.'—*Academy.*

E. F. Benson. DODO: A DETAIL OF THE DAY. By E. F. BENSON. *Sixteenth Edition. Crown 8vo.* 6s.

'A delightfully witty sketch of society.'—*Spectator.*
'A perpetual feast of epigram and paradox.'—*Speaker.*

E. F. Benson. THE RUBICON. By E. F. BENSON, Author of 'Dodo.' *Fifth Edition. Crown 8vo.* 6s.

Mrs. Oliphant. SIR ROBERT'S FORTUNE. By MRS. OLIPHANT. *Crown 8vo.* 6s.

'Full of her own peculiar charm of style and simple, subtle character-painting comes her new gift, the delightful story.'—*Pall Mall Gazette.*

Mrs. Oliphant. THE TWO MARYS. By MRS. OLIPHANT. *Second Edition. Crown 8vo.* 6s.

Mrs. Oliphant. THE LADY'S WALK. By Mrs. OLIPHANT. *Second Edition. Crown 8vo.* 6s.

'A story of exquisite tenderness, of most delicate fancy.'—*Pall Mall Gazette.*
'It contains many of the finer characteristics of her best work.'—*Scotsman.*
'It is little short of sacrilege on the part of a reviewer to attempt to sketch its outlines or analyse its peculiar charm.'—*Spectator.*

W. E. Norris. MATTHEW AUSTIN. By W. E. NORRIS, Author of 'Mademoiselle de Mersac,' etc. *Fourth Edition. Crown 8vo. 6s.*

''An intellectually satisfactory and morally bracing novel.'—*Daily Telegraph.*

W. E. Norris. HIS GRACE. By W. E NORRIS. *Third Edition. Crown 8vo. 6s.*

'Mr. Norris has drawn a really fine character in the Duke of Hurstbourne, at once unconventional and very true to the conventionalities of life.'—*Athenæum.*

W. E. Norris. THE DESPOTIC LADY AND OTHERS. By W. E. NORRIS. *Crown 8vo. 6s.*

'A budget of good fiction of which no one will tire.'—*Scotsman.*

W. E. Norris. CLARISSA FURIOSA. By W. E. NORRIS. *Crown 8vo. 6s.*

'As a story it is admirable, as a *jeu d'esprit* it is capital, as a lay sermon studded with gems of wit and wisdom it is a model.'—*The World.*

W. Clark Russell. MY DANISH SWEETHEART. By W. CLARK RUSSELL, Author of 'The Wreck of the Grosvenor,' etc. *Illustrated. Fourth Edition. Crown 8vo. 6s.*

Robert Barr. THE MUTABLE MANY. By ROBERT BARR, Author of 'In the Midst of Alarms,' 'A Woman Intervenes,' etc. *Second Edition. Crown 8vo. 6s.*

'Very much the best novel that Mr. Barr has yet given us. There is much insight in it, much acute and delicate appreciation of the finer shades of character and much excellent humour.'—*Daily Chronicle.*
'An excellent story. It contains several excellently studied characters, and is filled with lifelike pictures of modern life.'—*Glasgow Herald.*

Robert Barr. IN THE MIDST OF ALARMS. By ROBERT BARR. *Third Edition. Crown 8vo. 6s.*

'A book which has abundantly satisfied us by its capital humour. —*Daily Chronicle.*
'Mr. Barr has achieved a triumph whereof he has every reason to be proud.'—*Pall Mall Gazette.*

J. Maclaren Cobban. THE KING OF ANDAMAN : A Saviour of Society. By J. MACLAREN COBBAN. *Crown 8vo. 6s.*

'An unquestionably interesting book. It contains one character, at least, who has in him the root of immortality, and the book itself is ever exhaling the sweet savour of the unexpected.'—*Pall Mall Gazette.*

J. Maclaren Cobban. WILT THOU HAVE THIS WOMAN? By J. M. COBBAN, Author of 'The King of Andaman.' *Crown 8vo. 6s.*

Robert Hichens. BYEWAYS. By ROBERT HICHENS. Author of 'Flames,' etc. *Crown 8vo.* 6s.

'A very high artistic instinct and striking command of language raise Mr. Hichens' work far above the ruck.'—*Pall Mall Gazette.*
'The work is undeniably that of a man of striking imagination and no less striking powers of expression.'—*Daily News.*

Percy White. A PASSIONATE PILGRIM. By PERCY WHITE, Author of 'Mr. Bailey-Martin.' *Crown 8vo.* 6s.

'A work which it is not hyperbole to describe as of rare excellence.'—*Pall Mall Gazette.*
'The clever book of a shrewd and clever author.'—*Athenæum.*
'Mr. Percy White's strong point is analysis, and he has shown himself, before now, capable of building up a good book upon that foundation.'—*Standard.*

W. Pett Ridge. SECRETARY TO BAYNE, M.P. By W. PETT RIDGE. *Crown 8vo.* 6s.

'Sparkling, vivacious, adventurous.—*St. James's Gazette.*
'Ingenious, amusing, and especially smart.'—*World.*
'The dialogue is invariably alert and highly diverting.'—*Spectator.*

J. S. Fletcher. THE BUILDERS. By J. S. FLETCHER, Author of 'When Charles I. was King.' *Second Edition. Crown 8vo.* 6s.

'Replete with delightful descriptions.'—*Vanity Fair.*
'The background of country life has never, perhaps, been sketched more realistically.' —*World.*

Andrew Balfour. BY STROKE OF SWORD. By ANDREW BALFOUR. Illustrated by W. CUBITT COOKE. *Fourth Edition. Crown 8vo.* 6s.

'A banquet of good things.'—*Academy.*
'A recital of thrilling interest, told with unflagging vigour.'—*Globe*
'An unusually excellent example of a semi-historic romance.'—*World.*
'Manly, healthy, and patriotic.'—*Glasgow Herald.*

I. Hooper. THE SINGER OF MARLY. By I. HOOPER. Illustrated by W. CUBITT COOKE. *Crown 8vo.* 6s.

'Its scenes are drawn in vivid colours, and the characters are all picturesque.'— *Scotsman.*
'A novel as vigorous as it is charming.'—*Literary World.*

M. C. Balfour. THE FALL OF THE SPARROW. By M. C. BALFOUR. *Crown 8vo.* 6s.

'A powerful novel.'—*Daily Telegraph.*
'It is unusually powerful, and the characterization is uncommonly good.'—*World.*
'It is a well-knit, carefully-wrought story.'—*Academy.*

H. Morrah. A SERIOUS COMEDY. By HERBERT MORRAH. *Crown 8vo.* 6s.

H. Morrah. THE FAITHFUL CITY. By HERBERT MORRAH, Author of 'A Serious Comedy.' *Crown 8vo.* 6s.

L. B. Walford. SUCCESSORS TO THE TITLE. By Mrs. WALFORD, Author of 'Mr. Smith,' etc. *Second Edition. Crown 8vo.* 6s.

Mary Gaunt. KIRKHAM'S FIND. By MARY GAUNT, Author of 'The Moving Finger.' *Crown 8vo. 6s.*

'A really charming novel.'—*Standard.*
'A capital book, in which will be found lively humour, penetrating insight, and the sweet savour of a thoroughly healthy moral.'—*Speaker.*

M. M. Dowie. GALLIA. By MÉNIE MURIEL DOWIE, Author of 'A Girl in the Carpathians.' *Third Edition. Crown 8vo. 6s.*

'The style is generally admirable, the dialogue not seldom brilliant, the situations surprising in their freshness and originality, while the characters live and move, and the story itself is readable from title-page to colophon.'—*Saturday Review.*

J. A. Barry. IN THE GREAT DEEP. BY J. A. BARRY. Author of 'Steve Brown's Bunyip.' *Crown 8vo. 6s.*

'A collection of really admirable short stories of the sea, very simply told, and placed before the reader in pithy and telling English.'—*Westminster Gazette.*

J. B. Burton. IN THE DAY OF ADVERSITY. By J. BLOUN-DELLE-BURTON.' *Second Edition. Crown 8vo. 6s.*

'Unusually interesting and full of highly dramatic situations. —*Guardian.*

J. B. Burton. DENOUNCED. By J. BLOUNDELLE-BURTON. *Second Edition. Crown 8vo. 6s.*

'The plot is an original one, and the local colouring is laid on with a delicacy and an accuracy of detail which denote the true artist.'—*Broad Arrow.*

J. B. Burton. THE CLASH OF ARMS. By J. BLOUNDELLE-BURTON, Author of 'In the Day of Adversity.' *Second Edition. Crown 8vo. 6s.*

A brave story—brave in deed, brave in word, brave in thought.'—*St. James's Gazette.*
'A fine, manly, spirited piece of work.'—*World.*

W. C. Scully. THE WHITE HECATOMB. By W. C. SCULLY, Author of 'Kafir Stories.' *Crown 8vo. 6s.*

'It reveals a marvellously intimate understanding of the Kaffir mind, allied with literary gifts of no mean order.'—*African Critic.*

Julian Corbett. A BUSINESS IN GREAT WATERS. By JULIAN CORBETT. *Second Edition. Crown 8vo. 6s.*

'Mr. Corbett writes with immense spirit. The salt of the ocean is in it, and the right heroic ring resounds through its gallant adventures.'—*Speaker.*

L. Cope Cornford. CAPTAIN JACOBUS: A ROMANCE OF THE ROAD. By L. COPE CORNFORD. Illustrated. *Crown 8vo. 6s.*

'An exceptionally good story of adventure and character.'—*World.*

L. Daintrey. THE KING OF ALBERIA. A Romance of the Balkans. By LAURA DAINTREY. *Crown 8vo. 6s.*

M. A. Owen. THE DAUGHTER OF ALOUETTE. By MARY A. OWEN. *Crown 8vo. 6s.*

Mrs. Pinsent. CHILDREN OF THIS WORLD. By ELLEN F. PINSENT, Author of 'Jenny's Case.' *Crown 8vo.* 6s.

G. Manville Fenn. AN ELECTRIC SPARK. By G. MANVILLE FENN, Author of 'The Vicar's Wife,' 'A Double Knot,' etc. *Second Edition. Crown 8vo.* 6s.

L. S. McChesney. UNDER SHADOW OF THE MISSION. By L. S. MCCHESNEY. *Crown 8vo.* 6s.

> 'Those whose minds are open to the finer issues of life, who can appreciate graceful thought and refined expression of it, from them this volume will receive a welcome as enthusiastic as it will be based on critical knowledge.'—*Church Times.*

J. F. Brewer. THE SPECULATORS. By J. F. BREWER. *Second Edition. Crown 8vo.* 6s.

Ronald Ross. THE SPIRIT OF STORM. By RONALD ROSS, Author of 'The Child of Ocean.' *Crown 8vo.* 6s.

C. P. Wolley. THE QUEENSBERRY CUP. A Tale of Adventure. By CLIVE P. WOLLEY. *Illustrated. Crown 8vo.* 6s.

T. L. Paton. A HOME IN INVERESK. By T. L. PATON. *Crown 8vo.* 6s.

John Davidson. MISS ARMSTRONG'S AND OTHER CIRCUMSTANCES. By JOHN DAVIDSON. *Crown 8vo.* 6s.

H. Johnston. DR. CONGALTON'S LEGACY. By HENRY JOHNSTON. *Crown 8vo.* 6s.

R. Pryce. TIME AND THE WOMAN. By RICHARD PRYCE. *Second Edition. Crown 8vo.* 6s.

Mrs. Watson. THIS MAN'S DOMINION. By the Author of 'A High Little World.' *Second Edition. Crown 8vo.* 6s.

Marriott Watson. DIOGENES OF LONDON. By H. B. MARRIOTT WATSON. *Crown 8vo. Buckram.* 6s.

M. Gilchrist. THE STONE DRAGON. By MURRAY GILCHRIST. *Crown 8vo. Buckram.* 6s.

E. Dickinson. A VICAR'S WIFE. By EVELYN DICKINSON. *Crown 8vo.* 6s.

E. M. Gray. ELSA. By E. M'QUEEN GRAY. *Crown 8vo.* 6s.

MESSRS. METHUEN'S LIST

THREE-AND-SIXPENNY NOVELS
Crown 8vo.

DERRICK VAUGHAN, NOVELIST. By EDNA LYALL.
MARGERY OF QUETHER. By S. BARING GOULD.
JACQUETTA. By S. BARING GOULD.
SUBJECT TO VANITY. By MARGARET BENSON.
THE SIGN OF THE SPIDER. By BERTRAM MITFORD.
THE MOVING FINGER. By MARY GAUNT.
JACO TRELOAR. By J. H. PEARCE.
THE DANCE OF THE HOURS. By 'VERA.'
A WOMAN OF FORTY. By ESMÉ STUART.
A CUMBERER OF THE GROUND. By CONSTANCE SMITH.
THE SIN OF ANGELS. By EVELYN DICKINSON.
AUT DIABOLUS AUT NIHIL. By X. L.
THE COMING OF CUCULAIN. By STANDISH O'GRADY.
THE GODS GIVE MY DONKEY WINGS. By ANGUS EVAN ABBOTT.
THE STAR GAZERS. By G. MANVILLE FENN.
THE POISON OF ASPS. By R. ORTON PROWSE.
THE QUIET MRS. FLEMING. By R. PRYCE.
DISENCHANTMENT. By F. MABEL ROBINSON.
THE SQUIRE OF WANDALES. By A. SHIELD.
A REVEREND GENTLEMAN. By J. M. COBBAN.
A DEPLORABLE AFFAIR. By W. E. NORRIS.
A CAVALIER'S LADYE. By Mrs. DICKER.
THE PRODIGALS. By Mrs. OLIPHANT.
THE SUPPLANTER. By P. NEUMANN.
A MAN WITH BLACK EYELASHES. By H. A. KENNEDY.
A HANDFUL OF EXOTICS. By S. GORDON.
AN ODD EXPERIMENT. By HANNAH LYNCH.
SCOTTISH BORDER LIFE. By JAMES C. DIBDIN.

HALF-CROWN NOVELS
A Series of Novels by popular Authors.

HOVENDEN, V.C. By F. MABEL ROBINSON.
THE PLAN OF CAMPAIGN. By F. MABEL ROBINSON.
MR. BUTLER'S WARD. By F. MABEL ROBINSON.
ELI'S CHILDREN. By G. MANVILLE FENN.
A DOUBLE KNOT. By G. MANVILLE FENN.
DISARMED. By M. BETHAM EDWARDS.
A MARRIAGE AT SEA. By W. CLARK RUSSELL.
IN TENT AND BUNGALOW. By the Author of 'Indian Idylls.'

MY STEWARDSHIP. By E. M'QUEEN GRAY.
JACK'S FATHER. By W. E. NORRIS.
JIM B.
A LOST ILLUSION. By LESLIE KEITH.

Lynn Linton. THE TRUE HISTORY OF JOSHUA DAVIDSON, Christian and Communist. By E. LYNN LINTON. *Eleventh Edition. Post 8vo.* 1s.

Books for Boys and Girls

A Series of Books by well-known Authors, well illustrated.

THREE-AND-SIXPENCE EACH

THE ICELANDER'S SWORD. By S. BARING GOULD.
TWO LITTLE CHILDREN AND CHING. By EDITH E. CUTHELL.
TODDLEBEN'S HERO. By M. M. BLAKE.
ONLY A GUARD-ROOM DOG. By EDITH E. CUTHELL.
THE DOCTOR OF THE JULIET. By HARRY COLLINGWOOD.
MASTER ROCKAFELLAR'S VOYAGE. By W. CLARK RUSSELL.
SYD BELTON: Or, The Boy who would not go to Sea. By G. MANVILLE FENN.
THE WALLYPUG IN LONDON. By G. E. FARROW.

The Peacock Library

A Series of Books for Girls by well-known Authors, handsomely bound in blue and silver, and well illustrated.

THREE-AND-SIXPENCE EACH

A PINCH OF EXPERIENCE. By L. B. WALFORD.
THE RED GRANGE. By Mrs. MOLESWORTH.
THE SECRET OF MADAME DE MONLUC. By the Author of 'Mdle Mori.'
DUMPS. By Mrs. PARR, Author of 'Adam and Eve.'
OUT OF THE FASHION. By L. T. MEADE.
A GIRL OF THE PEOPLE. By L. T. MEADE.
HEPSY GIPSY. By L. T. MEADE. 2s. 6d.
THE HONOURABLE MISS. By L. T. MEADE.
MY LAND OF BEULAH. By Mrs. LEITH ADAMS.

MESSRS. METHUEN'S LIST 35

University Extension Series

A series of books on historical, literary, and scientific subjects, suitable for extension students and home-reading circles. Each volume is complete in itself, and the subjects are treated by competent writers in a broad and philosophic spirit.

Edited by J. E. SYMES, M.A.,
Principal of University College, Nottingham.

Crown 8vo. Price (with some exceptions) 2s. 6d.

The following volumes are ready:—

THE INDUSTRIAL HISTORY OF ENGLAND. By H. DE B. GIBBINS, D. Litt., M.A., late Scholar of Wadham College, Oxon., Cobden Prizeman. *Fifth Edition, Revised. With Maps and Plans.* 3s.

'A compact and clear story of our industrial development. A study of this concise but luminous book cannot fail to give the reader a clear insight into the principal phenomena of our industrial history. The editor and publishers are to be congratulated on this first volume of their venture, and we shall look with expectant interest for the succeeding volumes of the series.'—*University Extension Journal.*

A HISTORY OF ENGLISH POLITICAL ECONOMY. By L. L. PRICE, M.A., Fellow of Oriel College, Oxon. *Second Edition.*

PROBLEMS OF POVERTY: An Inquiry into the Industrial Conditions of the Poor. By J. A. HOBSON, M.A. *Third Edition.*

VICTORIAN POETS. By A. SHARP.

THE FRENCH REVOLUTION. By J. E. SYMES, M.A.

PSYCHOLOGY. By F. S. GRANGER, M.A. *Second Edition.*

THE EVOLUTION OF PLANT LIFE: Lower Forms. By G. MASSEE. *With Illustrations.*

AIR AND WATER. By V. B. LEWES, M.A. *Illustrated.*

THE CHEMISTRY OF LIFE AND HEALTH. By C. W. KIMMINS, M.A. *Illustrated.*

THE MECHANICS OF DAILY LIFE. By V. P. SELLS, M.A. *Illustrated.*

ENGLISH SOCIAL REFORMERS. By H. DE B. GIBBINS, D.Litt., M.A.

ENGLISH TRADE AND FINANCE IN THE SEVENTEENTH CENTURY. By W. A. S. HEWINS, B.A.

THE CHEMISTRY OF FIRE. The Elementary Principles of Chemistry. By M. M. PATTISON MUIR, M.A. *Illustrated.*

A TEXT-BOOK OF AGRICULTURAL BOTANY. By M. C. POTTER, M.A., F.L.S. *Illustrated.* 3s. 6d.

THE VAULT OF HEAVEN. A Popular Introduction to Astronomy. By R. A. GREGORY. *With numerous Illustrations.*

METEOROLOGY. The Elements of Weather and Climate. By H. N. DICKSON, F.R.S.E., F.R. Met. Soc. *Illustrated.*

A MANUAL OF ELECTRICAL SCIENCE. By GEORGE J. BURCH, M.A. *With numerous Illustrations.* 3s.

Messrs. Methuen's List

THE EARTH. An Introduction to Physiography. By EVAN SMALL, M.A. *Illustrated.*

INSECT LIFE. By F. W. THEOBALD, M.A. *Illustrated.*

ENGLISH POETRY FROM BLAKE TO BROWNING. By W. M. DIXON, M.A.

ENGLISH LOCAL GOVERNMENT. By E. JENKS, M.A., Professor of Law at University College, Liverpool.

THE GREEK VIEW OF LIFE. By G. L. DICKINSON, Fellow of King's College, Cambridge. *Second Edition.*

Social Questions of To-day

Edited by H. DE B. GIBBINS, D.Litt., M.A.

Crown 8vo. 2s. 6d.

A series of volumes upon those topics of social, economic, and industrial interest that are at the present moment foremost in the public mind. Each volume of the series is written by an author who is an acknowledged authority upon the subject with which he deals.

The following Volumes of the Series are ready:—

TRADE UNIONISM—NEW AND OLD. By G. HOWELL. *Second Edition.*

THE CO-OPERATIVE MOVEMENT TO-DAY. By G. J. HOLYOAKE. *Second Edition.*

MUTUAL THRIFT. By Rev. J. FROME WILKINSON, M.A.

PROBLEMS OF POVERTY. By J. A. HOBSON, M.A. *Third Edition.*

THE COMMERCE OF NATIONS. By C. F. BASTABLE, M.A., Professor of Economics at Trinity College, Dublin.

THE ALIEN INVASION. By W. H. WILKINS, B.A.

THE RURAL EXODUS. By P. ANDERSON GRAHAM.

LAND NATIONALIZATION. By HAROLD COX, B.A.

A SHORTER WORKING DAY. By H. DE B. GIBBINS, D.Litt., M.A., and R. A. HADFIELD, of the Hecla Works, Sheffield.

BACK TO THE LAND: An Inquiry into the Cure for Rural Depopulation By H. E. MOORE.

TRUSTS, POOLS AND CORNERS. By J. STEPHEN JEANS.

THE FACTORY SYSTEM. By R. W. COOKE-TAYLOR.

THE STATE AND ITS CHILDREN. By GERTRUDE TUCKWELL.

WOMEN'S WORK. By LADY DILKE, Miss BULLEY, and Miss WHITLEY.
MUNICIPALITIES AT WORK. The Municipal Policy of Six Great Towns, and its Influence on their Social Welfare. By FREDERICK DOLMAN.
SOCIALISM AND MODERN THOUGHT. By M. KAUFMANN.
THE HOUSING OF THE WORKING CLASSES. By E. BOWMAKER.
MODERN CIVILIZATION IN SOME OF ITS ECONOMIC ASPECTS. By W. CUNNINGHAM, D.D., Fellow of Trinity College, Cambridge.
THE PROBLEM OF THE UNEMPLOYED. By J. A. HOBSON, B.A.,
LIFE IN WEST LONDON. By ARTHUR SHERWELL, M.A. *Second Edition.*
RAILWAY NATIONALIZATION. By CLEMENT EDWARDS.

Classical Translations

Edited by H. F. FOX, M.A., Fellow and Tutor of Brasenose College, Oxford.

ÆSCHYLUS—Agamemnon, Chöephoroe, Eumenides. Translated by LEWIS CAMPBELL, LL.D., late Professor of Greek at St. Andrews, 5s.

CICERO—De Oratore I. Translated by E. N. P. MOOR, M.A. 3s. 6d.

CICERO — Select Orations (Pro Milone, Pro Murena, Philippic II., In Catilinam). Translated by H. E. D. BLAKISTON, M.A., Fellow and Tutor of Trinity College, Oxford. 5s.

CICERO—De Natura Deorum. Translated by F. BROOKS, M.A., late Scholar of Balliol College, Oxford. 3s. 6d.

LUCIAN—Six Dialogues (Nigrinus, Icaro-Menippus, The Cock, The Ship, The Parasite, The Lover of Falsehood). Translated by S. T. IRWIN, M.A., Assistant Master at Clifton ; late Scholar of Exeter College, Oxford. 3s. 6d.

SOPHOCLES—Electra and Ajax. Translated by E. D. A. MORSHEAD, M.A., Assistant Master at Winchester. 2s. 6d.

TACITUS—Agricola and Germania. Translated by R. B. TOWNSHEND, late Scholar of Trinity College, Cambridge. 2s. 6d.

Educational Books

CLASSICAL

PLAUTI BACCHIDES. Edited with Introduction, Commentary, and Critical Notes by J. M'COSH, M.A. *Fcap. 4to.* 12s. 6d.
'The notes are copious, and contain a great deal of information that is good and useful.'—*Classical Review.*

TACITI AGRICOLI. With Introduction, Notes, Map, etc. By R. F. DAVIS, M.A., Assistant Master at Weymouth College. *Crown 8vo.* 2s.

TACITI GERMANIA. By the same Editor. *Crown 8vo.* 2s.

HERODOTUS : EASY SELECTIONS. With Vocabulary. By A. C. LIDDELL, M.A. *Fcap. 8vo.* 1s. 6d.

SELECTIONS FROM THE ODYSSEY. By E. D. STONE, M.A., late Assistant Master at Eton. *Fcap. 8vo.* 1s. 6d.

PLAUTUS: THE CAPTIVI. Adapted for Lower Forms by J. H. FRESSE, M.A., late Fellow of St. John's, Cambridge. 1s. 6d.

DEMOSTHENES AGAINST CONON AND CALLICLES. Edited with Notes and Vocabulary, by F. DARWIN SWIFT, M.A., formerly Scholar of Queen's College, Oxford. *Fcap. 8vo.* 2s.

EXERCISES ON LATIN ACCIDENCE. By S. E. WINBOLT, Assistant Master at Christ's Hospital. *Crown 8vo.* 1s. 6d.

An elementary book adapted for Lower Forms to accompany the shorter Latin primer.
'Skilfully arranged.'—*Glasgow Herald.*
'Accurate and well arranged.'—*Athenæum.*

NOTES ON GREEK AND LATIN SYNTAX. By G. BUCKLAND GREEN, M.A., Assistant Master at Edinburgh Academy, late Fellow of St. John's College, Oxon. *Crown 8vo.* 3s. 6d.

Notes and explanations on the chief difficulties of Greek and Latin Syntax, with numerous passages for exercise.
'Supplies a gap in educational literature.'—*Glasgow Herald.*

GERMAN

A COMPANION GERMAN GRAMMAR. By H. DE B. GIBBINS, D.Litt., M.A., Assistant Master at Nottingham High School. *Crown 8vo.* 1s. 6d.

GERMAN PASSAGES FOR UNSEEN TRANSLATION. By E. M'QUEEN GRAY. *Crown 8vo.* 2s. 6d.

SCIENCE

THE WORLD OF SCIENCE. Including Chemistry, Heat, Light, Sound, Magnetism, Electricity, Botany, Zoology, Physiology, Astronomy, and Geology. By R. ELLIOTT STEEL, M.A., F.C.S. 147 Illustrations. *Second Edition. Crown 8vo.* 2s. 6d.

ELEMENTARY LIGHT. By R. E. STEEL. With numerous Illustrations. *Crown 8vo.* 4s. 6d.

ENGLISH

ENGLISH RECORDS. A Companion to the History of England. By H. E. MALDEN, M.A. *Crown 8vo.* 3s. 6d.

A book which aims at concentrating information upon dates, genealogy, officials, constitutional documents, etc., which is usually found scattered in different volumes.

THE ENGLISH CITIZEN: HIS RIGHTS AND DUTIES. By H. E. MALDEN, M.A. 1s. 6d.

A DIGEST OF DEDUCTIVE LOGIC. By JOHNSON BARKER, B.A. *Crown 8vo.* 2s. 6d.

MESSRS. METHUEN'S LIST

METHUEN'S COMMERCIAL SERIES

Edited by H. DE B. GIBBINS, D.Litt., M.A.

BRITISH COMMERCE AND COLONIES FROM ELIZABETH TO VICTORIA. By H. DE B. GIBBINS, D.Litt., M.A. 2s. *Second Edition.*

COMMERCIAL EXAMINATION PAPERS. By H. DE B. GIBBINS, D.Litt., M.A., 1s. 6d.

THE ECONOMICS OF COMMERCE. By H. DE B. GIBBINS, D.Litt., M.A. 1s. 6d.

FRENCH COMMERCIAL CORRESPONDENCE. By S. E. BALLY, Modern Language Master at the Manchester Grammar School. 2s. *Second Edition.*

GERMAN COMMERCIAL CORRESPONDENCE. By S. E. BALLY, 2s. 6d.

A FRENCH COMMERCIAL READER. By S. E. BALLY. 2s.

COMMERCIAL GEOGRAPHY, with special reference to the British Empire. By L. W. LYDE, M.A., of the Academy, Glasgow. 2s. *Second Edition.*

A PRIMER OF BUSINESS. By S. JACKSON, M.A. 1s. 6d.

COMMERCIAL ARITHMETIC. By F. G. TAYLOR, M.A. 1s. 6d.

PRÉCIS WRITING AND OFFICE CORRESPONDENCE. By E. E. WHITFIELD, M.A. 2s.

WORKS BY A. M. M. STEDMAN, M.A.

INITIA LATINA: Easy Lessons on Elementary Accidence. *Second Edition.* *Fcap. 8vo.* 1s.

FIRST LATIN LESSONS. *Fourth Edition. Crown 8vo.* 2s.

FIRST LATIN READER. With Notes adapted to the Shorter Latin Primer and Vocabulary. *Fourth Edition revised.* 18mo. 1s. 6d.

EASY SELECTIONS FROM CAESAR. Part I. The Helvetian War. 18mo. 1s.

EASY SELECTIONS FROM LIVY. Part I. The Kings of Rome. 18mo. 1s. 6d.

EASY LATIN PASSAGES FOR UNSEEN TRANSLATION. *Fifth Edition. Fcap. 8vo.* 1s. 6d.

EXEMPLA LATINA. First Lessons in Latin Accidence. With Vocabulary. *Crown 8vo.* 1s.

EASY LATIN EXERCISES ON THE SYNTAX OF THE SHORTER AND REVISED LATIN PRIMER. With Vocabulary. *Seventh and cheaper Edition re-written. Crown 8vo.* 1s. 6d. Issued with the consent of Dr. Kennedy.

THE LATIN COMPOUND SENTENCE: Rules and Exercises. *Crown 8vo.* 1s. 6d. With Vocabulary. 2s.

NOTANDA QUAEDAM: Miscellaneous Latin Exercises on Common Rules and Idioms. *Third Edition. Fcap. 8vo.* 1s. 6d. With Vocabulary. 2s.

LATIN VOCABULARIES FOR REPETITION: Arranged according to Subjects. *Sixth Edition. Fcap. 8vo.* 1s. 6d.

A VOCABULARY OF LATIN IDIOMS AND PHRASES. 18mo. Second Edition. 1s.
STEPS TO GREEK. 18mo. 1s.
EASY GREEK PASSAGES FOR UNSEEN TRANSLATION. Second Edition. Fcap. 8vo. 1s. 6d.
GREEK VOCABULARIES FOR REPETITION. Arranged according to Subjects. Second Edition. Fcap. 8vo. 1s. 6d.
GREEK TESTAMENT SELECTIONS. For the use of Schools. Third Edition. With Introduction, Notes, and Vocabulary. Fcap. 8vo. 2s. 6d.
STEPS TO FRENCH. Second Edition. 18mo. 8d.
FIRST FRENCH LESSONS. Second Edition. Crown 8vo. 1s.
EASY FRENCH PASSAGES FOR UNSEEN TRANSLATION. Third Edition revised. Fcap. 8vo. 1s. 6d.
EASY FRENCH EXERCISES ON ELEMENTARY SYNTAX. With Vocabulary. Second Edition. Crown 8vo. 2s. 6d.
FRENCH VOCABULARIES FOR REPETITION : Arranged according to Subjects. Sixth Edition. Fcap. 8vo. 1s.

SCHOOL EXAMINATION SERIES

EDITED BY A. M. M. STEDMAN, M.A *Crown 8vo.* 2s. 6d.

FRENCH EXAMINATION PAPERS IN MISCELLANEOUS GRAMMAR AND IDIOMS. By A. M. M. STEDMAN, M.A. *Ninth Edition.*
A KEY, issued to Tutors and Private Students only, to be had on application to the Publishers. *Fourth Edition. Crown 8vo. 6s. net.*
LATIN EXAMINATION PAPERS IN MISCELLANEOUS GRAMMAR AND IDIOMS. By A. M. M. STEDMAN, M.A. *Eighth Edition.*
KEY (*Third Edition*) issued as above. 6s. *net.*
GREEK EXAMINATION PAPERS IN MISCELLANEOUS GRAMMAR AND IDIOMS. By A. M. M. STEDMAN, M.A *Fifth Edition.*
KEY (*Second Edition*) issued as above. 6s. *net.*
GERMAN EXAMINATION PAPERS IN MISCELLANEOUS GRAMMAR AND IDIOMS. By R. J. MORICH, Manchester. *Fifth Edition.*
KEY (*Second Edition*) issued as above. 6s. *net.*
HISTORY AND GEOGRAPHY EXAMINATION PAPERS. By C. H. SPENCE, M.A., Clifton College. *Second Edition.*
SCIENCE EXAMINATION PAPERS. By R. E. STEEL, M.A., F.C.S., Chief Natural Science Master, Bradford Grammar School. *In two vols.* Part I. Chemistry ; Part II. Physics.
GENERAL KNOWLEDGE EXAMINATION PAPERS. By A. M. M. STEDMAN, M.A. *Third Edition.*
KEY (*Second Edition*) issued as above. 7s. *net.*

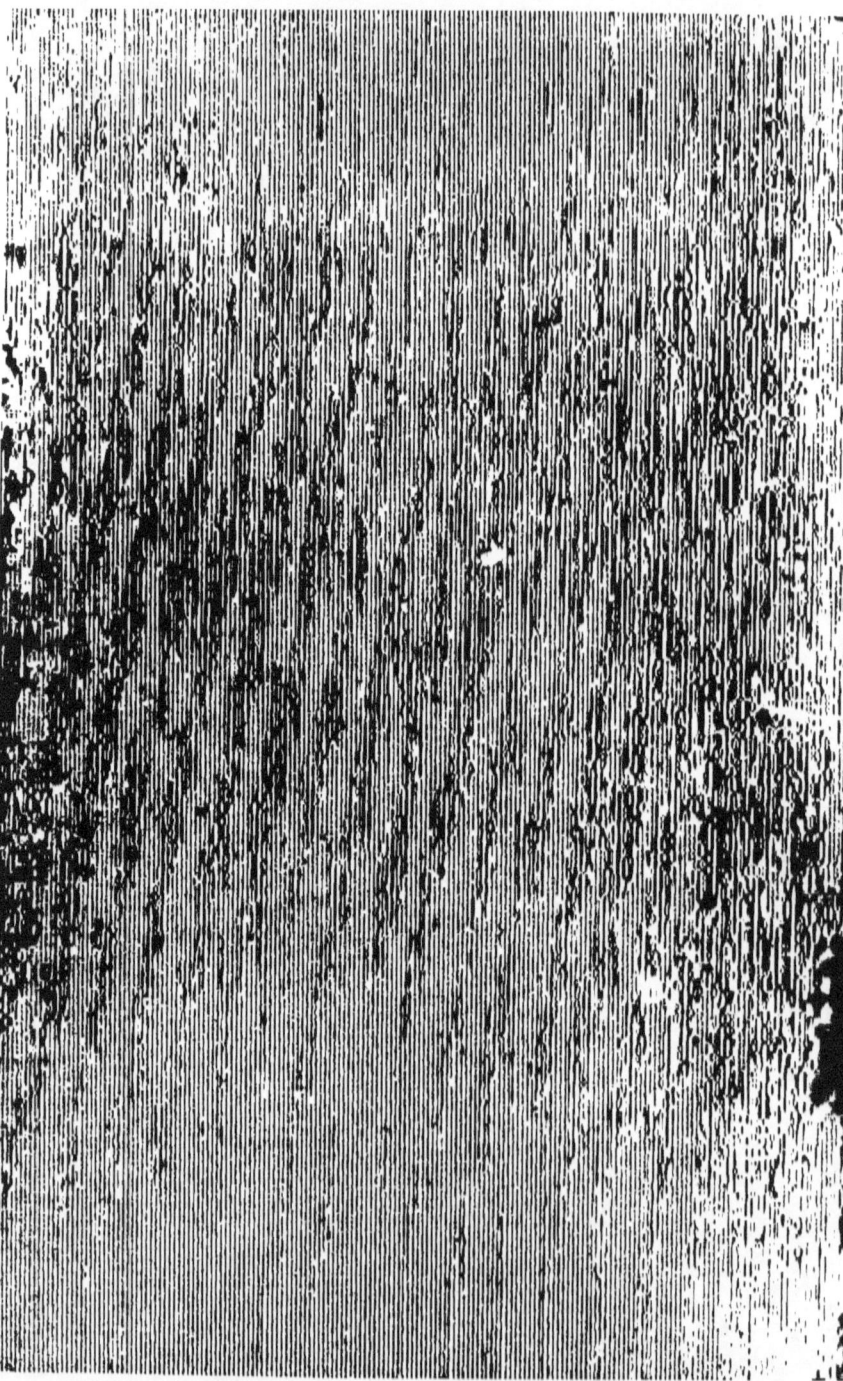

www.ingramcontent.com/pod-product-compliance
Lightning Source LLC
Chambersburg PA
CBHW020236240426
43672CB00006B/548